# EGYPTIAN BOOK OF THE DEAD HIEROGLYPH TRANSLATIONS USING THE TRILINEAR METHOD

Understanding the Mystic Path to Enlightenment Through Direct Readings of the Sacred Signs and Symbols of Ancient Egyptian Language With Trilinear Deciphering translation Method

## Vol. 4

by

Dr. Muata Ashby

©2019 Sema Institute

A Collection of Hieroglyphic Texts Translated by Dr. Muata Ashby from the Ancient Egyptian Books of The Dead

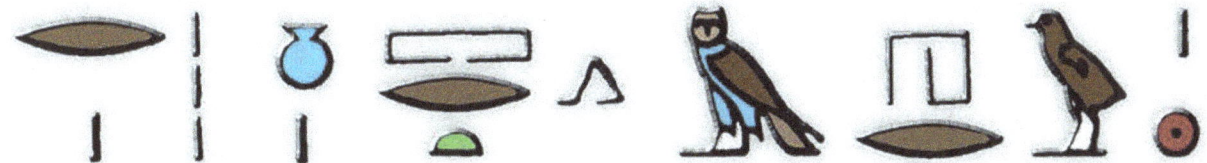

Cruzian Mystic Books

Sema Yoga

P.O.Box 570459

Miami, Florida, 33257

(305) 378-6253 Fax: (305) 378-6253

First U.S. edition 2019

All rights reserved. No part of this book may be used or reproduced in any manner whatsoever without written permission (address above) except in the case of brief quotations embodied in critical articles and reviews. All inquiries may be addressed to the address above.

The author is available for group lectures and individual counseling. For further information contact the publisher.

Ashby, Muata

EGYPTIAN BOOK OF THE DEAD HIEROGLYPH TRANSLATIONS USING THE TRILINEAR METHOD: Understanding the Mystic Path to Enlightenment through Direct Readings of the Sacred Signs and Symbols of Ancient Egyptian Language With Trilinear Deciphering Method

Volume 4.

ISBN: 1-884564-99-2

Library of Congress Cataloging in Publication Data

1 Egyptian Book of the Dead, 2 Egyptian Philosophy 3 Hieroglyphs 4 Meditation, 5 Self Help.

www,Egyptianyoga.com

www.Kemetuniversity.come

Egyptian Book of the Dead Hieroglyph Translations Volume 4

# Table of Contents

Table of Figures ................................................................................................................................. 7
PART 1: INTRODUCTION TO THE PERT-M-HERU ........................................................................ 10
Preface ............................................................................................................................................ 11
    A New Translation of the Prt M Hru ........................................................................................ 12
Author's Foreword ......................................................................................................................... 15
    Who Were the Ancient Egyptians and What is Yoga Philosophy? .......................................... 15
"Our people originated at the base of the mountain of the Moon, at the origin of the Nile river." ...... 16
        Who Am I? ............................................................................................................................ 20
Who am I? What is this mind which perceives? What is this universe made of? Is there a God? ................. 20
        Yoga Philosophy and the World Religious Philosophies Defined ..................................... 29
    The Tree Stages of Religion ...................................................................................................... 30
        Selected Spiritual Philosophies Compared ....................................................................... 31
Origins and Basis of Mysticism in the Rau nu Pert em Hru ........................................................ 34
    INTRODUCTION TO THE PHILOSOPHY OF The *PERT EM HERU* ................................................. 35
        Ancient Egyptian Religion as Yoga ...................................................................................... 36
        The Study of Yoga ................................................................................................................ 41
        The Stages of Human Spiritual Evolution and Aspiration ................................................. 46
    The Evolution of The Book of Coming Forth By Day ............................................................... 48
    The Elements of the Human Personality ................................................................................ 69
"Get thyself ready and make the thought in you a stranger to the world-illusion" ................... 70
Compendium of the Main Religious Traditions and Gods and Goddesses of Ancient Egyptian Spirituality .......... 73
    Ancient Egyptian Religion: The Spiritual Culture and the Purpose of Life: Shetaut Neter ...... 73
    Shetaut Neter ............................................................................................................................ 73
    Who is Neter in Kamitan Religion? .......................................................................................... 74
    Sacred Scriptures of Shetaut Neter ......................................................................................... 74

**SHETAUT ASAR-ASET-HERU** ............................................................................................................ 75
(c. 1580 B.C.E.-Roman Period) ...................................................................................................... 75
(c. 3,000 B.C.E. – PTOLEMAIC PERIOD) ......................................................................................... 75
    Neter and the Neteru ................................................................................................................ 76
        The Neteru ............................................................................................................................. 76

- The Neteru and Their Temples .................................................................................................................. 77
  - The Anunian Tradition ..................................................................................................................... 80
  - The Memphite Tradition .................................................................................................................. 81
  - The Theban Tradition ...................................................................................................................... 82
  - The Goddess Tradition .................................................................................................................... 83
  - Mehurt ("The Mighty Full One")The Asarian Tradition .................................................................... 83
  - The Aton Tradition .......................................................................................................................... 85
  - Akhnaton, Nefertiti and Daughters ................................................................................................. 85
  - The Mystical Creation Myth ............................................................................................................ 86
  - Prominent Ancient Egyptian Gods and Goddesses ......................................................................... 88
  - The Forces of Entropy ..................................................................................................................... 90
  - The Great Awakening of Neterian Religion ..................................................................................... 91
- The Human Personality and its Relationship to the Gods and Goddesses ........................................... 92
- The Mystical and Cosmic Implications of the Elements of the Personality .......................................... 93
- "Get thyself ready and make the thought in you a stranger to the world-illusion" .................................. 99
- TRANSLATION FORMATS USED FOR PRESENTING THE TRANSLATIONS WITH THE TRILINEAR METHOD ........... 102
  - Conventional Interlinear Format .................................................................................................. 102
  - Trilinear Contextual Format ......................................................................................................... 103
  - Reading the Philosophy Embedded in Ancient Egyptian Hieroglyphic Writings .......................... 105
  - ............................................................................................................................................... 107
- SECTION 2 ........................................................................................................................................... 107
- ANCIENT EGYPTIAN BOOK OF THE DEAD HIEROGLYPH TRANSLATIONS OF SELECTED CHAPTERS AND ASSOCIATED TEXTS ................................................................................................................................. 107
- PART 1: CREATION MYTH & THE ORIGIN OF MIND, THE FIELD OF HUMAN EXISTENCE & *EXPERIENCE* ............. 108
  - SELECTIONS FROM ANUNIAN CREATION MYTH A. Book of Knowing the forms of the Creator and defeating the principle of chaos/degradation/decay .................................................................. 109
  - Scripture of the Creation Version B-Book of Knowing the forms of the Creator and defeating the principle of chaos/degradation/decay .............................................................................................. 116
    - Ancient Egyptian Creation Myth B Continued: Origin of Feelings: Remy is the name of Ra source of vegetation, animals and people (endowed with sentiment (feelings). Sentiments give rise to {emotions}) ............................................................................................................................ 120
    - Invoke name of Ra and conquer Apep .................................................................................... 121

Ancient Egyptian Creation Myth B Continued: CREATION OF THE GODS AND GODDESSES THAT COMPOSE THE ELEMENTS OF NATURE AND THE COMPONENTS OF THE HUMAN PSYCHE ............ 122

Egyptian Book of the Dead: The relationship of the Soul of Ra and Osiris: Papyrus Ani-The Souls of Osiris and Ra meet in the netherworld. ............ 124

# PART 3: Body Conscience and Mental Complexes ............ 125

Selections from Papyrus Petersburg 1116A: Instruction for Mery-ka-ra ............ 126

Selections from Papyrus Petersburg 1116A: Instruction for Mery-ka-ra -continued ............ 128

Pert-M-Heru. Book of Enlightenment- Chapter of the Heart of Carnelian. Souls do the will of the Mind and experience its experiences as if they were its own ............ 130

Chap 17-The Wisdom of Body and Excrement ............ 134

# PART 4: WISDOM OF HARMONIZATION of the Human Personality and Overcoming Mental Complexes from the Pert-em-Heru ............ 135

Introduction to the Ka (mind), purity and the perpetual existence with waking conscience, from the Pyramid Texts of Pepi ............ 136

Chapter 156-Chapter of buckle of carnelian: Provisioning with Creative Power From the Feminine Divine ............ 137

Egyptian Book of the Dead Chapter 89. Chapter of Causing the Soul to come into Harmony with the Physical Body to Produce a Glorious Body ............ 140

Egyptian Book of the Dead Chapter XCI. "The Chapter of not letting the soul of a person be captive in " Neter-khert." (See pp. 114, 319, and pi. 17.) ............ 145

Pert-Im-Heru Chapter XCII. "The Chapter of opening the tomb to the soul and the" shadow, of coming forth by day, and of getting power over the legs." (See pp. 115, 319, and pi. 17.) ............ 148

# PART 5: SPECIAL DESCRIPTIONS OF SHEDY SPIRITUAL PRACTICES AS A PROCESS FOR RISING ABOVE COMPLEXES: PRIMER ON KEMETIC PSYCHOLOGY OF WELL-ADJUSTED (INTEGRATED) PERSONALITY TO PROMOTE SPIRITUAL ENLIGHTENMENT ............ 151

Ancient Egyptian Book of the Dead Chapter 78 – Transforming into a Hawk ............ 152

Ancient Egyptian Book of the Dead Chapter 78 – Transforming into a Hawk Verses-1, 22-24, 27-30 ............ 153

Egyptian Book of the Dead Chapter 78 – Transforming into a Hawk verses 10-13 ............ 153

Egyptian Book of the Dead Chapter 78 – Transforming into a Hawk verses 22-24 ............ 154

Egyptian Book of the Dead Chapter 78 – Transforming into a Hawk verses 27-30 ............ 155

Egyptian Book of the Dead Chapter 78 – Transforming into a Hawk Verses 58-64 ............ 156

Egyptian Book of the Dead Chapter 78 – Transforming into a Hawk verses 89-91 ............ 158

Verses from the Stele of Abu ............ 159

Egyptian Book of the Dead of Hunefer, The source of true happiness ............ 162

- Assorted Ancient Egyptian Texts Related to the Book of the Dead .................................................. 163
- Pyramid Texts -King Unas– Utterance 222.211b Born of Horus .................................................. 163
- The Movement of the Serpent Power According to the Ancient Egyptian Funerary Scripture ....................... 166
  - Section from Pert-m-Heru Chapter 15 .................................................. 168
- Hieroglyphic Scripture -Hymn to Goddess Net .................................................. 173
- The second HARPER'S SONG FROM THE TOMB OF NEFERHOTEP Theban Tomb No. 50 .................................................. 176
- Hymn to the Diadem- Bremner-Rhind Papyrus .................................................. 182

INDEX .................................................. 186

Other Books From C M Books .................................................. 192

Egyptian Book of the Dead Hieroglyph Translations Volume 4

# Table of Figures

Figure 1: A Papyrus Scroll of the Pert-m-Heru .................................................................................................. 10
Figure 2: An Ancient Egyptian tomb entrance at Sakkara (the land of Seker/Sokar-Asar). ................................ 14
Figure 3: A map of North East Africa showing the location of the land of *Ta-Meri* or *Kamut*, also known as Ancient Egypt. 16
Figure 4: The land of Ancient Egypt ................................................................................................................ 19
Figure 5: Scene from the *Prt m Hru* of Lady Ta-ameniu .................................................................................. 34
Figure 6: Above: Smai Heru-Set, ..................................................................................................................... 40
Figure 7: Coffin of Hent-Mehit, Singer (Chanter) of Amun, 21st dynasty showing anthropoid (human) features, texts and vignettes. ............................................................................................................................................. 50
Figure 8: Coffin of Hent-Mehit, Singer (Chanter) of Amun, 21st dynasty showing anthropoid (human) features, texts and vignettes. ............................................................................................................................................. 51
Figure 9: Coffin of Ipi-Ha-Ishutef Coffin texts version of Pyramid Texts that later appear in modified forms in the later papyrus *Prt m Hru* ................................................................................................................................ 53
Figure 10: Outer Coffin of Hapiankhtifi, 12th Dynasty, Middle Kingdom, ........................................................ 54
Figure 11: Above left: Forms of the God Djehuty (Djehuty)/Djehuty .............................................................. 68
Figure 12: Above right: Forms of the Goddess Maat/Maati ............................................................................ 68
**Figure 13: A two dimensional depiction of the elements of the personality.** ................................................ 92
Figure 14: The elements of the Individual human personality are derived from the Universal God Ra .......... 93

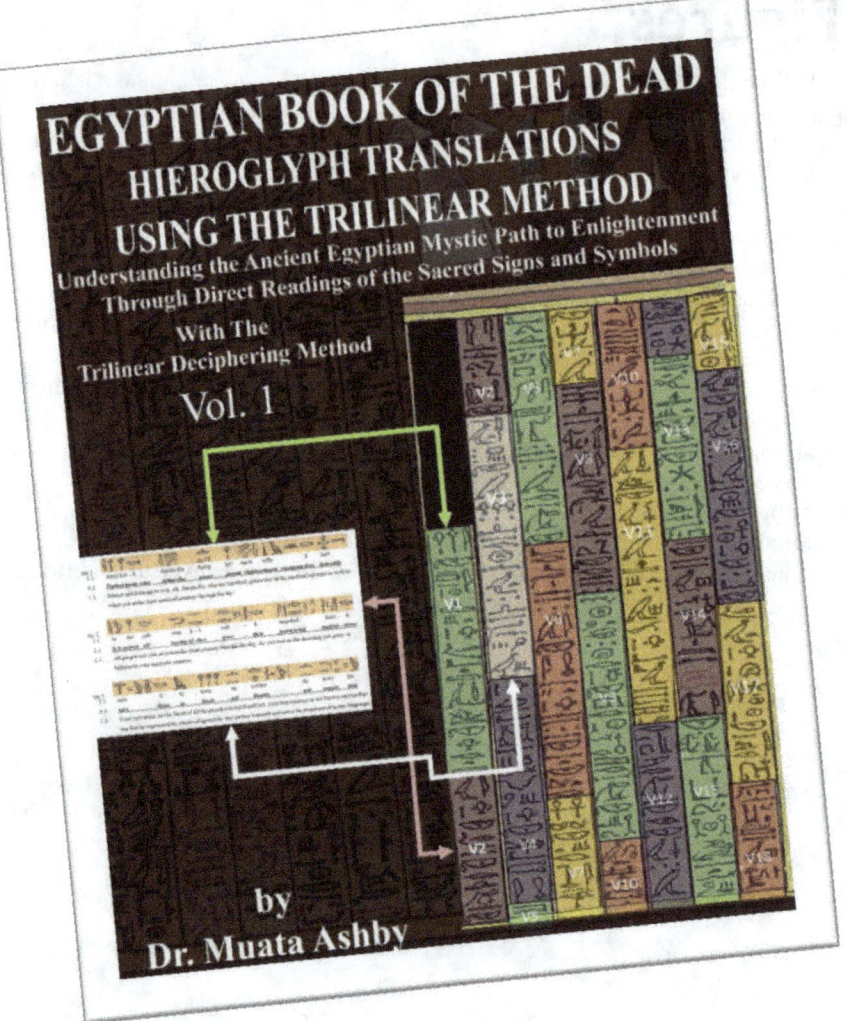

## ALSO AVAILABLE: Volume 1 + Volume 2 + Volume 3

This new volume contains original translations of Chapters of the Ancient Egyptian Book of the Dead (Book of Coming Forth By Day) displaying the Ancient Egyptian Hieroglyphs with word for word translations plus the innovative "Trilinear System", a technique developed by Dr. Muata Ashby to bring out the depths of the Kemetic/Neterian *Sebait* or Ancient Egyptian Mysteries philosophy. This is an ideal study guide for approaching the Ancient Egyptian Hieroglyphic writing in a step by step manner through three layers of descriptive translation. This volume includes translations presented at the annual Neterian Conferences over the last fifteen years and also includes new texts never before published. This book provides new and deeper and direct insights into the Egyptian Mysteries for beginning, advancing and advanced aspirants alike as it may be used as a philosophy study reference, a textbook, or as a reader for daily spiritual study or ritual worship.

# The True Name of The "Book of The Dead"

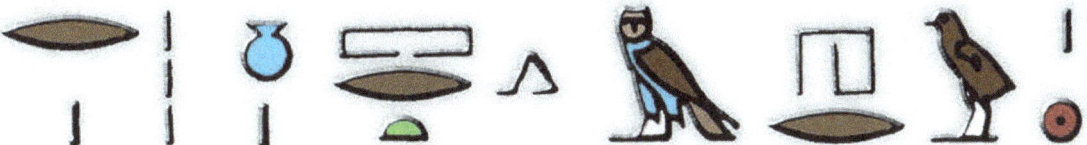

Rau nu pert m heru

=

The

"Chapters of going as light"

Or

## The

## "Book of Becoming Light"

Or

The

"Book of Enlightenment"

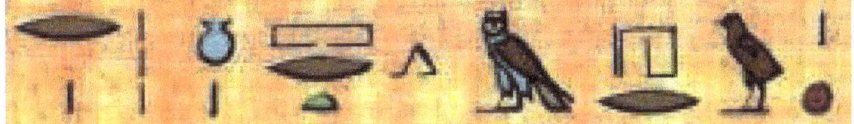

# PART 1: INTRODUCTION TO THE PERT-M-HERU

**Figure 1: A Papyrus Scroll of the Pert-m-Heru**

# Preface[1]

"The Egyptians neither entrusted their mysteries to everyone, nor degraded the secrets of divine matters by disclosing them to the profane, reserving them for the heir apparent of the throne, and for such of priests as excelled in virtue and wisdom."

—Clement of Alexandria (150?- 220?)

## The Three Levels of Religion and the Mysteries

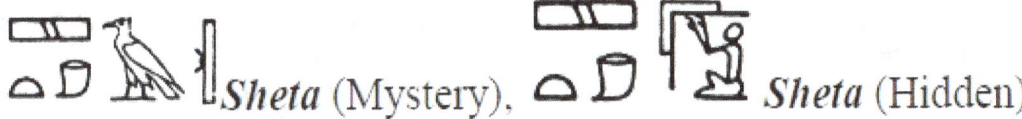

The first and most important teaching to understand in our study surrounds the Ancient Egyptian word "Sheti." Sheti comes from the root *Sheta*. The Ancient Egyptian word *Sheta* means something which is *hidden, secret, unknown*, or *cannot be seen or understood, a secret, a mystery*. What is considered to be inert matter also possesses "hidden" properties or *Shetau Akhet*. Rituals, Words of Power (Khu-Hekau, Mantras), religious texts and pictures are S*hetaut Neter* or *Divine Mysteries*. *Shetat* or *Seshetat* are the secret rituals in the cults of the Egyptian Gods. *Shetai* is the *Hidden God, Incomprehensible God, Mysterious One,* and *Secret One.* One name of the soul of the Ancient Egyptian god Amun is *Shet-ba* (The One whose soul is hidden). The name Amun itself signifies "The Hidden One," "*Shetai.*" Sheti (spiritual discipline) is to go deeply into the mysteries, to study the mystery teachings and literature profoundly, to penetrate the mysteries. *Nehas-t* signifies: "resurrection" or "spiritual awakening." The body or *Shet-t* (mummy) is where a human being focuses attention to practice spiritual disciplines. When spiritual discipline is perfected, the true Self or *Shti* (he who is hidden in the coffin) is revealed.

**Shetaut Neter**

(Secrets about the Divine Self)

The *Book of Coming Forth By Day* represents the second level of Shetaut Neter. Shetaut Neter means "the way or wisdom of the hidden Divinity which is behind all Creation." Religion has three levels of practice. The first is the myth, which includes the traditions, stories and everything related to it. The next stage is the ritualization of the myth. The final stage is the metaphysical philosophy behind the teachings given in the myth. The book *The Asarian Resurrection,* presented the complete myth of Asar (Asar or Osiris), Aset (Isis) and Heru (Horus). The *Book of Coming Forth By Day* represents stage two, the

---

[1] Taken from the book Egyptian Book of the Dead by Muata Ashby ©2000

ritualization of the myth of Asar, and through the practice of the rituals contained in the book it is possible to feel, think, act and ultimately experience the same fate of Asar, spiritual enlightenment. Thus, a spiritual aspirant is to understand that {he/she} has incarnated on earth and has been dismembered by egoistic thoughts and actions. However, by gaining an understanding of the hidden mysteries, it is possible to reach a state of beatitude and resurrection, just as Asar.[2]

Therefore, a serious spiritual aspirant should see every aspect of {his/her} life as a ritual in which the soul within them (Asar) is struggling to be reborn again. This spiritual rebirth is accomplished by the practices of listening to the teachings, practicing them and meditating upon them. With the understanding of the hidden knowledge, you can see that all of nature around you is Divine. This includes plants, animals, planets and stars, food, other people, etc. So, through your understanding of the myth and how it relates to your life, and by living your life according to this understanding (ritual), you can lead yourself to discover and realize (mystical experience) the deeper truth behind your own being. This is the true practice of religion. If you understand the superficial teachings of a religious myth, and you practice its rituals blindly without understanding the deeper implications, you will not obtain the higher realization. Your practice will be at the level of dogma. This is why there is so much religious conflict in the world today. At the level of dogma, each religion has different myths and rituals and therefore, little if any, common ground upon which to come together. The results of this misunderstanding and ignorance have been personal disillusionment and wars. Yet, at the mystical or metaphysical level, all religions are actually pointing towards the same goal, that of spiritual realization.

# A New Translation of the Prt M Hru

Why do we need a new translation of the *Ancient Egyptian Book of the Dead*?[3] If you have picked up a Christian Bible lately, you will notice that you do not have the original text. In fact, the present versions are centuries removed from the original scriptures which comprised the original texts. The Bible is one of the primary sources containing information regarding the beliefs of the Christian faith. It is a compilation of selected portions of writings[4] by different authors, written over a period of 1,000-2,000 years (1,500 B.C.E.- 200 A.C.E.). It is composed of two main sections, the Old Testament and the New Testament, which are made up of smaller books. The original form of the Old Testament is in the ancient Hebrew language. Later, about 250 B.C.E., the Old Testament was translated into Greek. The original form of the New Testament is in the ancient Aramaic, Greek and Hebrew. These forms serve as the primary "original" texts of the Bible. However, since most of the people of the world do not understand ancient Aramaic, Hebrew or Greek, it became necessary to make translations of the Bible into forms that people of modern times could understand. Translations of the Bible pose important problems because the church and religious scholars admittedly[5] do not understand the meanings of some of the ancient Hebrew words in part or at all. Present day English speaking people would not even be able to understand the original King James Version of the Bible which was written only 387 years ago,

---

[2] See the book *The Mystical teachings of the Ausarian Resurrection: Initiation Into the Third Level of Shetaut Asar* by Muata Ashby
[3] Pert m Hru-Book of Coming Forth By Day
[4] The Bible does not include the entire group of scriptures that were written in biblical times. See the book *Christian Yoga* by Muata Ashby
[5] By general admission; confessedly.

much less scriptures that were written over 1,700 years ago. However, the essence of a teaching can be discerned and brought forth by those who are initiated into the correct understanding and practice of religious philosophy in its three steps[6]. This is why updates to the translations are necessary.

However, at the same time, the necessity for translations opens the door to corruption and misunderstanding, as some translators may want to present a certain view of the scriptures to prove their own points or to mislead others, or they simply may not produce a correct translation because they do not understand the philosophy which the original Sages were trying to impart. Many people do not see the spiritual scriptures as books of spiritual principles being imparted through metaphors. Rather, they insist that they are to be believed word for word or not at all. If this is the case, and if certain words, customs or ideas cannot be understood by theologians and scholars, as they have already admitted, there is bound to be some misunderstanding. For example, people in modern industrialized countries live with modern plumbing and aqueducts. Their concerns are different than people thousands of years ago worrying about the annual Nile flood or rains for watering their crops. Since ancient spiritual scriptures are most often enveloped in mythology which has been blended with historic events and personalities, these will inevitably contain some information related by expressions that only people living in those times would understand. If the scriptures are interpreted strictly in historical or literal terms, they will become the object of many different interpretations and consequently, arguments and misinterpretation as well. For this reason, the religious beliefs of the translator of the particular text in question may or may not be in agreement with the original scriptural meaning, and may consequently influence the translation. Therefore, the reader should exercise caution when choosing a translation to use for study. Another important consideration is that the translator should be a practitioner of the philosophy as well, that is, one who is involved with the culture of the text. In this way, by living the teachings, they can draw from the feel of the teaching and thereby bring to bear the inner insight which comes from the Divine source.

Since languages and culture change over time, it becomes necessary to update translations on a regular basis. Another important factor is that there are new discoveries that arise from time to time which alter the understanding of the use of some terms or elucidate a new meaning of the old text, which in turn affects the understanding of the meaning of the teachings. Although revision work has been incorporated into this volume, its most important contribution relates to the interpretation of the scriptures from the point of view of a living mystical tradition.

Unlike the Bible whose original texts were translated into many languages, the *Ru Pert Em Heru (Prt m Hru)* has not suffered removal from its original form, but from convention to suit modern culture. What I mean is that the pervasiveness of the Bible and its various versions has caused a situation in which many people, including scholars, have come to believe the Bible as being historically accurate, and the final authority on spiritual teachings. They also view the modern versions as being true to the original versions. While the study of the *Prt m Hru* has been mostly confined to scholars and a limited number of interested people, it has suffered from being interpreted by scientists instead of religious scholars and practitioners of the philosophy. Thus, the translations, while being accurate in many respects, have lost the deeper meaning which was originally intended. Yet, this meaning is as real today as it was seven thousand years ago when the *Pyramid Texts* were carved in stone, but it can only be discovered if the translation and interpretation has a spiritual basis.

---

[6] Myth, Ritual and Metaphysical (Mysticism).

**Figure 2: An Ancient Egyptian tomb entrance at Sakkara (the land of Seker/Sokar-Asar).**

# Author's Foreword

Who Were the Ancient Egyptians and What is Yoga Philosophy?

The Ancient Egyptian religion (*Shetaut Neter*), language and symbols provide the first "historical" record of Yoga Philosophy and Religious literature. Egyptian Yoga is what has been commonly referred to by Egyptologists as Egyptian "Religion" or "Mythology," but to think of it as just another set of stories or allegories about a long lost civilization is to completely miss the greatest secret of human existence. Yoga, in all of its forms and disciplines of spiritual development, was practiced in Egypt earlier than anywhere else in history. This unique perspective from the highest philosophical system which developed in Africa over seven thousand years ago provides a new way to look at life, religion, the discipline of psychology and the way to spiritual development leading to spiritual Enlightenment. Egyptian mythology, when understood as a system of Yoga (union of the individual soul with the Universal Soul or Supreme Consciousness), gives every individual insight into their own divine nature and also a deeper insight into all religions and Yoga systems.

Diodorus Siculus (Greek Historian) writes in the time of Augustus (first century B.C.):

"Now the Ethiopians, as historians relate, were the first of all men and the proofs of this statement, they say, are manifest. For that they did not come into their land as immigrants from abroad, but were the natives of it and so justly bear the name of autochthones (sprung from the soil itself), is, they maintain, conceded by practically all men..."

"They also say that the Egyptians are colonists sent out by the Ethiopians, Asar having been the leader of the colony. For, speaking generally, what is now Egypt, they maintain, was not land, but sea, when in the beginning the universe was being formed; afterwards, however, as the Nile during the times of its inundation carried down the mud from Ethiopia, land was gradually built up from the deposit...And the larger parts of the customs of the Egyptians are, they hold, Ethiopian, the colonists still preserving their ancient manners. For instance, the belief that their kings are Gods, the very special attention which they pay to their burials, and many other matters of a similar nature, are Ethiopian practices, while the shapes of their statues and the forms of their letters are Ethiopian; for of the two kinds of writing which the Egyptians have, that which is known as popular (demotic) is learned by everyone, while that which is called sacred (hieratic), is understood only by the priests of the Egyptians, who learnt it from their Fathers as one of the things which are not divulged, but among the Ethiopians, everyone uses these forms of letters. Furthermore, the orders of the priests, they maintain, have much the same position among both peoples; for all are clean who are engaged in the service of the gods, keeping themselves shaven, like the Ethiopian priests, and having the same dress and form of staff, which is shaped like a plough and is carried by their kings who wear high felt hats which end in a knob in the top and are circled by the serpents which they call asps; and this symbol appears to carry the thought that it will be the lot who shall dare to attack the king to encounter death-carrying stings. Many other things are told by them concerning their own antiquity and the colony which they sent out that became the Egyptians, but about this there is no special need of our writing anything."

The Ancient Egyptian texts state:

"Our people originated at the base of the mountain of the Moon, at the origin of the Nile river."

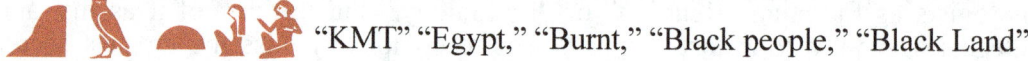 "KMT" "Egypt," "Burnt," "Black people," "Black Land"

In describing the Ancient Egyptians of his time, Herodotus (Greek historian c. 484-425 BC) said: *"The Egyptians and Nubians have thick lips, broad noses, wooly hair and burnt skin... ...And the Indian tribes I have mentioned, their skins are all of the same color, much like the Ethiopians... their country is a long way from Persia towards the south..."* Diodorus, the Greek historian (c. 100 B.C.) said the following, *"And upon his return to Greece, they gathered around and asked, "tell us about this great land of the Blacks called Ethiopia." And Herodotus said, "There are two great Ethiopian nations, one in Sind (India) and the other in Egypt."* Thus, from these accounts we gather that the Ancient Egyptian peoples were of dark complexion, i.e. of African origin and they had close ties in ancient times with the peoples of India.

*Where is the land of Egypt?*

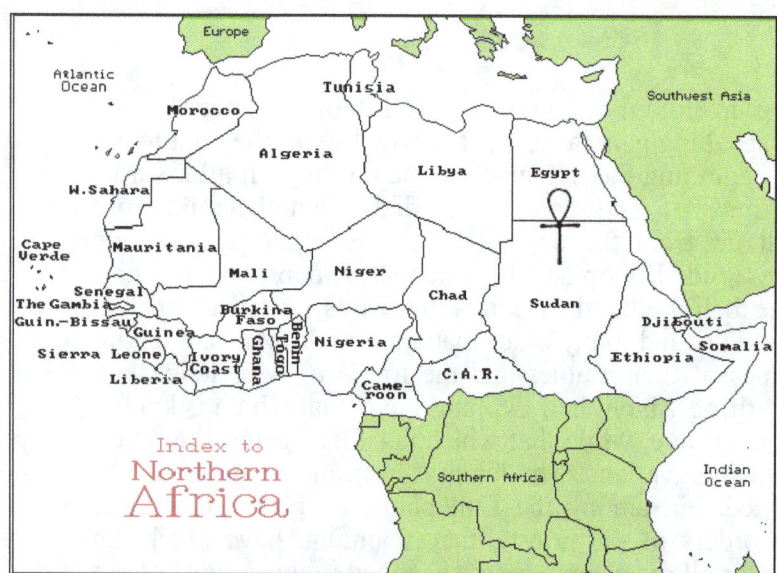

**Figure 3: A map of North East Africa** showing the location of the land of *Ta-Meri* or *Kamut,* also known as Ancient Egypt.

The Ancient Egyptians lived for thousands of years in the northeastern corner of the African continent in the area known as the Nile Valley. The Nile river was a source of dependable enrichment for the land and allowed them to prosper for a very long time. Their prosperity was so great that they created art, culture, religion, philosophy and a civilization which has not been duplicated since. The Ancient Kamitans (Egyptians) based their government and business concerns on spiritual values and therefore, enjoyed an orderly society which included equality between the sexes, and a legal system based on universal spiritual laws. The *Prt m Hru* is a tribute to their history, culture and legacy. As historical insights unfold, it becomes clearer that modern culture has derived its basis from Ancient Egypt, though the credit is not often given, nor the integrity of the practices maintained. This is another important reason to study Ancient Egyptian Philosophy, to discover the principles which allowed their civilization to prosper over a period of thousands of years in order to bring our systems of government, religion and social structures to a harmony with ourselves, humanity and with nature.

Christianity was partly an outgrowth of Judaism, which was itself an outgrowth of Ancient Egyptian culture and religion. So who were the Ancient Egyptians? From the time that the early Greek philosophers set foot on African soil to study the teachings of mystical spirituality in Egypt (900-300 B.C.E.), Western society and culture was forever changed. Ancient Egypt had such a profound effect on Western civilization as well as on the native population of Ancient India (Dravidians) that it is important to understand the history and culture of Ancient Egypt, and the nature of its spiritual tradition in more detail.

The history of Egypt begins in the far reaches of history. It includes The Dynastic Period, The Hellenistic Period, Roman and Byzantine Rule (30 B.C.E.-638 A.C.E.), the Caliphate and the Mamelukes (642-1517 A.C.E.), Ottoman Domination (1082-1882 A.C.E.), British colonialism (1882-1952 A.C.E.), as well as modern, Arab-Islamic Egypt (1952- present).

Ancient Egypt or Kamit, was a civilization that flourished in Northeast Africa along the Nile River from before 5,500 B.C.E. until 30 B.C.E. In 30 B.C.E., Octavian, who was later known as the Roman Emperor, Augustus, put the last Egyptian King, Ptolemy XIV, a Greek ruler, to death. After this Egypt was formally annexed to Rome. Egyptologists normally divide Ancient Egyptian history into the following approximate periods: The Early Dynastic Period (3,200-2,575 B.C.E.); The Old Kingdom or Old Empire (2,575-2,134 B.C.E.); The First Intermediate Period (2,134-2,040 B.C.E.); The Middle Kingdom or Middle Empire (2,040-1,640 B.C.E.); The Second Intermediate Period (1,640-1,532 B.C.E.); The New Kingdom or New Empire (1,532-1,070 B.C.E.); The third Intermediate Period (1,070-712 B.C.E.); The Late Period (712-332 B.C.E.).

In the Late Period the following groups controlled Egypt. The Nubian Dynasty (712-657 B.C.E.); The Persian Dynasty (525-404 B.C.E.); The Native Revolt and re-establishment of Egyptian rule by Egyptians (404-343 B.C.E.); The Second Persian Period (343-332 B.C.E.); The Ptolemaic or Greek Period (332 B.C.E.- c. 30 B.C.E.); Roman Period (c.30 B.C.E.-395 A.C.E.); The Byzantine Period (395-640 A.C.E) and The Arab Conquest Period (640 A.C.E.-present). The individual dynasties are numbered, generally in Roman numerals, from I through XXX.

The period after the New Kingdom saw greatness in culture and architecture under the rulership of Ramses II. However, after his rule, Egypt saw a decline from which it would never recover. This is the period of the downfall of Ancient Egyptian culture in which the Libyans ruled after The Tanite (XXI) Dynasty. This was followed by the Nubian conquerors who founded the XXII dynasty and tried to restore Egypt to her past glory. However, having been weakened by the social and political turmoil of wars, Ancient Egypt fell to the Persians once more. The Persians conquered the country until the

Greeks, under Alexander, conquered them. The Romans followed the Greeks, and finally the Arabs conquered the land of Egypt in 640 A.C.E to the present.

However, the history which has been classified above is only the history of the "Dynastic Period." It reflects the view of traditional Egyptologists who have refused to accept the evidence of a Predynastic period in Ancient Egyptian history contained in Ancient Egyptian documents such as the *Palermo Stone, Royal Tablets at Abydos, Royal Papyrus of Turin,* the *Dynastic List* of *Manetho,* and the eye-witness accounts of Greek historians Herodotus (c. 484-425 B.C.E.) and Diodorus. These sources speak clearly of a Predynastic society which stretches far into antiquity. The Dynastic Period is what most people think of whenever Ancient Egypt is mentioned. This period is when the pharaohs (kings) ruled. The latter part of the Dynastic Period is when the Biblical story of Moses, Joseph, Abraham, etc., occurs (c. 2100? - 1,000? B.C.E). Therefore, those with a Christian background generally only have an idea about Ancient Egypt as it is related in the Bible. Although this biblical notion is very limited in scope, the significant impact of Ancient Egypt on Hebrew and Christian culture is evident even from the biblical scriptures. Actually, Egypt existed much earlier than most traditional Egyptologists are prepared to admit. The new archeological evidence related to the great Sphinx monument on the Giza Plateau and the ancient writings by Manetho, one of the last High Priests of Ancient Egypt, show that Ancient Egyptian history begins earlier than 10,000 B.C.E. and may date back to as early as 30,000-50,000 B.C.E.

It is known that the Pharaonic (royal) calendar based on the Sothic system (star Sirius) was in use by 4,240 B.C.E. This certainly required extensive astronomical skills and time for observation. Therefore, the history of Kamit (Egypt) must be reckoned to be extremely ancient. Thus, in order to grasp the antiquity of Ancient Egyptian culture, religion and philosophy, we will briefly review the history presented by the Ancient Egyptian Priest Manetho and some Greek Historians.

The calendar based on the Great Year was also used by the Ancient Egyptians. The Great Year is based on the movement of the earth through the constellations known as the precession of the Equinoxes and confirmed by the History given by the Ancient Egyptian Priest Manetho in the year 241 B.C.E. Each Great Year has 25,860 to 25,920 years and 12 arcs or constellations, and each passage through a constellation takes 2,155 – 2,160 years. These are the "Great Months." The current cycle or year began around the year 10,858 B.C.E. At around the year 36,766 B.C.E., according to Manetho, the Creator, Ra, ruled the earth in person from his throne in the Ancient Egyptian city of Anu. By this reckoning our current year (2,000 A.C.E.) is actually the year 38,766 based on the Great Year System of Ancient Egyptian history.

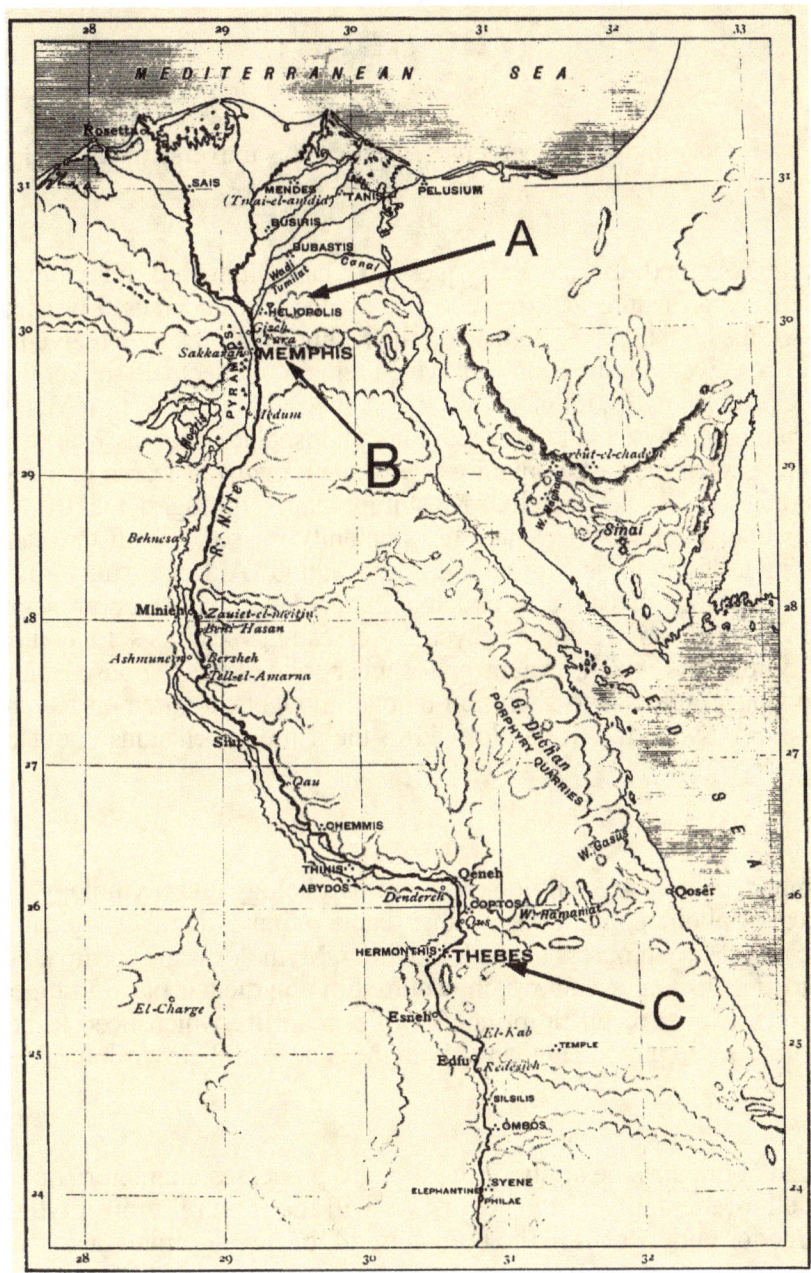

**Figure 4: The land of Ancient Egypt**

Egypt is located in the north-eastern corner of the African Continent. The cities wherein the theology of the Trinity of Amun-Ra-Ptah was developed were: A- Anu (Heliopolis), B-Hetkaptah (Memphis), and C-Waset (Thebes). The cities wherein the theology of the Trinity of Asar-Aset-Heru was developed were A- Anu, D-Abydos, E- Philae, F- Edfu, G-Dendera, and H- Ombos.

# Who Am I?

Who am I? What is this mind which perceives? What is this universe made of? Is there a God?

Throughout history, these and many other questions have followed humanity from generation to generation. The need of human nature to experience, to evolve and understand has led to the invention of philosophies which assist the human mind in grasping the realities it seems to perceive in the world as well as those which it seems to perceive with the heart, but which remain intellectually unknowable. In ancient times these philosophies developed as myths, religions, yoga systems and in modern times they have taken the form of sciences called psychology, physics and non-religious philosophies such as Marxism and existentialism. Yet with all the developments of the past, humanity as a whole remains in search of the answers to happiness, health and peace. Has religion and science failed? Most importantly, throughout all the teachings embodied in religions and the discoveries of modern science, has humanity missed out on the benefits of religion and science? Is there anything useful in these endeavors for humankind? A deeper study into the history, meaning and practice of ancient teachings reveals a remarkable concordance with modern scientific discoveries. In essence, modern sciences such as Quantum Physics are leading scientists to contemplate life and our understanding of reality in terms which ancient philosophers and Sages espoused thousands of years ago. Science is a discipline which professes to shun non-rational thoughts, a common feature to both mythology and religion. So how is it possible that it would lead to the same conclusions about existence as mystical religions and Yoga philosophy?

Two of the most important areas we will look into are psychology and mythology. We will look at these from a yogic or mystical-symbolic point of view rather than a rational, literal or logical way. The reasons for doing this will become clear as we progress through the study. Mythology and spiritual symbolism were never intended to be understood as factual events which occurred in a particular place in time exclusively. Rather, they are to be understood as ever recurring principles of human life which need to be understood in their deepest sense in order for them to provide humanity with the benefit of their wisdom.

Psychology has been defined as the study of the thought processes characteristic of an individual or group (mind, psyche, ethos, mentality). In this work we will focus on religious mythology as a psychological discipline for understanding the human mind, its development and transformation. Mythology can be understood as a language, however, it is a unique kind of language. Certain languages are similar because they are part of a family of languages. For example: Italian and Spanish. This similarity makes it possible for a person whose native language is Spanish to understand the meanings of some Italian words so as to somewhat be able to follow along a conversation in Italian. Mythology is much more intelligible than an ordinary human language. Mythology is more akin to music in its universality. If the key elements of this language are well understood, it is possible to understand and relate any mythological system to another and thereby gain the understanding of the message being imparted. Setting up your own personal spiritual program will require that you develop a profound understanding of the psychological principles upon which ancient mythology is based in order to discover your special path on the spiritual journey.

In order to gain insight into the *"Psycho-Mythology"* or psychological implications of religious and spiritual mythology which promote the psycho-spiritual transformation of the individual leading to the attainment of

Enlightenment, we must first define what is meant by the terms psycho and mythology. Here, the term *psycho* must be understood as far more than simply that which refers to the mind and its thoughts. We will be using *psycho* to mean everything that constitutes human consciousness in all of its stages and states. *Mythology* here refers to the codes, messages, ideas, directives and beliefs which affect the psyche through the conscious and unconscious mind of an individual, specifically those effects which result in transpersonal or transcendental changes in the personality as well as those which constitute anti-yogic, anti-transcendental movements.

While our study begins with Egyptian Mythology, Religion and Yoga Philosophy, it also necessarily relates to all mythologies, religions and philosophies around the world. Briefly, Egyptian religion is the oldest recorded religion in this historical era and in our book, *Egyptian Yoga*, we compiled the correlations between the religion which developed in Egypt and those which developed later around other parts of Africa as well as in Asia.[7] It becomes evident that what has been called Egyptian Mythology is in reality a highly sophisticated and advanced system of Yoga Philosophy. Yoga is a system of personal transformation by which we are able to discover our true Self wherein lies the answers to all of our questions about the purpose of our existence, who we are, how to overcome adversity and promote prosperity, and why we are in the situations of life in which we find ourselves. Most importantly, the idea is not to amass mountainous amounts of wisdom teachings but to discover their meanings and how to apply them in ordinary life to rise above it, as a lotus rises above the muddy waters without retaining a single drop of the dirty water on its petals. If this does not occur, then one is not practicing philosophy, religion or yoga, but something else. Initiation is therefore the process of coming into a philosophy and way of life which allows you to become free of any restrictions or impediments to your happiness. It is also a process of discovering how to end pain and suffering in life. Thus, it is a process of becoming established in your own inner support and inner peace without depending on the world.

## What is Human Existence and What is its Purpose?

Human life is a process in which a human being experiences various situations, ranging from pain and suffering to happiness and pleasure, between the time span of birth and death. From a yogic point of view, all human situations are painful because they are distractions from the true source of bliss and abiding happiness within the heart. Attachment to objects and relationships outside of oneself seems like the normal course of human life, but the masses of people adopt this mode of existence out of ignorance. Ignorance of what? Ignorance of their deeper Self. If they had knowledge of the deeper Self within, there would be no need to seek personal fulfillment through worldly achievements, worldly possessions or worldly relationships. This endless search leads every ignorant human being to engage in various situations and entanglements, which in the beginning seem to hold the possibility of bringing about a happy circumstance, but which invariably leads to pain, suffering and frustration. A mature human being discovers that ordinary human life cannot satisfy the inner need of the soul because it is unpredictable and transient. So what should one live for? Did not the Ancient Egyptians build wondrous monuments and innovations in science, medicine, government, social order, etc.? They did not withdraw from the world, but they did not seek spiritual fulfillment through the world either. This is the first key to understanding Ancient Egyptian culture and spiritual philosophy.

You do not have to turn on the television or read a newspaper to see the miserable condition of most people. Think about your own life. Has there been any situation where happiness was abiding? Have you experienced any relationship with someone who never disappointed you or caused you pain? Has there been any possession you acquired which did not lose its power to bring you happiness or that you did not become bored with, even though it made you happy to possess it in the beginning? Even those people who say they are

---

[7] The term Asia includes Europe.

happy with life as it is are deluding themselves into believing that the happy moments balance the painful ones. This is not true because even the happy moments are setting you up for some painful disappointment in the future, because all worldly situations and relationships come to an end. Thus, by living in accordance with the ignorant philosophy of life, your happy moments cause longing for more happy moments, and when these are not possible, there is disappointment and frustration. The longing and frustration does not end at the time of death. When the body dies, the mind continues to hold the deep rooted desires for worldly fulfillment and this causes the soul to be impelled toward countless new lifetimes of karmic entanglements in search of worldly fulfillment. All of this occurs out of ignorance of one's true Self.

> "The visible world is ephemeral, the spirit world is forever; gain strength from this since nothing physical can destroy you."

> "Labor not after riches first, and think thou afterwards wilt enjoy them. He who neglects the present moment, throws away all that he hath. As the arrow passes through the heart, while the warrior knew not that it was coming; so shall his life be taken away before he knoweth that he hath it."

> "There is no happiness for the soul in the external worlds since these are perishable, true happiness lies in that which is eternal, within us."

> **FROM: THE STELE OF ABU:** "Be chief of the mysteries at festivals, know your mouth, come in Hetep (peace), enjoy life on earth but do not become attached to it; it is transitory."

—Ancient Egyptian Proverbs

Becoming free from the clutches of ignorance is not as simple as learning about its cause. Even if you are honest and truly believe in the philosophy of yoga and mystical spirituality, all of your mental efforts to negate the ignorance will fail in the beginning. This is because your mind has spent many hours over a period of days, months, years, lifetimes and eons, believing in the illusion of human life. Even if you were to understand that it is your worldly attachments which are causing you mental agitation and suffering, the process of attaining Enlightenment is not as simple as saying, "O.K. since my possessions are distracting me and causing me agitation and worry, I will give them up and have peace." Even if you were to find yourself without possessions, your mind would be grieving over their loss, or preoccupied with how to regain them or how to survive without them.

Even if you give everything up and go to a distant cave away from civilization, you cannot escape from the world. There will still be ants and mosquitoes to bite you, cold weather, rain, wild animals, and the restless wandering of your mind thinking of the life you left! Initiation into spiritual life is the process of learning an art of living which leads to freedom even while involved in the world. Your goal is to become as the lotus which rises up from the muddy waters, able to exist in the world without being soiled by it, and having discovered the bliss of inner spiritual discovery, always abiding in that wondrous glory in any situation which life presents to you. Once the teachings of spirituality are understood and you have a firm conviction as to their reality, then you can begin the process of making them your reality. Spiritual realization requires sustained effort over a period of time wherein spiritual disciplines are directed towards overturning the mountainous creations, which the mind has produced in the past due to ignorance. The mind is like a river. Ignorant ideas are like logs, rocks, branches and dams in the river which block, divert or distort the flow of water. With the correct equipment (correct understanding and practice of the spiritual disciplines) and through sustained effort, the obstacles to spiritual realization can be removed allowing the river of the mind to flow freely toward the ocean of self-discovery. As the second stage in the practice of religion (ritualism), the *Prt m Hru* also encompasses the disciplines of spiritual practice which are in modern times recognized by the name "Yoga," especially the Yoga of Righteous action. These will be discussed in detail later.

If you have developed enough spiritual sensitivity to understand that there is no abiding peace or happiness to be found in ordinary human existence, you are qualified to study the deeper mysteries of spiritual life. This is the process of Initiation, which leads from ignorance to Enlightenment and self-discovery. It is the process by which a human being living an ordinary life is taught how to lead an extraordinary life and to attain superhuman expanded (enlightened) consciousness. Where is there an inexhaustible source of bliss and happiness, which does not depend on external factors? Where is it possible to find unending peace and tranquility and a joy which is not subject to external conditions of either prosperity or adversity? The initiatic process shows the way.

In order for the teachings of mystical spirituality to come true in your life, you must make them the central force in your life. You must center your life around them and infuse them into every aspect of your life. In this way you will become transformed into the ideal of what the teachings describe: an Enlightened human being. It is not possible to gain higher spiritual understanding of the practices in any other way except to live them. Thus initiation is a way of life and not a single event. It is a continuous process which leads to greater and greater awareness and expansion, culminating in the highest levels of Self-Knowledge, Stage Three of Religion.

Before proceeding with the main body of this work, it would be helpful to establish some working definitions for the disciplines which will be discussed in order to provide a common basis for understanding the journey we will undertake. These terms will be further defined and explored throughout the course of this work.

**Philosophy**

Philosophy has been defined as the speculative inquiry concerning the source and nature of human knowledge and a system of ideas based on such thinking. In this work, the idea of philosophy will be confined to the modes of thinking employed for the purpose of transforming the human mind, leading it to achieve transpersonal states of consciousness. In its original sense, philosophy is a mental discipline for leading a person to enlightenment. In modern times this lofty notion of philosophy has come to be regarded as unscientific speculation or even as an opinion or belief of one person or group versus another. Specifically, we will look at Kemeticism[8] as a philosophy of psychological transformation.

---

[8] Term coined by the author to signify Kemetic, based on the ancient words Kemet or Kamit, used in Ancient Egypt to describe the land and inhabitants of North-East Africa, meaning Ancient Egyptian- related to Ancient Egyptian culture, religion and mysticism. **"KMT" "Egypt", "Burnt", "Land of Blackness", "Land of the Burnt People."** This term is most appropriately used to refer to the religion of Ancient Egypt in order to relate it to the culture of ancient times.

"Never forget, the words are not the reality, only reality is reality; picture symbols are the idea, words are confusion."[9]

"The Self {ultimate reality} is not known through study of scriptures, nor through subtlety of the intellect, nor through much learning; but by him who longs for it is it known."[10]

One caveat which any true philosophy must follow is the understanding that words in themselves cannot capture the ultimate essence of reality. Words can be a trap to the highly developed intellect. Therefore, we must always keep in mind that words and philosophical discourse can only point the way to the truth. In order to discover the truth, we must go beyond all words, all thoughts, and all of our mental concepts and philosophies, because the truth, as *Hermetic* and *Vedanta* philosophy would say, can only be experienced; it cannot be encapsulated in any way, shape or form.

The study of philosophy in its highest form is to assist the student in understanding {his/her} own mind in order to be able to transcend it, and thus, experience the "transcendental" reality which lies beyond words, thoughts, concepts and mental notions. Mental conceptions are based on our own worldly experiences. They help us to understand the world as the senses perceive it. However, clinging to these experiences as the only reality precludes our discovery of other forms of reality or existence which lies beyond the capacity of the senses. A dog's olfactory sense and the vision of a hawk are much superior to that of the human being.

However, the human has one advantage which is superior to all senses and scientific instruments, the intuitional mind when it is purified by the practice of Yoga philosophy and disciplines. Ancient mystical philosophical systems have as their main goal the destruction of the limited concepts and illusions of the mind. In essence, the philosophies related to understanding nature and a human being's place in it were the first disciplines which practiced what would today be called Transpersonal Psychology, that is, a system of psychology which assists us in going beyond the personal or ego-based aspects of the psyche in order to discover what lies beyond (trans) the personal (relating to the personality).

**Metaphysics**

Metaphysics is the branch of philosophy that systematically investigates first causes of nature, the universe and ultimate reality. The term comes from the Greek "*meta physika*," meaning "after the things of nature." In Aristotle's works, he envisioned that the first philosophy came after the physics. Metaphysics has been divided into *ontology*, or the study of the essence of being or that which is or exists, and *cosmology*, the study of the structure and laws of the universe and the manner of its creation.

---

Another term, "Egyptian Yoga" meaning Smai Tawi, has bee introduced previously. Howevber, the proper name of Ancient Egyptian Religion is "Shetaut Neter," meaning "the hidden way of the Divine Self" (i.e. God).

[9] Hermetic proverb. Hermeticism is the later development of Kemetic Philosophy.
[10] Indian Vedantic proverb.

From time immemorial, philosophers, such as those who wrote the Ancient Egyptian Creation myths, to Greek philosophers such as Plato and Aristotle, to more modern philosophers such as Whitehead and Kant, have written on metaphysics. Skeptics, however, have charged that speculation which cannot be verified by objective evidence is useless. However, these skeptics do not realize that what they consider as "objective reality" is not objective at all, since objectivity is based on the perceptions of the senses, and as just discussed, modern science itself has proven that the human senses cannot perceive the phenomenal universe as it really is. Further, the objective information that can be gathered by scientific instruments is only valid under certain conditions. This makes it relative and not absolute information. Thus, what people ordinarily consider to be real and abiding is not. Einstein's proof of relativity confirms this. There must be something real beyond the phenomenal world which sustains it. The search for that higher essence is the purpose of philosophy and metaphysics. Therefore, the value of metaphysical and mystical philosophy studies is evident.

**Psychology**

Psychology, as used by ordinary practitioners of society, has been defined as the study of the thought processes characteristic of an individual or group (mind, psyche, ethos, mentality). In this work we will focus on Kemeticism as a psychological discipline for understanding the human mind, its source, higher development and transformation. However, Mystical Psychology in reality does not relate only to the mind since a human being is composed of several complex aspects. The term personality, as it is used in Yoga, implies mind, body and spirit, as well as the conscious, subconscious and unconscious aspects of the mind. Therefore, the discipline of psychology must be expanded to include physical as well as spiritual dimensions. Once again, modern medical science has, within the last twenty years, acknowledged the understanding that health cannot be treated as a physical problem only, but as one which involves the mind, body and spirit. Likewise, spiritual teaching must be related as a discipline which involves not only the soul of an individual, but the mind and body as well – in other words, the entire human being.

**Yoga**

The literal meaning of the word Yoga is to *"yoke"* or to *"link"* back. The implication is to link back individual consciousness (human personality) to its original source, the original essence: Universal Consciousness. In a broad sense Yoga is any process which helps one to achieve liberation or freedom from bondage to the pain and spiritual ignorance of ordinary human existence. So whenever you engage in any activity with the goal of promoting the discovery of your true Self, be it studying the spiritual wisdom teachings, exercising, fasting, meditation, breath control, rituals, chanting, prayer, etc., you are practicing yoga. If the goal is to help you to discover your essential nature as one with God or the Supreme Being, Consciousness, then it is Yoga.

Yoga (Sanskrit for "union") is a term used for a number of disciplines, the goal of each being to lead the practitioner to attain union with Universal Consciousness. Present day Indian Yoga philosophy is based on several Indian texts such as the *Upanishads, Bhagavad Gita* and the *Yoga-sutras* of Patañjali, and several other Yoga treatises developed in India. The practice of Yoga generally involves meditation, moral restraints, and the awakening of energy centers (in the body) through specific postures (asanas) or physical exercises, and breathing exercises. All Yoga disciplines are devoted to freeing the soul or individual self from worldly (mental) restraints. They have become popular in the West as a means of self-control and relaxation.

The specific form of *"yoking"* or to *"linking"* back that was practiced in Ancient Egypt was called "Smai Tawi" or union of the two lands, i.e. the opposites, the Higher and lower aspects of self or soul and Spirit.

**Religion**

All religions tend to be deistic at the elementary levels. Most often it manifests as an outgrowth of the cultural concepts of a people as they try to express the deeper feeling which they perceive, though not in its entirety. Thus, deism is based on limited spiritual knowledge. Deism, as a religious belief or form of theism, holds that God's action was restricted to an initial act of creation, after which he retired (separated) to contemplate the majesty of his work. Deists hold that the natural creation is regulated by laws put in place by God at the time of creation and inscribed with perfect moral principles. A deeper study of religion will reveal that in its original understanding, it seeks to reveal the deeper essential nature of creation, the human heart and their relation to God, which transcends the deistic model or doctrine. The term religion comes from the Latin *"Relegare"* which uses the word roots *"Re"* which means *"Back"* and *"Ligon"* which means *"to hold, to link, to bind."* Therefore, the essence of true religion is the same as yoga, that is, of linking back, specifically, linking the soul of its follower back to its original source: God. So, although religion in its purest form is a Yoga system, incorporating the yoga disciplines within its teachings, the original intent and meaning of the religious scriptures are often misunderstood, if not distorted. This occurs because religions have developed in different geographic areas. As a result, the lower levels of religion which are mixed with culture (historical accounts, stories and traditions) have developed independently, and thereby appear to be different from each other on the surface. This leads to confusion and animosity among people who are ignorant of the true process of religious movement. Religion consists of three levels: *myth, ritual and mystical experience*. If the first two levels are misunderstood or accepted literally, the spiritual movement will fail to proceed to the next higher level. In order for a religious experience to lead one to have a mystical experience, all three levels of religion must be completed. This process will be fully explained throughout the text of this volume.

**Mysticism**

Mysticism is a spiritual discipline for attaining union with the Divine through the practice of deep meditation or contemplation, and other spiritual disciplines such as austerity, detachment, renunciation, etc. In this aspect, Mysticism and Yoga are synonymous.

**Dualism**

Similar to Deism, Dualism is the belief that all things in nature are separate and real, and that they exist independently from any underlying essence or support. It is the belief in the pairs of opposites wherein everything has a polar counterpart. For example: male - female, here - there, hot - cold, etc. While these elements seem real and abiding to the human mind, mystical philosophers throughout history have been claiming that this is only an outer expression of the underlying essence from which they originate. In reality, the underlying essence of all things is non-dual and all-encompassing. It is the substratum of all that exists. Modern science has been confirming this view of matter. The latest experiments in quantum physics show that all matter is composed of energy. Most importantly for this study, dualism is a state of mind that occurs at an immature level of mental understanding of reality. It is akin to egoism and egoistic tendencies which tend to make a person see {himself/herself} as separate and distinct from the world and from other living beings. Through the study and practice of mystical spiritual teachings, dualism is replaced with non-dualism and salvation, spiritual enlightenment, then occurs. Therefore, salvation or resurrection is related to a non-dualistic view of existence and bondage and death are related to dualism and egoism.

A dualistic view of life can lead to agitation, suffering and even catastrophic events in human experience because the mind is trained to see either good or evil, acceptable or unacceptable, you or me, etc., and not the whole of creation composed of many parts. In the dualistic state of mind, the attitudes of separation and exclusivism are exaggerated. These render the mind agitated. Mental agitation prevents the mind from achieving greater insights into the depths of spiritual teachings. Thus, agitated people are usually frustrated and unable to discover inner peace and spiritual fulfillment.

When societal institutions such as the church rationalize and even sanction dualism, then egoistic sentiments hold sway over the heart of human beings. In this sense, dualism and egoism go hand in hand. When universal love and humility are replaced by egoism and arrogance, then it becomes possible to hurt others and to hurt nature. When we forget our common origin and destiny, we easily fall into the vast pit of egoism. We see ourselves as an individual in a world of individuals, fighting a battle of survival for wealth in order to gain pleasures of the senses, rather than seeing ourselves as divine beings who are made in the same image, with the same frailties and potential. This degraded condition opens the doors to the deep-rooted fears and sense of inadequacy which translate into anger, resentment, hatred, greed and all negative tendencies in the human personality. The concept of dualism is the basis of the atrocities and injustices that have been committed in the history of the world. Under its control, human beings seek to control others and nature, and to satisfy their inner urges through violence because they cannot control themselves and express their deeper needs in constructive ways. In the Indian Vedantic tradition, duality or *dvaita* is seen as the greatest error of the human mind. For this reason all of the disciplines of Vedanta, Shetaut Neter, Yoga, Buddhism, Taoism and other forms of creation-centered spirituality are directed toward developing a correct understanding of human existence. When the underlying unity behind the duality is discovered, there can be no violence or ill will against others. This is the basis of non-violence. Harmony and spiritual enlightenment then arise spontaneously. Egoism now gives way to universal love and peace.

**Spiritual Transformation**

Transformation here is to be understood as not merely a change in specific behavior patterns or a change in feeling based on temporary circumstances, but as a complete re-orientation of the psychology of the individual. This re-orientation will lead to a permanent improvement in behavior and genuine metamorphosis of the innermost levels of the mind. Specifically, we will focus on Kemeticism as a system for psychological transformation wherein the individual ceases to be a limited individual, subject to the foibles and follies of human nature, and attains the state of transcendence of these failings.

**Mythology**

Most people hold the opinion that mythology is a lie, an illusion, fiction or fantasy. Mythology can be best understood as a language. However, it is a unique kind of language. An ordinary language is sometimes similar to another because it is a part of a family of languages. For example, Italian and Spanish words are similar. This similarity makes it possible for a person whose native language is Spanish to understand the meanings of some Italian words and somewhat follow along a conversation in Italian. Even so, mythology is much more intelligible than this. Mythology is more akin to music in its universality. If the key elements of this language of mythology are well understood, then it is possible to understand and relate any mythological system to another and thereby gain the understanding of the message being imparted.

**Enlightenment**

Enlightenment is the central topic of our study and the coveted goal of all practitioners of Yoga and Religion. Enlightenment is the term used to describe the highest level of spiritual awakening. It means attaining such a level of spiritual awareness that one discovers the underlying unity of the entire universe as well as the fact that the source of all creation is the same source from which the innermost Self within every human heart arises.

All forms of spiritual practice are directed toward the goal of assisting every individual to discover the true essence of the universe both externally, in physical creation, and internally, within the human heart, as the very root of human consciousness. Thus, many terms are used to describe the attainment of the goal of spiritual knowledge and the eradication of spiritual ignorance. Some of these terms are: *Enlightenment, Resurrection, Salvation, The Kingdom of Heaven, Christ Consciousness, Cosmic Consciousness, Moksha or Liberation, Buddha Consciousness, One With The Tao, Self-realization, Know Thyself, Heruhood, Nirvana, Sema, Yoga,* etc.

# Yoga Philosophy and the World Religious Philosophies Defined

Yoga philosophy and disciplines have developed independently as well as in conjunction with religious philosophies. It may be accurate to say that Yoga is a science unto itself which religions have used and incorporated into their religious philosophies and practices by relating the yogic principles to symbols such as deities, gods, goddesses, angels, saints, etc. The following is a brief description of yoga philosophy in comparison to the philosophies which developed alongside it.

**Yoga Philosophy**

Human consciousness and universal consciousness are in reality one and the same. The appearance of separation is a mental illusion. Yoga is the mystical and mindful (thoughtful, aware, observant) union of individual and universal consciousness by integrating the aspects of individual personality, thereby allowing the personality to be purified so that it may behold its true essence.

**Vedanta Philosophy**

Spiritual Philosophy of Mystical Psychology of Ancient India.

1- Absolute Monism: Only God is reality. All else is imagination.

2- Modified Monism: God is to nature as soul is to body.

**Monotheism**

Monotheism means the belief in the existence of a single God in the universe. Christianity, Judaism, and Islam are the major monotheistic religions. It must be noted here that the form of monotheism espoused by the major Western religions is that of an exclusive, personified deity who exists in fact and is separate from creation. In contrast, the monotheism of Ancient Egyptian, Hindu and Gnostic Christian traditions envisions a single Supreme Deity that is expressed as the Supreme Deity of all other traditions, as well as the phenomenal world. It is not exclusive, but universal.

**Polytheism**

Polytheism means the belief in or worship of many gods. Such gods usually have specific attributes or functions.

**Totemism**

Totemism is the belief in the idea that there is a relationship between kinship groups and specific animals and plants. Many scholars believe that religions which use these symbols are primitive because they are seen as worshipping those animals themselves. However, when the mythology behind the beliefs is examined more closely, the totems are understood as symbols of specific tutelary deities which relate the individuals to a group, and also to the greater workings of nature, and ultimately, to God.

**Pantheism**

1- Absolute Pantheism: Everything there is, is God. God and Creation are one.

2- Modified Pantheism: God is the reality or principle behind nature.

**Panentheism**

Term coined by KC F. Krause (1781-1832) to describe the doctrine that God is immanent in all things but also transcendent, so that every part of the universe has its existence in God, but He is more than the sum total of the parts.

**Kemeticism: Shetaut Neter: Ancient Egyptian Philosophy - Egyptian Yoga**


1-Monotheistic Polytheism - Ancient Egyptian religion encompasses a single and absolute Supreme Deity that expresses as the cosmic forces (gods and goddesses), human beings and nature.

## *Hinduism and Mahayana Buddhism*
1-Monotheistic Polytheism.


# The Tree Stages of Religion

While on the surface it seems that there are many differences between the philosophies, upon closer reflection there is only one major division, that of belief or non-belief. Among the believers there are differences of opinion as to how to believe. This is the source of all the trouble between religions. This is because ordinary religion is deistic, based on traditions and customs which are themselves based on culture. Since culture varies from place to place and from one time in history to another, there will always be some variation in spiritual traditions. These differences will occur not only between cultures, but even within the same culture. An example of this is Christianity with its myriad of denominations.

Therefore, those who cling to the idea that religion has to be related to a particular culture and its specific practices or rituals will always have some difference with someone else's conception. In the three stages of religion, Myth, Ritual and Mysticism, culture belongs to the myth stage of religious practice, the most elementary level.

# Myth → Ritual → Mysticism

An important theme, which will be developed throughout this volume, is the complete practice of religion, that is, in its three aspects, *mythology, ritual* and *metaphysical* or the *mystical experience* (mysticism - mystical philosophy). At the first level a human being learns the stories and traditions of the religion. At the second level rituals are learned and practiced. At the third level a spiritual aspirant is led to actually go beyond myths and rituals and to attain the ultimate goal of religion. This is an important principle, because many religions present different aspects of philosophy at different levels, and an uninformed onlooker may label it as primitive or idolatrous, etc., without understanding what is going on. For example, Hinduism and Ancient Egyptian Religion present polytheism and duality at the first two levels of religious practice. However, at the third level, mysticism, the practitioner is made to understand that all of the gods and goddesses being worshipped do not exist in fact, but are in reality aspects of the single, transcendental Supreme Self. This is evident in the Prt M Hru.

In the area of Yoga Philosophy and the category of Monism, there are little, if any, differences. This is because these disciplines belong to the third level of religion wherein mysticism reaches its height. The goal of all mysticism is to transcend the phenomenal world and all mental concepts. Ordinary religion is a part of the world and the mental concepts of people, and must too be ultimately transcended.

## Selected Spiritual Philosophies Compared

The Sages of ancient times created philosophies through which it might be possible to explain the origins of creation, as we saw above. Then they set out to create disciplines which could lead a person to discover for themselves the spiritual truths of life and thereby realize the higher reality which lies beyond the phenomenal world. These disciplines are referred to as religions and spiritual philosophies (mysticism-yoga). Below is a basic listing of world religious and spiritual philosophies.

## Table 1: Religious Philosophies

| RELIGIOUS PHILOSOPHIES | | | | |
|---|---|---|---|---|
| **Shetaut Neter** | **Vedanta** | **Samkhya** | **Buddhism** | **Yoga** |
| Non-dualist metaphysics. God manifests as nature and cosmic forces (neteru). Union with the Divine through wisdom, devotion and identification with the Divine. | Non-dualist metaphysics. God alone exists. Union with the Divine through wisdom, devotion and identification with the Divine. | Dualist Philosophy. Discipline of understanding what is real (God) from what is unreal (transient world of time and space). | Union with the Absolute through extinction of desire. | Mystical tradition: union of individual consciousness with the Absolute Consciousness (God) through cessation of mental activity by wisdom, devotion and identification with the Divine.<br><br>Example<br>☐<br><br>Egyptian Yoga<br><br>Indian Yoga<br><br>Christian Yoga<br><br>Buddhist Yoga<br><br>Chinese (Taoist) Yoga |

**Table 2: Religious Categories**

| Religious Categories | | | | |
|---|---|---|---|---|
| Theism<br><br>Belief in a God which will save you. | Atheism<br><br>Salvation by doing what makes you happy. There is no God, only existence, which just happened on its own without any help. | Ethicism<br><br>Salvation by performing the right actions. | Ritualism<br><br>Salvation by performing the correct rituals. | Monism<br><br>Salvation by understanding that all is the Self (God). |
| ⬇ | ⬇ | ⬇ | ⬇ | ⬇ |
| <u>Example</u><br><br>Orthodox Christian<br><br>Orthodox Islam<br><br>Orthodox Judaism | <u>Example</u><br><br>Epicureans<br><br>Charvacas<br><br>Atheists<br><br>Existentialists<br><br>Stoics<br><br>Humanists | <u>Example</u><br><br>Zoroastrianism<br><br>Jainism<br><br>Confucianism<br><br>Aristotelianism | <u>Example</u><br><br>Brahmanism<br><br>Priestcraft | <u>Example</u><br><br>Taoism<br><br>Spinoza<br><br>Cabalism<br><br>Sufism<br><br>Idealism<br><br>Christian Science<br><br>Gnosticism<br><br>Gnostic Christianity<br><br>Vedanta<br><br>Shetaut Neter<br><br>Buddhism |

# Origins and Basis of Mysticism in the Rau nu Pert em Hru

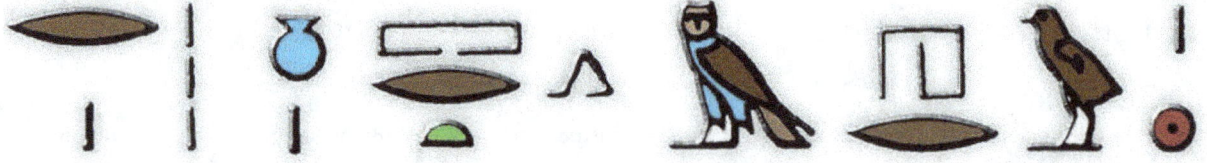

**Figure 5: Scene from the *Prt m Hru* of Lady Ta-ameniu**

## INTRODUCTION TO THE PHILOSOPHY OF The *PERT EM HERU*

## *What is The* Rau nu Pert em Hru?

The scriptures presented in this volume come from the extensive body of texts known as the *Egyptian Book of the Dead*. These texts span the entire history of Ancient Egypt, beginning with the *Pyramid Texts* in the early Dynastic period. These were followed by the *Coffin Texts*, which were followed by the late dynastic texts which were recorded on a variety of different media, of which the most popularly known is papyrus.

The teachings of mystical spirituality are contained in the most ancient writings of Egypt, even those preceding the Dynastic or Pharaonic period (4,500 B.C.E.-600 A.C.E). The most extensive expositions of the philosophy may be found in the writings, which have in modern times been referred to as "The Egyptian Book of the Dead."

It was originally known as "Rau nu Prt M Hru" or "Rau nu *Pert Em Heru*" or "Reu nu *Pert Em Heru*."

> *Rau*= words, teachings, liturgy, *nu* = of, *Prt* or *Pert* = going out, *em* or *m* = as or through, *Hru* or *Heru* = Spiritual Light or Enlightened Being (the God Heru). This may therefore be translated as: ***"The Word Utterances for Coming into the Spiritual Light (Enlightenment) or Becoming one with Heru."***

Thus, the *Rau nu Pert Em Heru* is a collection of words used to affirm spiritual wisdom and to direct a human being towards a positive spiritual movement. Each *Rau* or *Ru* contains affirmations of mystical wisdom that enables a human being to understand and experience that particular aspect of Divinity. The collection of these verses has been referred to as "Chapters," "Utterances" or "Spells" by Egyptologists. While the teachings presented in the *Rau nu Pert Em Heru* may be thought of as being presented in Chapters and referred to as such, they must also be thought of as special words which, when understood, internalized and lived, will lead a person to spiritual freedom. In this volume we will refer to the groupings of subjects as "Chapters" which may be better defined for our usage here as: a collection of Hekau -words of power- which impart a spiritual teaching and affirm that teaching, and by their repeated utterance make it a reality. The term "Ru" may be used as a shortened version of "Rau." It was not until after 1,500 B.C.E. that the collections of Ru were compiled in the form of papyrus scrolls and standardized to some degree. However, this process of standardization was not as rigid as the canonization of the books of the Bible, which had been separate scriptures relating to Christianity and Judaism prior to around the year 350 A.C.E.

In Egyptian mythology, Hru is not only a reference to the god who is the son of Aset and Asar (Isis and Osiris), but Hru also means "Day" and "Light." In fact, Day and Light are two of the most important attributes of the god Heru who is understood as the highest potential of every human being. Therefore, the title may also read as **"The Book of Coming Forth by (into) the Day," "The Guide for Becoming Heru," "The Chapters for Coming into the Light,"** or **"The Book of Enlightenment."** The writings were named "The Egyptian Book of the Dead" by modern Egyptologists who obtained them from the modern day dwellers of the area (northeast African Arabs) who said they were found buried with the Ancient Egyptian dead. In the interest of simplicity and consistency, the name "*Pert Em Heru*" will be used throughout this text.

The *Pyramid Texts* and the *Book of Coming Forth By Day* are similar in scripture and purpose. It is correct to understand that the texts referred to as the *Book of Coming Forth By Day* evolved out of the *Pyramid Text* writings. This is because the *Pyramid Texts* are the early form of the well-known texts, which have been called the *Book of Coming Forth By Day*. The *Pyramid Texts* are hieroglyphic writings contained in the pyramid tombs[11] of the kings of the early Dynastic period. Both are collections of utterances, originally recorded in hieroglyphic, which lead the initiate to transform {his/her} consciousness from human to divine, by purifying the mind with wisdom about the neteru (gods and goddesses, divine forces in the universe), and through the practice of rituals which promote personality integration and thus, spiritual transformation. Each of these constitute major treatises of Ancient Egyptian philosophy and together constitute an advanced, holistic system of spiritual development. All of these have as the main purpose to effect the union of the individual human being with the Transcendental Self. This philosophy of spiritual transcendence and enlightenment did not begin with the dawn of the Dynastic period in Ancient Egypt. The evidence from ancient texts and the history of Manetho show that the Ancient Egyptian history, which is known about, is only the descendent of a much more ancient era of Egyptian civilization.[12]

# Ancient Egyptian Religion as Yoga

## The Ancient Egyptians Practiced Yoga

> **yo·ga** (y½"g...) *n*. **1.** Also **Yoga**. A Hindu discipline aimed at training the consciousness for a state of perfect spiritual insight and tranquility. **2.** A system of exercises practiced as part of this discipline to promote control of the body and mind. **--yo′gic** (-g¹k) *adj*.
>
> —American Heritage Dictionary

Most people have heard of Yoga as an exercise, however, Yoga is a vast science of human psychology and spiritual transformation which includes physical and mental health as the prerequisite for further progress. Yoga, in all of its disciplines, was practiced in Ancient Egypt (Kemet, Kamut, Kamit or Ta-Meri) and is the subject of the Ancient Egyptian Mysteries. Yoga, as it was practiced in Ancient Egypt, included the disciplines of virtuous living, dietary purification, study of the wisdom teachings and their practice in daily life, psychophysical and psycho-spiritual exercises and meditation. Practitioners of Indian Yoga, Buddhist Yoga and Chinese Yoga (Taoism) today refer to all of these disciplines as Yogic disciplines. Therefore, the Ancient Egyptians were the first practitioners of Yoga Philosophy in our history. Through a process of gradually blending these in the course of ordinary life, an individual can effect miraculous changes in {her/his} life and thereby achieve the supreme goal of all existence, the goal of Yoga: Union with the Higher Self.

---

[11] Not to be confused with the Pyramids in Giza.
[12] See the book *Cycles of Time* by Muata Ashby

## The Term "Egyptian Yoga" and The Philosophy Behind It

Egyptian Yoga is what has been commonly referred to by Egyptologists as Egyptian "Religion" or "Mythology," but to think of it as just set of stories or allegories about a long lost civilization is to completely miss the greatest secrets of human existence. As previously discussed, Yoga in all of its forms was practiced in Egypt earlier than anywhere else in our history. This unique perspective from Africa provides a new way to look at life, religion and the discipline of psychology. Perhaps most importantly though, Egyptian mythology, when understood as a system of Yoga, gives every individual insight into their own divine nature. This is its true worth.

The teachings of Yoga are at the heart of *Prt m Hru*. As explained, the word "Yoga" is a Sanskrit term meaning to unite the individual with the Cosmic. The term has been used in certain parts of this book for ease of communication since the word "Yoga" has received wide popularity especially in western countries in recent years. The Ancient Egyptian equivalent of yoga is: *"Smai." Smai* (Sma, Sema, Sama) means union, and the following determinative terms give it a spiritual significance, at once equating it with the term "Yoga" as it is used in India. When used in conjunction with the Ancient Egyptian symbol which means land, *"Ta,"* the term "union of the two lands" arises.

*Smai Tawi*

(From Chapter 4 of the *Prt m Hru*)

In Chapter 4[13] and Chapter 17[14] of the *Prt m Hru,* a term "Smai Tawi" is used. It means "Union of the two lands of Egypt," ergo "Egyptian Yoga." The two lands refer to the two main districts of the country (North and South) In ancient times Egypt was divided into two sections or land areas. These were known as Lower and Upper Egypt. In Ancient Egyptian mystical philosophy, the land of Upper Egypt relates to the divinity Heru (Horus), who represents the Higher Self, and the land of Lower Egypt relates to Set, the divinity of the lower self. So **Smai Tawi** means "the union of the two lands" or the "Union of the lower self with the Higher Self. The lower self relates to that which is negative and uncontrolled in the human mind, while the Higher Self relates to that which is above temptations and is good in the human heart. Thus, we also have the Ancient Egyptian term **Smai Heru-Set,** or the union of Heru and Set. So Smai Tawi or Smai Heru-Set are the Ancient Egyptian words which can be translated as "**Egyptian Yoga.**"

---

[13] Commonly referred to as Chapter 17
[14] Commonly referred to as Chapter 176

Above from left to right are the symbols of Egyptian Yoga: *Sma, nfr, nkh, and htp*. The Ancient Egyptian language and symbols provide the first "historical" record of Yoga Philosophy and Religious literature. The Indian culture of the Indus Valley Dravidians and Harappans appear to have carried it on and expanded much of the intellectual expositions in the form of the Vedas, Upanishads, Puranas and Tantras, the ancient spiritual texts of India.

The hieroglyph Sma, "Sema," represented by the union of two lungs and the trachea, symbolizes that the union of the Higher Self and lower self leads to the One.

The hieroglyph, nfr, "Nefer," close in pronunciation to "Neter" (God), expressed by the union of the heart and the trachea symbolizes: That which is the most beautiful thing, the highest good, and the greatest achievement.

The hieroglyph, nkh, "Ankh," symbolizes the union of the male (cross-temporal) and the female (circle-eternal) aspects of oneself, leading to the transformation into an androgynous being. Thus, the two become One. The Ankh was also later used in Christianity and Hinduism as a symbol of divinity. Therefore, the Ankh is the unifying symbol, which links Egypt, India and Christendom.

The hieroglyph htp, "Hetep," symbolizes supreme peace, the final abode of all who satisfy the desire of their soul, union with its Higher Self: YOGA. Egyptian Yoga encompasses many myths and philosophies, which lead to the reunion of the soul with its Higher Self. Ancient Egyptian religion involves three major theological branches based on the Trinity (Amun-Ra-Ptah) which emanates out of the Hidden and nameless Transcendental Divinity. This Divinity is variously known under the following names: Nameless One, Nebertcher or Neberdjer, Tem, Neter Neteru, Amun, Asar, Ra, Kheper, and Aset. These names are to be understood as being synonymous. They refer to the same idea of an Absolute Supreme Being or transcendental reality from which the phenomenal world arises, as land rises out of an ocean.

The central and most popular character within Ancient Egyptian Religion of Asar is Heru, who is an incarnation of his father, Asar. Asar is killed by his brother Set who, out of greed and demoniac (Setian) tendency, craved to be the ruler of Egypt. With the help of Djehuty (Djehuty), the God of wisdom, Aset, the great mother and Hetheru, his consort, Heru prevailed in the battle against Set for the rulership of Kemet (Egypt). Heru's struggle symbolizes the struggle of every human being to regain rulership of the Higher Self and to subdue the lower self. With this understanding, the land of Egypt is equivalent to the {Kingdom/Queendom} concept of Christianity.

The most ancient writings in our historical period are from the Ancient Egyptians. These writings are referred to as hieroglyphics. Also, the most ancient civilization known was the Ancient Egyptian civilization. The proof of this lies in the ancient Egyptian Sphinx, as previously discussed. The original name given to these writings by the Ancient Egyptians is *Medtu Neter,* meaning "the writing of God" or *Neter Medtu* or "Divine Speech." These writings were inscribed in temples, coffins and papyruses and contained the teachings in reference to the spiritual nature of the human being and the ways to promote spiritual emancipation, awakening or resurrection. The Ancient Egyptian proverbs presented in this text are translations from the original hieroglyphic scriptures. An example of hieroglyphic text is presented on the front cover.

Egyptian Philosophy may be summed up in the following proverbs, which clearly state that the soul is heavenly or divine and that the human being must awaken to the true reality, which is the Spirit, Self.

*"Self-knowledge is the basis of true knowledge."*

*"Soul to heaven, body to earth."*

*"Man is to become God-like through a life of virtue and the cultivation of the spirit*

*through scientific knowledge, practice and bodily discipline."*

*"Salvation is accomplished through the efforts of the individual.*

*There is no mediator between man and {his/her} salvation."*

*"Salvation is the freeing of the soul from its bodily fetters, becoming a God through knowledge and wisdom, controlling the forces of the cosmos instead of being a slave to them, subduing the lower nature and through awakening the Higher Self, ending the cycle of rebirth*

*and dwelling with the Neters who direct and control the Great Plan."*

## The Ancient Egyptian Symbols of Yoga

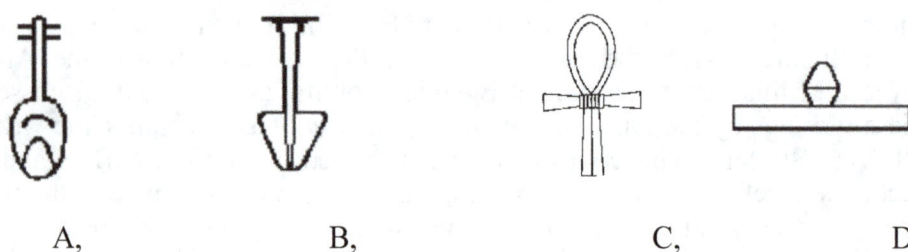

A,        B,        C,        D

The theme of the arrangement of the symbols above is based on the idea that in mythological and philosophic forms, Egyptian mythology and philosophy merge with world mythology, philosophy and religion. The hieroglyphic symbols at the very top (†) mean: **"Know Thyself," "Self-know**edge *is the basis of all true knowledge"* and (±) abbreviated forms of **Smai tawi,** signifies "Egyptian Yoga." The next four below represent the four words in Egyptian Philosophy, which mean **"YOGA."** They are: (A) **"Nefer"**(B) **"Sema"** (C) **"Ankh"** and (D) **"Hetep."**

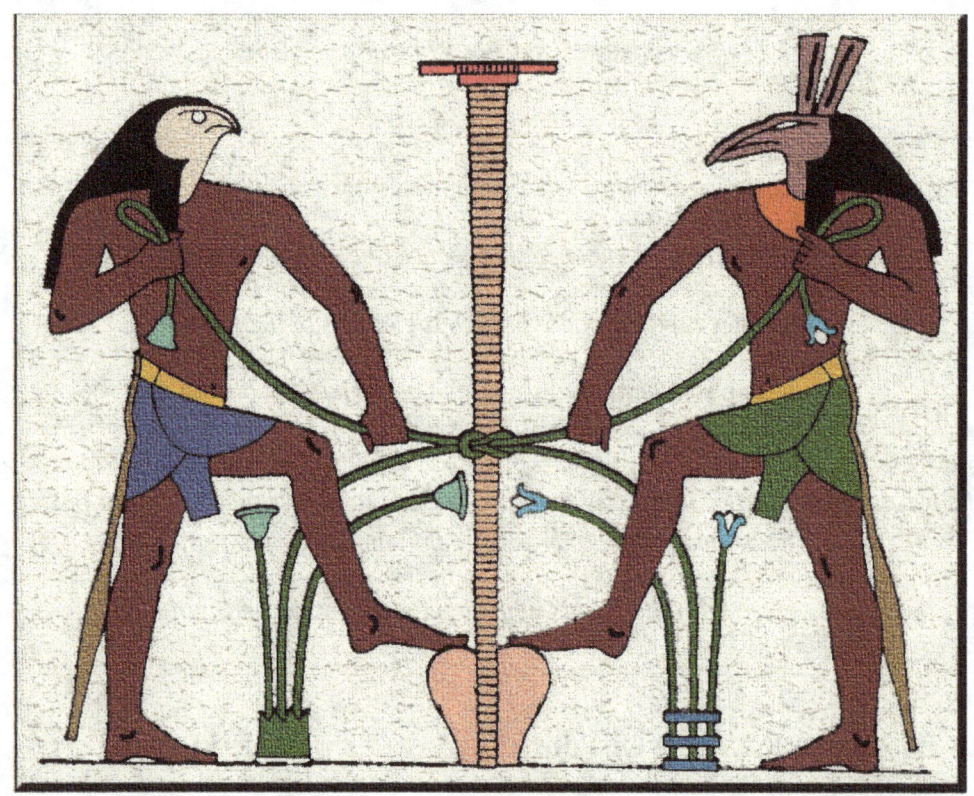

**Figure 6: Above: Smai Heru-Set,**

Heru and Set join forces to tie up the symbol of Union (Sema –see (B) above). The Sema symbol refers to the Union of Upper Egypt (Lotus) and Lower Egypt (Papyrus) under one ruler, but also at a more subtle level, it refers to the union of one's Higher Self and lower self (Heru and Set), as well as the control of one's breath (Life Force) through the union (control) of the lungs (breathing organs). The character of Heru and Set are an integral part of the *Pert Em Heru*.

# The Study of Yoga

The study and practice of Yoga involves three distinct phases. These are: *Listening to the wisdom teachings, Reflecting on those wisdom teachings and making them an integral part of your life, and Meditation, the art of transcending ordinary human awareness and consciousness.* Since a complete treatise on the theory and practice of yoga would require several volumes, only a basic outline will be given here.[15]

When we look out upon the world, we are often baffled by the multiplicity, which constitutes the human experience. What do we really know about this experience? Many scientific disciplines have developed over the last two hundred years for the purpose of discovering the mysteries of nature, but this search has only engendered new questions about the nature of existence. Yoga is a discipline or way of life designed to promote the physical, mental and spiritual development of the human being. It leads a person to discover the answers to the most important questions of life such as Who am I?, Why am I here? and Where am I going?

As stated earlier, the literal meaning of the word *Yoga* is to *"Yoke"* or to *"Link"* back, the implication being to link the individual consciousness back to the original source, the original essence, that which transcends all mental and intellectual attempts at comprehension, but which is the essential nature of everything in Creation, termed "Universal Consciousness. While in the strict sense, Yoga may be seen as a separate discipline from religion, yoga and religion have been linked at many points throughout history and continue to be linked even today. In a manner of speaking, Yoga as a discipline may be seen as a non-sectarian transpersonal science or practice to promote spiritual development and harmony of mind and body thorough mental and physical disciplines including meditation, psycho-physical exercises, and performing action with the correct attitude.

The teachings which were practiced in the Ancient Egyptian temples were the same ones later intellectually defined into a literary form by the Indian Sages of Vedanta and Yoga. This was discussed in our book *Egyptian Yoga: The Philosophy of Enlightenment*. The Indian Mysteries of Yoga and Vedanta represent an unfolding and intellectual exposition of the Egyptian Mysteries. Also, the study of Gnostic Christianity or Christianity before Roman Catholicism will be useful to our study since Christianity originated in Ancient Egypt and was also based on the Ancient Egyptian Mysteries.

The question is how to accomplish these seemingly impossible tasks? How to transform yourself and realize the deepest mysteries of existence? How to discover "Who am I?" This is the mission of Yoga Philosophy and the purpose of yogic practices. Yoga does not seek to convert or impose religious beliefs on any one. Ancient Egypt was the source of civilization and the source of religion and Yoga. Therefore, all systems of mystical spirituality can coexist harmoniously within these teachings when they are correctly understood.

---

[15] See the book *Egyptian Yoga: The Philosophy of Enlightenment* by Muata Ashby

The goal of yoga is to promote integration of the mind-body-spirit complex in order to produce optimal health of the human being. This is accomplished through mental and physical exercises which promote the free flow of spiritual energy by reducing mental complexes caused by ignorance. There are two roads which human beings can follow, one of wisdom and the other of ignorance. The path of the masses is generally the path of ignorance which leads them into negative situations, thoughts and deeds. These in turn lead to ill health and sorrow in life. The other road is based on wisdom and it leads to health, true happiness and enlightenment.

Our mission is to extol the wisdom of yoga and mystical spirituality from the Ancient Egyptian perspective and to show the practice of the teachings through our books, videos and audio productions. You may find a complete listing of other books by the author, in the back of this volume.

The Discipline of the Yoga of Wisdom is imparted in three stages:

1-<u>Listening</u> to the wisdom teachings on the nature of reality (creation) and the nature of the Self.

2-<u>Reflecting</u> on those teachings and incorporating them into daily life.

3-<u>Meditating</u> on the meaning of the teachings.

Note: It is important to note here that the duplicate teaching which was practiced in the Ancient Egypt Temple of Aset[16] of **<u>Listenin</u>**g to, **<u>Reflectin</u>**g upon, and **<u>Meditatin</u>**g upon the teachings is the same process used in Vedanta-Jnana Yoga of India of today. **The Yoga of Wisdom** is a form of Yoga based on insight into the nature of worldly existence and the transcendental Self, thereby transforming one's consciousness through development of the wisdom faculty.

## *The Egyptian Yoga Perspective on Death and its Influence on Gnostic Christianity*

Egyptian Yoga is the philosophy and disciplines based on Ancient Egyptian mysticism which promote spiritual enlightenment. Spiritual enlightenment means a movement towards transcending death. In this context, death is not regarded as a miserable event, but a transition into a higher form of being if one's earthly life had been lived in accordance with the teachings of Maat. In ancient times, the Ancient Egyptians were often referred to by people in neighboring countries as "the most religious people of all the world" because they seemed to constantly affirm spiritual principles in every aspect of their lives. This is not to be considered as a fanatical existence, the way we would look at cults or obsessed fundamentalist religious groups of our time. The Ancient Egyptians recognized the fact that there is a higher reality beyond the physical. Since all living beings must die someday, and move into that other reality, it makes sense to seek to understand, and become comfortable with death, and to revere the Supreme Divinity which was discovered to be the author and sustainer of all creation. Therefore, death should not be viewed as a pathetic event, but as an inevitable occurrence for which one should be prepared, and can even look forward to.

The creators of Ancient Egyptian mythology and religion recognized that if people live their lives independent of spiritual acknowledgment, life will lose its focus and human beings will lose their way. They will get caught up in the pettiness of human life and their egoism will lead them to untold

---

[16] See the book *The Wisdom of* Aset by Dr. Muata Ashby

sufferings both in life on earth as well as beyond. Therefore, life should be a process of affirming the spiritual reality, and even a worship of the Divine. In this manner life itself becomes a spiritual movement towards enlightenment, a process of promoting prosperity and peace. For more insights into the nature of death in light of *Prt m Hru* philosophy, see the sections of this book entitled "Readings for the Guidance of the Dying Person and their Relatives" and "Readings for the Guidance of the Spiritual Aspirant."

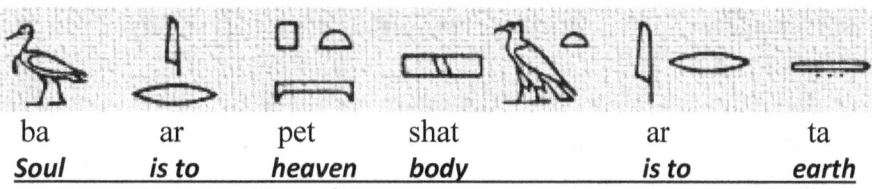

| ba | ar | pet | shat | ar | ta |
|---|---|---|---|---|---|
| *Soul* | *is to* | *heaven* | *body* | *is to* | *earth* |

From the Prt m Hru of the *Pyramid Texts* (3,200-2,575 B.C.E.)

The passage above shows that the fundamental teaching from the ancient period of Ancient Egyptian mystical philosophy never held a hope for a "physical resurrection." This understanding was carried over into Gnostic Christianity, which developed in Ancient Egypt during the Roman Period, and became a source for controversy between the Gnostic Christians and the Orthodox Christians. The main difference between Orthodox Christianity and other religions seems to have been the insistence on a physical resurrection from the dead. While other religions proclaimed a spiritual transformation of some kind, the Orthodox Christians fervently believed and still believe in a mysterious bodily resurrection from the grave. The Gnostic *Gospel of Philip* strongly refutes the Catholic view of a bodily resurrection, calling these notions ridiculous and misunderstood by the orthodox community. The following excerpt from the Gnostic *Gospel of Phillip* brings home this point.

"Those who say that the Lord died first and then rose up are in error, for he rose up and then died. We are to receive the resurrection while we live."

Many Egyptologists have suggested that the Ancient Egyptians embalmed their dead with the idea that the dead person would attain immortality, and that the Ancient Egyptians believed that the physical body, which was mummified, would rise up again someday. This idea spurred many Hollywood[17] movies. The statements above, from the early and late periods of Ancient Egyptian culture, clearly show that the Ancient Egyptians never sought a bodily resurrection or eternal life in the physical body. They understood death as a passageway to the next existence, and just as the physical body needs nourishment, the spiritual body was also provided for by means of the subtle essence of the solid food that was buried with the mummy.

The Catholic Christian Church Fathers gradually moved away from a mystical interpretation of Christianity and formed a religious doctrine based on a bodily resurrection from death, leading to one's existence in heaven at the right hand of the Father. The Gnostic Christian leaders disagreed with this view. The same predicament was experienced in Islamic countries during the years immediately following the death of Muhammad (also Mohammed).

---

[17] Hollywood, Calif., area of greater Los Angeles known throughout the world as the home of the US movie industry.

The problem of human existence is the forgetfulness of the Divine essence of the Self and the identification with the body as the Self. Through concern with the body and its needs and desires, the true Self becomes identified with worldly concerns and the fulfillment of desires of the body, mind and senses. This is the development of the ego and individual soul. This identification with the desires of the body is what leads the soul to further ignorance of its true Self. It is the pursuit of desires that keeps the mind occupied with worldly thoughts such as the fear of disease and death of the body, the pursuit of pleasure and happiness, and the eradication of things which cause displeasure.

Gnosticism, Hinduism, Buddhism, Taoism and Ancient Egyptian Religion all emphasize the need to practice detachment and dispassion toward the body. These disciplines relieve the pressure of the lower desires, which impel a person to run after the illusions of life. These traditions hold that only through detachment is it possible to calm the mind enough for it to perceive the transcendental reality.

The constant preoccupation with the body is incessantly reinforced through many years of living with family and others in society. Such body consciousness leads to the conviction that the psychophysical complex (mind and body) is indeed the Self. It is this idea that is to be dispelled through the spiritual discipline of constantly turning towards the Divine (through the various disciplines of Yoga) instead of to the body and to the world of illusion.

This process becomes easier to understand through reflection on the fact that the body is composed of physical elements, which are themselves, transient. The body you have today is not the same as the one you had nine years ago. Every cell in your body has been regenerated. Even your bones are different. As surely as people are born, just as surely their body will someday cease to exist. Is it wise to hold onto something that you will definitely lose at some point in time? Impermanence is a given fact of life. Flowers grow, live and die. Insects grow, live and die. Yet people accept these changes. Why is it that people do not cry when the flower dies, or when a leaf falls from a tree and dies or for every creature in nature that has died? The fact is that it is not only death that causes fear, but attachment to that which died and has met the "unknown." So fear of death is due to ignorance of one's true nature.

Likewise, people hold on to life, no matter how miserable a situation they may be in, because they don't know any other way of thinking or acting, and also because they have the illusion that there is a chance they may find happiness someday or they may somehow come into some money. Wealth is a big illusion. You can read the papers and see how wealth destroys a person's peace of mind through the endless worries associated with acquiring, investing and protecting it.

Matthew 19

23. Then said Jesus to his disciples, Verily I say to you, That it is hard for a rich man to enter into the kingdom of heaven.

24 And again I say to you, It is easier for a camel to go through the eye of a needle, than for a rich man to enter into the Kingdom of God.

—Christian Bible

"Labor not after riches first, and think thou afterwards wilt enjoy them. He who neglects the present moment, throws away all that he hath. As the arrow passes through the heart, while the warrior knew not that it was coming; so shall his life be taken away before he knoweth that he hath it."

—Ancient Egyptian Proverb

An even greater illusion comes into play when a person tries to figure out which part of the body contains the soul. There is no body part which contains the soul or which can be considered to be the "Self." No body part can be called "me," yet somehow the conglomerate of thoughts, memories, physical body and senses is understood to be "me." This error or misunderstanding is the cause of human misery and pain because it involves the soul in the mishaps and troubles of the mind-body complex and its attending desires. If the mind and senses were transcended, these problems along with individual identification with the body-mind would cease, and the true Self would be discovered to be infinite and eternal. This is the discovery of the Saints and Sages. For this reason they have proclaimed that the soul has been overtaken by ignorance of its true Self, and due to this ignorance, it is subject to experience the pain of human existence.

A simple philosophical study of the body reveals the error in thinking that the body is the Self. If the senses fail to perceive, or a limb or organ ceases to operate, consciousness is still there. The awareness of being alive remains even if the perceptions of the senses or nerves fail. The practice of spirituality involves discovering that which transcends the body, as well as learning how to become attached to that transcendent reality as the truth, rather than remaining attached to the physical body and its desires and impulses, as well as to one's emotions throughout the ups and downs of human existence.

The world of unenlightened human existence is likened to being out in the middle of the ocean when there is a raging storm. The desires are the waves thrashing the mind about. Spiritual practice is the boat, which allows a person to weather the storm of the world with its ever-changing situations. It gives the power to move forward in life and not be disturbed by the choices, desires and unpredictability of the world-process.

# The Stages of Human Spiritual Evolution and Aspiration

## *The Format of this Book*

This book is written in a format which follows the manner prescribed for human spiritual evolution. Therefore, the following section will detail the ancient teachings of spiritual evolution and aspiration so that the reader may consciously be aware of the process which this book is striving to engender. The scribes of ancient times did not have a set order for the Utterances of the *Books of Coming Forth By Day*. They were prepared in accord with the needs, special inclinations and interests of those who requested that one be made for them. Many translators of the various Chapters or Utterances of Coming Forth By Day in modern times have also placed the utterances in accordance with their own understanding of the intent of the priests/priestesses. What follows is a compilation of the most important mystical utterances. It is a special sequence which is synchronous with the universal principles of spiritual evolution. The chapter numbers given by traditional Egyptologists will be provided as footnotes preceding each chapter for easy reference.

In Yoga philosophy, spiritual evolution is described as follows: Listening, Reflection and Meditation. All of the five major categories of yoga described before (Yoga of Wisdom, Yoga of Devotional Love, Yoga of Meditation, Tantric Yoga and Yoga of Selfless-Righteous Action.) can be found in the *Ru Prt m Hru*. A spiritual aspirant listens to the teachings, reflects upon their meaning and then enters into deep meditation on them.

**Table 3: The Stages of Spiritual Evolution**

| The Stages of Spiritual Evolution | In the Shetaut Neter (Egyptian Yoga) system, there are three stages of spiritual evolution. |
|---|---|
| 1- ***Aspiration***- Students who are being instructed on a probationary status, and have not experienced inner vision. The important factor at this level is awakening of the Spiritual Self, that is, becoming conscious of the divine presence within one's self and the universe by having faith that there is a spiritual essence beyond ordinary human understanding. | 1- **The Mortals:** *Students who were being instructed on a probationary status, but had not experienced inner vision.* |
| 2- ***Striving***- Students who have attained inner vision and have received a glimpse of Cosmic Consciousness. The important factor at this level is purgation of the self, that is, purification of mind and body through a spiritual discipline. The aspirant tries to totally surrender "personal" identity or ego to the divine inner Self which is the Universal Self of all Creation. | 2- **The Intelligences:** *Students who had attained inner vision and had received a glimpse of Cosmic Consciousness.* |
| 3- ***Established***- Students who have become IDENTIFIED with or UNITED with GOD. The important factor at this level is illumination of the intellect, that is, experience and appreciation of the divine presence during reflection and meditation, Union with the Divine Self, the divine marriage of the individual with the universal. | 3- **The Creators or Beings of Light:** *Students who had become IDENTIFIED with or UNITED with the light (GOD).* |

The three steps of spiritual practice (myth, ritual and mystical philosophy and experience) which complete the practice of religion, follow the formats described above closely. Many students of Ancient Egyptian religion have focused on the religious stories of Ancient Egypt as mythical fables or superstitious rantings from a long lost civilization. In the Egyptian Yoga Book Series, we successfully show how the teachings of mystical spirituality were carefully woven into and throughout Ancient Egyptian Mythology. Ancient Egyptian Religion centers around the understanding that every human being has an immortal soul and a mortal body. Further, it holds that creation and the human soul have the same origin. How can this momentous teaching be proven and its reality experienced? This is the task of Mystical Spirituality (religion in its three phases and/or the practice of Yoga disciplines).

Thus, it is evident that the *Ru Prt m Hru* utilizes the universal principles of mystical spirituality and mystical religion. The *Prt m Hru* lays heavy emphasis on Ritual, Spiritual Wisdom and the Mystical Union with the Divine. One more subheading may be added, that is, Mythology. The spiritual wisdom is to be studied and deeply reflected upon, and this will lead to a transformation in one's personality. This process constitutes the journey that a spiritual aspirant must follow in order to go from mortality to immortality. However, in ancient times, the first level of religion, the myth, was well known by all people in Ancient Egyptian society. So the first Yogic step of listening to the teachings or the first step of religion, learning the myth, was more part of the socialization of the culture. A person would learn it as they were growing up and would not require an introduction such as has been presented in the first part of this book. Therefore, their practice would be more advanced than a present day aspirant. They would go right into the practice of the rituals, and begin to learn the mystical implications of these as they relate to the myth of Asar, Aset and Heru, which they already knew so well. Thus, we will combine the universal principles of mystical spirituality and mystical religion and arrange this volume in accordance with the following criteria. Part 1 will treat the following subjects: Presentation of the myth upon which the *Prt m Hru* is based, Gloss on the Myth, Gloss on the Philosophy behind the Myth and the *Prt m Hru*. Part 2 will present the translated scripture of *Prt m Hru* as follows: Awakening, Wisdom and Ritual, Transformation- affirmations for reflection and advancement, and Mystical Union.

## The Evolution of The Book of Coming Forth By Day
### *Phases of Ancient Egyptian Literature*

| | |
|---|---|
| Myths (Pre-Dynastic Period) Shetaut Asar-Aset-Heru The Myth of Asar, Aset and Heru | Books of Coming Forth By Day Example of famous papyruses: Papyrus of Any Papyrus of Hunefer |
| Shetaut Atum-Ra The Myth of Creation | Papyrus of Kenna Greenfield Papyrus, Etc. |
| Pyramid Texts (c. 5,000 B.C.E. or prior) | Monumental Inscriptions and Theological Treatises |
| Pyramid of Unas Pyramid of Teti, Pyramid of Pepi I, Pyramid of Mernere, Pyramid of Pepi II | Example: Temple of Seti 1. Temple of Aset, Temple of Hetheru, Shabaka Inscription, Stele of Djehuty (Djehuty) Nefer, Hymns of Amun, etc. Hermetic Texts |
| Wisdom Texts (c. 3,000 B.C.E. – Ptolematic Period) Precepts of Ptahotep Instructions of Any Instructions of Amenemope Etc. | |
| Coffin Texts (c. 2040 B.C.E.-1786 B.C.E.) | |
| Papyrus Texts (c. 1570 B.C.E.-Roman Period)[18] | |

---

[18] After 1570 BC they would evolve into a more unified text, the Egyptian Book of the Dead.

Egyptian Book of the Dead Hieroglyph Translations Volume 4

# The Ancient Egyptian Scriptures

**Pyramid Texts 5,000 B.C.E.**

**Coffin Texts 3,500 B.C.E.**

**Papyrus Texts 2500 B.C.E.-300 A.C.E**

## The Origins of the Scriptures of Prt m Hru

As mentioned earlier, the texts which comprise the *Rau nu Prt m Hru* originate in the far distant past. In the form of the *Pyramid Texts* they were codified as utterances which when understood and practiced could lead the practitioner to reach expanded levels of consciousness. This was symbolically referred to as gaining power over the gods and goddesses and becoming a Glorified Soul. The antiquity of the scriptures is attested to by some of the rubrics used on some chapters. For example, the rubrics for some of the versions of Chapters 31 and 36 state that they *were originally found* (not created) *by Hertataf(Hardedef) at Khemenu, the city of the god Djehuty (Djehuty), while on a tour of inspection of the temples of Egypt.* Some variants assign the finding to *Semti*, who was a king in the first Dynasty. For this and other reasons it can be said that the scriptures originated in Pre-dynastic times, but were codified in Dynastic times.

The common view of the *Pyramid Texts* is that they are the earliest known versions of the "Book of the Dead." They seem to be compositions of scripture which refer to a king who is part of a ritual wherein offerings are given in the temple and spells are uttered or chanted for the purpose of attaining power or control over the spirits of the dead and over the gods and goddesses. This has been the traditional interpretation by Egyptologists and others who have not had the opportunity to study and practice the mystical teachings from around the world. If these studies are entered into with an open mind and if one is willing to read the texts within the context of mysticism, and an expanded belief in the potential of human experience, a much different understanding arises from the literal interpretations which have been provided thus far. From a mystical perspective, it must be understood that the utterances of the "*Prt m Hru*" were not only for individuals as they were approaching the time of death or who had already died, but they also incorporated rituals designed to engender a mystical experience in the participants. These initiates were not waiting or just preparing for the time of death to use the knowledge in the Netherworld. They were interested in discovering the mysteries of the other world even while still alive. Thus, the book is not for the dead, but for those who truly want to become alive. Therefore, earliest known versions of the texts are compositions of scripture which refer to an initiate who is part of a ritual wherein offerings are given and special words are recited, uttered or chanted for the purpose of transforming the consciousness of that individual, to attain power or control over the spirits of the demons (the egoistic tendencies) and over the gods and goddesses (virtuous qualities).

We will not attempt to provide a literal translation of the texts since this would lead to intellectual stagnation. It would be like reading a poem and trying to apply its meaning literally and critiquing it on its grammatical merits. Mystical literature should be understood as a grand metaphor which seeks to explain the origins of creation and humanity, along with providing an understanding of the transcendental modes of consciousness and the human experience. These modes may be termed as *Higher Consciousness, God, The Supreme Being, Universal Soul, Supreme Consciousness, etc.*

**Figure 7: Coffin of Hent-Mehit, Singer (Chanter) of Amun, 21st dynasty showing anthropoid (human) features, texts and vignettes.**

So a mystical teaching, while existing in an historical context, is in reality not concerned with history or ordinary human reality, since these are, in the end, transient, illusory and irrelevant to the attainment of higher consciousness. Therefore, while certain historical information is needed to set a context for our study in relation to world history, an emphasis will be placed on revealing the mystical meaning contained in it, because it is this meaning alone that will lead the spiritual aspirant to attain the goal of mysticism, that of transcending ordinary human consciousness and discovering the deeper realities that lie within the heart. In this sense the *Prt m Hru* is absolutely true and factual in every detail. Mystical teachings are primarily concerned with the here and now as well as the transcendental wisdom, and not specifically with any particular historical event. The use of mythological stories and ritual traditions should not be confused with history. Myths are used by Sages in order to convey mystical teachings about the human condition and the mysteries of the human heart. Thus, any study which does not affirm the transcendental nature of a myth is relegated to understanding only the superficial (exoteric) meaning of a teaching.

In the earlier times, the teachings of the Medtu Neter (Divine Speech- Egyptian Mysteries) and Shetaut Neter (The Secret Way of the Spirit) were inscribed in the mortuary pyramids of the wealthy nobles. These texts are called *Pyramid Texts.* Later, the texts were inscribed on the mortuary coffins themselves. These texts are referred to as *Coffin Texts.* The next evolution in the codification of the Ancient Egyptian teachings was the use of papyrus paper.

The versions of the *Prt m Hru* which were recorded in the later periods of Ancient Egyptian history are not exactly the same as those which were inscribed in the earliest periods. While most of the teachings of the later versions can be traced to earlier origins, many new utterances were added by different priests and priestesses. Therefore, the exposition of the teachings represents an evolution in mystical thought which in many ways was refined and expanded over a period of more than 5,000 years.

Thus, the later versions are a combination of ancient, original teachings and more modern expansions and additions to the teachings, which were not part of the original. The earlier texts did not include vignettes. The addition of vignettes is an important evolution in the transmission of the teaching since it adds a new dimension to the visual quality of the scripture. The vignettes first appear in the *Coffin Text* period.

**Figure 8: Coffin of Hent-Mehit, Singer (Chanter) of Amun, 21st dynasty showing anthropoid (human) features, texts and vignettes.**

Certain scriptures, such as Chapters 16 and 143, were always included in a vignette (illustrated, embellished with pictures) form, and never included text. Along with this, it should be understood that the teachings presented in the book itself are implicit, meaning that there is a certain amount of understanding which one must already have in order to fully understand the book even before picking it up for the first time. Also, once the book is picked up and studied it must be understood that its wisdom is not only transmitted by words, but also through the visual or pictorial nature of the scripture itself. The process of initiation serves to provide the student with information about the symbols and the subtle meanings or nuances of the philosophy. This is why, with the exception of Chapter 4[19], there are few explanations or glosses in the text itself. Certain Chapters, such as Chapter 33[20], are like compilations and refinements of earlier concepts. While containing their principles, there are no groupings of utterances in the earlier works which compile the *Negative Confessions* or *Precepts of MAAT* and the concepts or laws

---

[19] Generally referred to as Chapter 17
[20] Generally referred to as Chapter 125

which must be followed in order to be pure of heart, as found in the later papyrus versions of the *Prt m Hru*. This aspect of the later versions does not represent a new concept or innovation, but a refinement and an expansion of that which was present at the inception of the teaching and first recorded in the form of the *Pyramid Texts*.

## The Order of The Chapters

The collection of writings in the *Prt m Hru,* dedicated to spiritual enlightenment, are separate but complementary passages which may or may not relate directly to each other. The original format of the texts which are now referred to as the "Book of the Dead" was a collection of related texts which may be described as injunctions, admonitions or affirmations, hymns, litanies and chants related to promoting and bringing into reality the spiritual enlightenment of the individual initiate. These early texts are now known as the *Pyramid Texts.* These passages may be accurately referred to as "Chapters" or "Utterances." However, the ancient term was "Rw" (**roo** or **rau**, meaning "group of words to be spoken"). It is notable that the text and illustrations within the various papyri do not always coincide and that different scrolls contain the same utterances in different orders. This points to the fact that there is no correct order in which the utterances must be presented nor is there a prescribed number of utterances which must be included in a volume in order for it to be considered a complete book. Also, the hieroglyphic scripture could be written in either a vertical or horizontal form, from right to left or left to right, and some chapters have variants, making their length variable. Some chapters, like Chapter 10, even obtain special instructions expressing the need to copy the texts as it is found, when making new scrolls of the *Prt m Hru*. Thus, some chapters like 4 and 31, have a short and long version. Consequently, there was no set length for a papyrus scroll of the *Prt m Hru*. Its length could range from a few feet to 70 or 80 feet or more in length. In ancient times certain chapters would be chosen by individuals in accordance with their feeling or the direction of their spiritual preceptors (priests and priestesses).

**Figure 9: <u>Coffin of Ipi-Ha-Ishutef</u>** Coffin texts version of Pyramid Texts that later appear in modified forms in the later papyrus *Prt m Hru*

**Figure 10: Outer Coffin of Hapiankhtifi, 12th Dynasty, Middle Kingdom,**

Pert-m-Heru from *Pyramid Texts* (3,200-2,575 B.C.E.):

Verse 1.
1.1.  ba    ar    pet    shat    ar    ta

**1.2.  Soul is to heaven body is to earth**

1.3.  The soul belongs to heaven and the body belongs to the earth.

Pert-m-Heru from *Papyrus Texts* (332 B.C.E.- c. 30 B.C.E.):

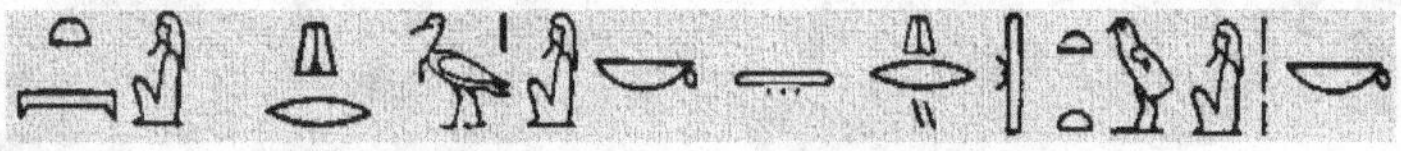

Verse 1.
1.1.  pet    kher    ba - k    ta    khery    tutu - k

**1.2.  heaven under jurisdiction soul thine, earth jurisdiction of image - thine**

1.3.  heaven has control over the soul and is where your soul goes, earth has control over the physicality of the personality and is where the image of your soul, the physical body stays.

As the hieroglyphic scriptures above show, there are some concepts which existed in the earliest era of Kamitan/Kemetic culture which were maintained, over a period of thousands of years, down to the very late era. There are some utterances, chapters and concepts, which appear in most or all of the surviving copies. Some of these include Chapter 1, which pertains to coming forth by day, Chapter 9[21], which pertains to being triumphant over the enemies and understanding the deeper mystical wisdom about the nature of the Divine, and Chapter 36[22] which pertains to coming forth into the ultimate light, implying transformation from mortal human life into immortality and oneness with the Divine.

This presentation represents a new look at the *Prt m Hru*, the Ancient Egyptian compilation for scriptures dedicated to the purpose of attaining spiritual enlightenment, more fully translated: Ancient Egyptian Book of Coming Out of the World and Into Spiritual Enlightenment. It is the fruit many years of research into the mythology, mystical philosophy and culture of Yoga in Ancient Egypt. Also, it is the fruit of inner work by the author in the form of meditation on and spiritual practice of the teachings contained in the *Prt m Hru*. It is highly recommended that the reader should study the following volumes by the author first, before reading the *Prt m Hru* text in Part 2 of this volume. This advice is given because the teachings for coming into enlightenment which are contained in the *Prt m Hru* were not designed to be read by those who have not been initiated into the philosophy of Maat and Shetaut Neter. Therefore, it is suggested that the reader study the extensive introduction in Part 1 of this volume and also acquire the following volumes by the author as a further introduction to the mystical wisdom teachings of Ancient Egyptian Yoga Philosophy: *The Asarian Resurrection, The Ancient Egyptian Bible* and

---

[21] Generally referred to as Chapter 17
[22] Generally referred to as Chapter 30

*The Mystical Teachings of the Asarian Resurrection.* The translation presented here is original, by the author, based on the original hieroglyphic texts. It is not intended as a literal, word for word treatise but as a prose translation in common English for better understanding. This format will better convey the meaning in terms that people in modern culture can more easily comprehend.

The *Rau nu Prt m Hru* is not a Bible, in the strict understanding of the term, from a religious-mythological point of view. As previously mentioned, religion has three levels of practice. First, there is the mythology upon which the religion is based. The text(s) that presents the story and basic beliefs of the religion is what constitutes the Bible of the particular religion. For example, in Christianity the religion is based on the myths related to the story of Jesus. This is what is presented in the Christian Bible, the myth. The words that are uttered in the church mass every Sunday are later developments of the tradition based on the myth. They represent the second stage of religion, the *Ritual* stage. In the same way, the myth that the *Ru Prt m Hru* is related to the story of Asar, his incarnation on earth, his death and resurrection but the myth is not told in the *Prt M Hru* texts themselves. The scripture which relates the story of Asar is the Bible, proper, of Ancient Egypt.[23] Therefore, the Bible of Ancient Egypt is the collection of scriptures containing the myth(s) related to the divinity. These were compiled in the book *The Asarian Resurrection: The Ancient Egyptian Bible.* However, the utterances contained in the *Prt M Hru* book deal with the rituals related to the myth, i.e. the resurrecting Asar, the central teaching of the myth of Asar. This was explained in the books *The Asarian Resurrection: The Ancient Egyptian Bible* and *The Mystical Teachings of the Asarian Resurrection* also by the author. The *Prt m Hru* constitutes the utterances that are to be read, recited or chanted as a means of taking the teachings of the myth to the next level of practice, the ritual.

As occurs with the *Christian Bible*, *The Bhagavad Gita* and other texts, many people do not see the *Prt m Hru* as a book of spiritual principles and affirmations for transforming the mind. Rather, they insist that it is to be believed word for word. If this is the case, and if certain words, customs or ideas cannot be understood by theologians and scholars the *Prt m Hru,* it will become the object of many different interpretations and consequently, arguments. For this reason, the religious beliefs of the translator of the texts, which may or may not be in agreement with the original scriptural meaning, may influence the translation and therefore, the reader should exercise caution when choosing a translation to use for study. In the case of the *Prt m Hru*, scholars have consistently attempted to deny and downplay any mystical significance that may be found in the texts. This has served to minimize the understanding of the text and degrade the overall meaning of the spiritual philosophy behind it.

Another factor is that since languages change over time, it is necessary to update the translations on a regular basis. Present day English speaking people would not be able to understand the original King James Version of the Bible which was written only 387 years ago, much less scriptures that were written over 1,700 years ago. However, the essence of a teaching can be discerned and brought forth by those who are initiated into the correct understanding and practice of religious philosophy in its three steps[24]. This is why updates to the translations by qualified scholars are necessary. Another important factor is that there are new discoveries that arise from time to time which may alter the timelines of the *Prt m Hru*, the Christian Bible and other texts or elucidate a new meaning of the old text, which in turn may affect the meaning of the teachings. This has been a major task which this volume, **Mysticism of the Prt m Hru: The Book of Enlightenment,** has attempted to perform in reference to the scriptures presented.

---

[23] See the book *The Ausarian Resurrection: The Ancient Egyptian Bible* by Muata Ashby.
[24] Myth, Ritual and metaphysical (Mysticism).

The question and struggle is to determine how best to provide a translation without reinterpreting the text. Some translators provide a word-for-word translation which means that each word is translated individually, but this is often difficult to understand since the nuances of the culture, inflections and grammar of ancient times is pretty much alien to modern society. Some translators work individually, while others work in committees. It is thought that committees would do a better job since its individual members would be less susceptible to deviation from the original texts. Some translators work individually, but their work is checked by a committee. In contrast to the Christian Bible, the *Prt m Hru* has been translated relatively few times (a few dozen) in the last 175 years. However it faces some of the problems that the Biblical scriptures face. There are several thousand Christian Bibles produced for people in various languages. Unfortunately, some of these Bibles were produced by translators who were not checked by any committee. Others could not even read the original texts, but gave their rendition anyway, and still others were simply paraphrased by people who thought they were conveying a meaning, but instead deviated from the original texts substantially. Some may want to promote a conservative agenda or a liberal agenda. Others may want to highlight a particular doctrine or political view over another, etc. So under these circumstances, it is not surprising that in the days of slavery in America, when Christian slave owners wanted to justify their ownership of slaves, some Bibles were produced espousing interpretations of scriptures and commentaries on those scriptures which promoted sexist and racist ideas. Paraphrases can convey the meaning of certain texts more easily than the word for word translations, but can also more easily reflect the doctrinal viewpoints of the translators. Therefore, it is important to know who has produced the book and if they have or had any ulterior motives or hidden agendas in their work. Many people feel that when they pick up a Christian Bible, they are holding the "Word of God." This idea has been engrained in the minds of many people for so many years that most do not question the contents of the Bible they are reading, and even become hostile when their illusions are challenged. They brand anyone who deviates from the concepts they have accepted as blasphemers or worse. All the while they are filling themselves with ignorance which will hurt their own spiritual evolution and accordingly, humanity as a whole.

Like the Christian Bible translations, the translations of the *Ancient Egyptian Book of Coming into Enlightenment* poses important problems because the meanings of some of the ancient symbols are not understood in part or at all by the scholars. This is due, in part, to the fact that the use of the hieroglyphic language died out in the middle of the first millennia of the common era (around 500 A.C.E.). This break in the initiatic tradition accounts for some of the loss in terms of the meanings of rare glyphs. However, just as modern language adopts new terms and allows others to fall out of usage, the Ancient Egyptian language as it is understood today can still convey the teachings with remarkable lucidity.

The third level of religion is mysticism. This level requires that the practitioner of the rituals understand the myth and its ultimate purpose. Thus, this volume contains a compendium of the myth. However, there is no substitute for the complete text with reproductions of the vignettes prepared by the Ancient Egyptian Sages themselves which have been compiled in the book *The Asarian Resurrection: The Ancient Egyptian Bible.* Along with that volume it is recommended that the serious student study the detailed commentary of the myth in the book, *The Mystical Teachings of the Asarian Resurrection* as well as the lecture series on the Asarian Resurrection, available on audio tape by Dr. Muata Ashby.

## *The Versions of the* Prt m Hru

The Ancient Egyptian scriptures today referred to as the "Book of the Dead" evolved through at least three phases, stages or editions. These are referred to by most Egyptologists as "recensions" or "versions" (editions). This classification generally follows a historical outline of the development of the central universities of Ancient Egypt. In ancient times there were four main centers of philosophical scholarship. These were the main Temple in the city of Anu (Greek-Heliopolis), the main Temple in the city of Waset (Greek-Thebes), the main Temple in the city of Hetkaptah (Greek-Memphis) and the Temple in the city of Abdu, the center of the worship of Asar. Anu, Waset and Hetkaptah were the capital cities of the country in different historical periods. These were the schools attended by the Greek students of philosophy, Pythagoras being one of the most famous. Abdu remained as the spiritual center of Asarian(Osiris) worship throughout history.

The *Pyramid Texts* are regarded by Egyptologists as being the first versions of the *Prt m Hru*. This is known as the **Anunian Recension,** and it is regarded as containing 759 utterances (chapters). These are regarded as belonging to the *Old Kingdom Period,* (cultural period of development- Dynasties 1-5). The next grouping of writings of the *Prt m Hru are referred to as Coffin Texts*. They are regarded as belonging to the *Middle Kingdom Period* (Dynasties 11-12). They were inscribed on wooded coffins and include complete utterances from the *Pyramid Texts* along with completely new ones. These texts are regarded as containing 1,185 invocations (utterances, chapters). In the city of Waset the priests/priestesses created a new version of *Prt M Hru*. These are usually referred to as the **Wasetian (Theban) recension** of the *Prt m Hru*. The **Wasetian Recension** adopted several texts from the older recension but added many more new ones. This recension is found on papyrus scrolls and one of its principal features are the extensive vignettes. In the very late period (after 600 B.C.E.), most papyri included a possible total of 192 chapters. These are usually referred to as the **Saite Recension** (Greco-Roman Period). This edition was written in hieratic text, including vignettes and contained only a few Hymns and sections of Chapter 33 which concern the Great Judgment and the Confessions of Innocence (42 principles of Maat).

The entire panorama of Ancient Egyptian theology can be thought of as a university system. Within a university, many colleges may be found. Each may specialize in a particular aspect of a subject while working harmoniously with other subjects presented in the other colleges within the university system. Likewise, the theology of Ancient Egypt emerged all at once but aspects of it were developed in different periods, by different schools or colleges which emerged within Ancient Egyptian history with the purpose of emphasizing and espousing particular perspectives of the theology, thereby popularizing certain teachings and divinities at different times. The earlier edition of the *Prt m Hru* originated in the College of Anu and was based on the Supreme Being in the form of "Ra." The next important edition developed in Waset. It was based on the Supreme Being in the form of "Amun" or "Amun-Ra." Both the Anunian and Wasetian teachings are to be regarded as emphasizing more of a devotional aspect of spiritual practice. They are referred to as "Theban Theology." The College of Hetkaptah (Memphis) developed a tradition that was based on the Supreme Being in the form of "Ptah." The Memphite teachings are referred to independently as "Memphite Theology" and are to be regarded as emphasizing more of a philosophical and psychological aspect of spiritual practice and were not used in exactly the same manner as the writings now referred to as the collection of chapters known as "Book of the Dead." The teachings of the Temple in the city of Abdu are a direct extension of the Anunian teachings, as they deal with the mythology related to the grandson of Ra, i.e. Asar. The later editions will be discussed at length in the following sections, as well as in the glosses and notes throughout this book.

The **Anunian edition** was inscribed in the pyramids of the early kings of Ancient Egypt in hieroglyphics. It is thus known as the *Pyramid Texts*. Some parts of it were inscribed in coffins, papyri, tombs, and steles. It should be noted that while this period roughly corresponds to 5,000 B.C.E.- 3,000 B.C.E., this is only the period in which the writings were codified (set down in hieroglyphic text). There are archeological and anthropological indications that the teachings existed prior to this period, in the vast reaches of so called "pre-history" referred to as the "Pre-dynastic" period.

The **Wasetian edition** (Theban-cultural period of development- Dynasties 18-20) can be found on papyri in hieroglyphics. The writings were partitioned into chapters with titles, but were still not given any definite order in the collection. These texts can be found after the cultural period of the 20$^{th}$ dynasty in hieroglyphic text as well as hieratic text.

Another version is recognized, called **Saite** or **Ptolemaic edition.** The Ptolemies were the Greek descendants of one of Alexander the Great's generals who took control of Egypt after Alexander had died. It is the latest cultural period of Ancient Egyptian history in which the country was besieged by outside conquering nations (Persians, Greeks, and especially the Romans) as well as internal social disintegration due to wars, breakdowns in social order and periods of civil unrest, martial law or the absence of government order altogether. In this edition, the chapters were arranged in a definite order and were written in hieroglyphics as well as hieratic text. However, this order was not absolutely rigid, nor did all the papyri follow what might be considered a sequential pattern for reading and studying purposes. It was considered sufficient that the chapters be present in the scroll (Ancient Egyptian book form).

The texts used for this present translation rely on the older versions (*Pyramid Texts* and *Coffin Texts*) in reference to the general themes of Kemetic spirituality content and as a method of determining the proper order of the collection of writings. Since the papyrus versions are summaries of the writings of the *Coffin Texts*, which are themselves expansions on the *Pyramid Texts*, the later versions (papyrus versions) are good sources in reference to the titles and format of separation of the chapters as well as the presentation of vignettes and the conciseness of writing in the presentation of certain concepts, for in the later versions, there is to be found a refinement of the verses which appeared in the earlier texts. The collection presented in this volume represent the most mystical chapters taken from all versions of the *Prt m Hru*. In this volume, when discussing writings from the *Pyramid Texts*, they will be referred to as "utterances." When discussing writings from the *Coffin Texts*, they will be referred to as "invocations," and when discussing the Papyrus Texts they will be referred to as "chapters." It should be noted that the use of the words *invocations, utterances*, or *chapters* can be confusing since in the *Pyramid Text* and *Coffin Text* writings, utterances can be as short as one sentence or as long as a long essay akin to the chapters of the later texts.

Due to the lack of diligence in transcribing the texts in ancient times, some of the chapters were duplicated within the same scroll, sometimes exactly the same way and at other times with grammatical errors, errors in meaning or minor changes that are inconsequential to the overall mystical importance of the teaching. In later papyruses, many innovations and expansions and sometimes even embellishments on the scripture can be found. These are not always in keeping with the intent of the original scriptures, those at the inception of the teaching. In these cases the errors, duplications or concepts not in keeping with the original scriptures and which may even be considered degradations in the philosophy, such as the *ushabti*[25] (*Coffin Text* 472) teachings or the predilection to remain in the Sekhet Hetep (enjoying heavenly pleasures) as opposed to moving forward into the Sekhet Yaru and on to discover and become one with Asar, have been either repaired, incorporated into one chapter or omitted altogether. Some of these discrepancies can also be accounted for by the vast periods of time since the scriptures were created, and also the intervening periods of social disturbances which have occurred. Keeping this in mind, it is remarkable that despite the minor discrepancies, the scriptures of Coming Forth from the early period of the *Pyramid Texts* to the Late period of the *Papyrus Texts* in the Ptolemaic and Roman Conquest Periods, display a faultless concordance of mythology and yogic mystical philosophy.

The occurrence of errors in the *Prt m Hru* should not be surprising to the student of Ancient Egyptian scripture. In fact, all scriptures from around the world including the Bible, the Koran, Bhagavad Gita, The Tao, and others, in themselves or their related scriptures, contain errors, both grammatical and/or contradictions in meaning. This is due to the vast amount of writing as well as the vast intervening periods of time between the writings, the versions, compilations etc., of the same scripture. The refinement of any scripture, as any book, depends on not writing, but rewriting. Those scriptures written independently and by different personalities at different times are bound to display inconsistencies. These should not be a basis for viewing that scripture in a negative light, but should promote understanding and a keen eye which knows how to sift truth from untruth. Added to these issues is the fanatical reverence of some aspirants. Some people have developed the opinion that simply because a text is ancient, that it must necessarily be correct in every detail. Further, many people believe that if a text is not ancient, it cannot be authentic or correct. This of course translates to the implication that modern day Sages are not to be revered as the Sages in ancient times. These are of course, misconceived ideas of the ignorant. In fact, the teachings are to be imparted by living spiritual teachers and authentic spiritual teachers have always updated and interpreted the teachings. This was true in ancient times and continues to be true today.

A true spiritual aspirant is not like an orthodox, narrow-minded personality who must believe that every single word in a particular scripture is "exactly" correct, or otherwise wrong and must be discarded altogether. An Ancient Egyptian proverb admonishes that true spiritual aspirant goes to the "essence of the meaning" without being distracted by minor concerns in grammar or correspondences of unimportant aspects of the scripture which have little bearing on the essence of the teachings.

"Strive to see with the inner eye, the heart. It sees the reality not subject to emotional or personal error;
it sees the essence. Intuition then is the most important quality to develop."

"Never forget: the words are not the reality, only reality is reality;
picture symbols are the idea, words are confusion."

"It takes a strong disciple to rule over the mountainous thoughts
and constantly go to the essence of the meaning; as mental complexity increases,
thus will the depth of your decadence and challenge both be revealed."

—Ancient Egyptian Proverbs

---

[25] See the section of this book entitled "The choice of chapters" in Part II of this volume.

## Language, Pronunciation, Spelling and Meaning

The authors of all of the world's scriptures were divinely inspired, however, they worked with the limited instrument of the human personality, which is in itself prone to error. This was true in ancient times as it continues to be true in modern times. The pursuit of perfection in life is not found in a perfectly written scripture. In any case, none exist, for one person's perfection can be another person's garbage. What is good for one person is not necessarily good for another. People have different tastes, opinions, etc., because they come from different walks of life, and not because one thing is intrinsically better than the other. Therefore, while one person likes one scripture over another, this does not mean that one is better than another. It simply means that one scripture appeals to one person's sensibilities, based on their cultural background, personality inclinations, etc. Further, just as it is impossible to know the exact pronunciations of words in old English, and yet it is possible to understand what writers like Chaucer and Shakespeare meant, it is unnecessary to know the exact pronunciations of Ancient Egyptian words where the meaning is well established. The teaching of the Ancient Egyptian *Myth of Ra and Aset*[26] bears out the importance of the essence of meaning as opposed to the spoken words. Further, since Ancient Egyptian language experienced at least three major periods of evolution (Old Kingdom, Middle Kingdom and New Kingdom), when determining pronunciations, like the spellings, we are faced with period differences, regional differences and personality differences. Some texts have different spellings for the same word within the same papyrus. Add to this the differences between colloquy[27] and script, the ever-changing regional accents and expressions, and the question then becomes which pronunciations are we talking about, the ancient or late ones, the ones of the north or those of the west, etc.? Remarkably, the hieroglyphic texts underwent less changes than one might expect given the excessively long period of time for its usage, the longest in the world at over 5,000 years! Consider that it has only been since the beginning of the eighteenth century that western culture "standardized" language. Were it not for this, modern English speaking people might not understand the English speeches and writings of George Washington. Pronunciations can be approximated in many ways: correlating to Greek words, which correspond to the Ancient Egyptian, correlating to Coptic words derived from Ancient Egyptian, extrapolating from known words, etc. However, these will always be approximations and a spiritual aspirant should not spend too much time with this issue, but rather on understanding the philosophy behind the words, for no matter how they are pronounced or spelled, the essence remains intact and effective, and the essence is the meaning. The following Hermetic[28] proverbs give insight into the feelings of the Ancient Egyptian Sages on the question of pronunciation and meaning.

"Keep this teaching from translation in order that such mighty Mysteries might not come to the Greeks and to the disdainful speech of Greece, with all its **looseness and its surface beauty**, taking all the strength out of the solemn and the strong - the energetic speech of Names."

Ancient Egyptian literature has its own style and feeling, and the *usage* of the Kemetic language is exhorted above other languages because it is precise and more importantly, concise in its descriptions and terms, with a minimum of flowery language (*looseness and surface beauty*) while achieving a certain poetic sentiment. The absence of superfluous parts of speech in a language will consequently allow the language to be more direct and concise and thus, less subject to misinterpretation. This injunction is

---

[26] See the book Mysticism of the Goddess by Dr. Muata Ashby
[27] **col·lo·quy** (kŏl'ə-kwē) *n., pl.* **col·lo·quies**. **1.** A conversation, especially a formal one. **2.** A written dialogue.
[28] Ancient Egyptian philosophy in the Greek-Roman period.

relating the idea that Kemetic grammar, the system of inflections, syntax, and word formation of the language, is simple, containing a minimum of prepositions[29] and adjectives to embellish a subject. Many Greeks who came to Ancient Egypt were not interested in changing their ways to suit the teaching, but rather wanted to suit the teachings to their lifestyles without making the fundamental changes that are necessary to attain enlightenment. In modern times, many people use Kemetic symbols and may even utter certain Ancient Egyptian words, but do so without true feeling or insight because they do not *live* the culture. In essence, they continue to be worldly people while appearing to adopt some spiritual philosophy, and therefore, their efforts fall far short of what is necessary to make the teachings effective. Thus, it is all right to translate the word *Asar* (Kemetic) into *Osiris* (Greek), as long as the meaning remains intact. However, this can only occur if one is deeply involved in the culture and if one is led by an authentic spiritual teacher. The objection above is not on the basis of pronunciation, but that in translating it the Greeks apparently wanted to make the terms into something other than what they were supposed to be. Thus, just as it is virtually impossible for a twentieth century English speaking person to communicate with a ninth century English speaking person, it would be more than likely that an Egyptologist of our time could not communicate verbally with an Ancient Egyptian person, but could communicate by writing hieroglyphs back and forth. The meaning, which transcends words and their time period of usage, is higher than the words themselves.

This is emphasized in the second proverb below where the objection is raised, because when the translation is made into Greek, the meaning is often lost. The language is taken but not the teaching (*the teachings keepeth clear the meaning of the words*). The meaning gives value to the words and thus, any words are useful in describing the transcendental essence. For example, the word "Neberdjer" from Ancient Egypt, "Brahman" from India, "Tao" from China, etc., have the same meaning, the Transcendental Absolute. A Chinese person using the word "Tao" will discover the same truth as the person who follows Kemetic Philosophy using the word "Neberdjer." Thus, meaning is more important than grammar or pronunciation since the mind assigns meaning first and pronunciation afterwards. Further, the medium of words cannot fully capture the perfection of thought because it is a limited medium. The fullness of the true essence of the Divine cannot be captured by any concept and words cannot capture the totality of any idea. However, sound and pronunciation do have legitimate purposes and uses in spiritual study and especially in the study of the Kemetic language.

## The Language of Names

> "Unto those who come across these words, their composition will seem most simple and clear; but on the contrary, as this is unclear, and has the true meaning of its words concealed, it will be still unclear, when, afterwards, the Greeks will want to turn our tongue into their own - for this will be a very great ***distorting and obscuring*** of even what has heretofore been written. Turned into our own native tongue, ***the teachings keepeth clear the meaning of the words***. For that its very ***quality of sound, the very power of Egyptian names***, have in themselves the bringing into act of what is said."

The Kemetic language is special in many ways because it reflects many universal cosmic principles of sound. An example of this is the Ancient Egyptian word "*mut.*" Mut means mother and it is reflected in "mata" of the Hindu language, "madre' of Spanish, "mother" in English, etc. The "m" sound is a

---

[29] In some languages, a word placed before a substantive and indicating the relation of that substantive to a verb, an adjective, or another substantive, as English *at, by, in, to, from,* and *with*. (American her. Dic.)

universal "seed sound" principle of motherhood. However, this is not an absolute rule because other words are used as well. The use of names in the Kemetic language is important because they act as keys to unlocking the mysteries of life, but this is true only for those initiated into the philosophy. In Kemetic philosophy, words are seen as abstract representatives of phenomenal reality. Since the mind is the only reality and the external world only reflects a conceptualized form based on an idea in God's mind, words are a higher reality when compared to the physical world and all Kemetic words are names for objects and/or concepts. In fact, Creation is a concept given a name and not an absolute, abiding reality in and of itself.

By studying the phonetic and pictorial (Kemetic language is not only phonetic, but also illustrative) etymology (the origin and development of a linguistic form) and etiology (the study of causes or origins) of names and applying the initiatic science, it is possible to decipher the mysteries of Creation by discovering the teachings embedded in the language by the Sages of Ancient Egypt.

For example, the Kemetic word "Pa" is central to understanding the deeper essence of nature, divinity and the gods and goddesses of the *Prt m Hru*. In the study of the word "Pa," philosophy as well as pictorial and phonetic associations must be considered. Along with this, the variations in spellings act to expand the possible associations and thereby also the appropriate meaning in the given usage. Sometimes the very same words may be used, but its usage in different texts denotes a slight difference in the nuance of the meaning in accordance with the usage. This aspect of assigning the proper meaning of a word which is used even with the same spelling but in different contexts in different or even the same Kemetic scriptures, is an artistic development which comes to a translator with time. Thus, there is no right or wrong interpretation, but there is greater and greater approximation to the higher intended truth behind the teaching as research moves forward. Also, it should be remembered that research here implies not only studying books, but also meditation and introspection, as well as living in accordance with the philosophy.

# Table 4: Study of the Kemetic Word "Pa"

| The Etymological, Etiological, Phonetic and Pictorial Study of the Kemetic word "Pa" | Meaning |
|---|---|
| A- | A- **Pa**- demonstrative, this, the, to exist |
| B- | B- **Pau** - Primeval Divinity- The Existing One |
| C- | C- **Paut**- Primeval time - remote ages- beginning time |
| D- | D- **Paut**- stuff, matter, substance, components which make something up. |
| E- | E- **Pauti**- The Primeval God; Primeval Divinity who is self-Created; Dual form relates to rulership of Upper and Lower Egypt |
| F- | F- **Pauti-u**- Primeval Divinity with male or |

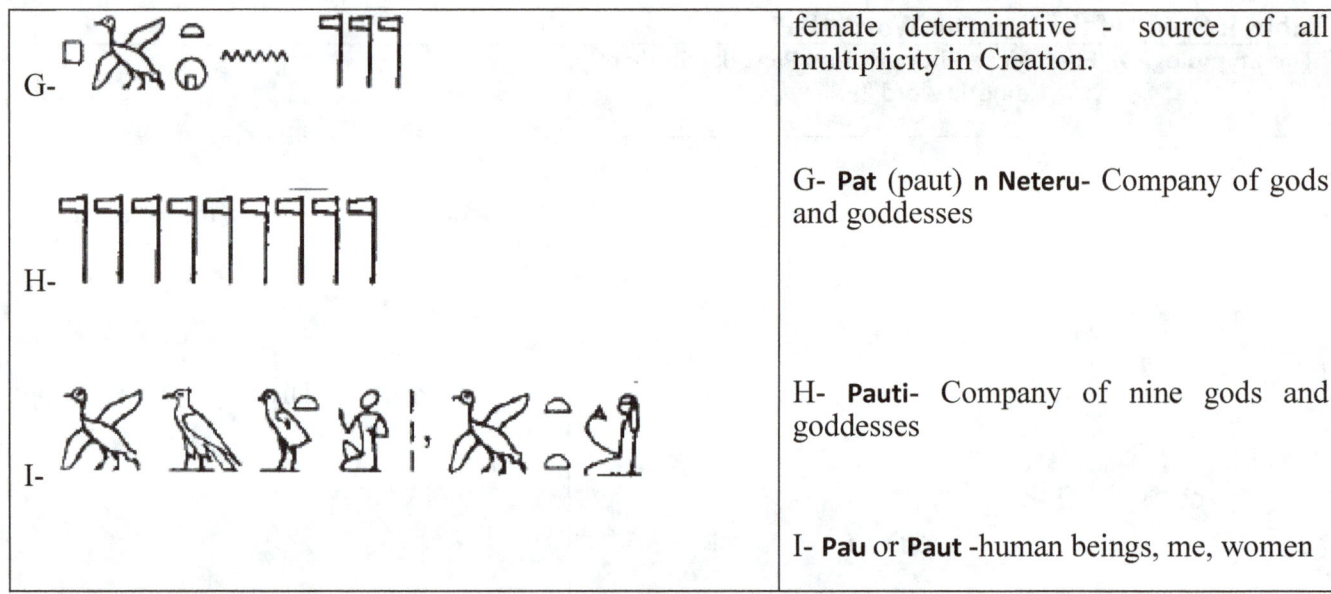

The Ancient Egyptian words and symbols related to the Company of Gods and Goddesses (Pauti) indicate several important mystical teachings. The root of the Ancient Egyptian word Pauti is *Pa* (Figure A). Pa means "to exist." Thus, Creation is endowed with the quality of existence as opposed to non-existence. *Pau* (Figure B) is the next progression in the word. It means the *Primeval Divinity*, the source of Creation. *Paut* (Figure C and D) is the next evolution of the word, Pau, meaning *primeval time* and *the very substance out of which everything is created is the one and the same*. *Pauti* is the next expression of **Pa** and it has two major meanings. It refers to the *Primeval Divinity* or Divine Self (God) (Figure E). *Pautiu* refers to *Pauti* but in plural, as well as being a gender specific term implying, *the Divinity as the source of the multiplicity in creation*. In the Ancient Egyptian language, like Spanish for example, all objects are assigned gender. Also, Pauti refers to the deities who comprise the *Company of Gods and Goddesses* (Figure G and H). **Paut** (men) or **Pautet** (women) also refers to *living beings*, especially *human beings* (Figure I).

Therefore, the most important teaching relating to the nature of Creation is being given here. The gods and goddesses of the creation are not separate principles or entities. They are in reality one and the same as the Primeval Divinity. They are expressions of that Divine Self. However, they are not transformations of or evolutions from the Divine Self, but the very same Divine Self-expressing as Creation. So even though God is referred to as a primordial deity who did something a long time ago or set into motion various things, in reality God and Creation are one and the same. Ra is the "God of the primeval time" as well as the gods and goddesses of Creation which sustain it all the time. With this understanding, it is clear to see that God is not distant and aloof, observing Creation from afar. The Divine Self is the very basis of Creation and is in every part of it at all times. This is why the terms *Pa-Neter* and *neteru* are also used to describe the Divine. Pa-Neter means "The Supreme Being" and neteru means "the gods and goddesses." Also, the word "neteru" refers to creation itself. So neter-u emanates from Neter. Creation is nothing but God who has assumed various forms or neteru: trees, cake, bread, human beings, metal, air, fire, water, animals, planets, space, electricity, etc. This is a profound teaching which should be reflected upon constantly so that the mind may become enlightened to its deeper meaning and thereby discover the Divinity in nature.

The Divine Self is not only in Creation but is the very essence of every human being as well. Therefore, the substratum of every human being is in reality God as well. The task of spiritual practice and Yoga is to discover this essential nature within your own heart. This can occur if one reflects upon this teaching and realizes its meaning by discovering its reality in the deepest recesses of one's own experience. When this occurs, the person who has attained this level of self-discovery is referred to as having become enlightened. They have discovered their true, divine nature. They have discovered their oneness with the Divine Self.

In conclusion, it must be understood that Kemetic language is synonymous with Kemetic philosophy. As such, when speaking, one must adhere to truth. The ultimate truth is, that when we speak of objects, we are in reality speaking about principles, deeper basis of which is the Divine Self. When words are spoken, they immediately take on the first level of reality as they engender an image in the mind of the listener. When a listener acts upon what has been heard, the speech takes on a reality in the physical plane. Therefore, the speech is a reflection of an idea, a concept, and the physical reality is a reflection of speech. The cause underlying the concept is the real name of a thing, its higher reality, and this essence has no name or form in its potentiality, but only in its relative manifestation. This relative manifestation is the world of time and space and all living and non-living objects in it. Therefore, we have three levels of reality, the thought, the word and the actual object existing in the physical world. However, these are only relative realities since they are all ephemeral in nature and not abiding. The creative essence (God-transcendental consciousness) which gave power to the thought, the concept, is the source and substratum which lends temporary reality to the projection (thought, the word and the actual object).

Flowery and imprecise language as well as language that praises worldliness as opposed to the Divine (ex. language that promotes arrogance, pride and the illusion that human existence is abiding) distracts the mind away from this great practice. Thus, it becomes an agent of ignorance and confusion, fostering and sustaining a deluded notion of reality. This is the higher teaching which is otherwise espoused as *Maakheru* –"Truth of Speech." Therefore, truth is a higher reality in relation to words, language or symbols, etc. Thus, while one should endeavor to be as accurate as possible, understanding the meaning of the words and their teaching is more important than their pronunciation or spelling. The following Ancient Egyptian proverbs extol the ideals just introduced.

"If you are in authority, then you should do perfect things, those which will be remembered by posterity. Never listen to the words of flatterers or words that fill you with pride and vanity."

"Words cannot give wisdom if they stray from the truth."

"Words are not the reality, only reality is reality;

picture symbols are the idea,

words are confusion."

As one can imagine, studying the phonetic and pictorial etymology of names can be an extensive discipline and learning the Kemetic language entails much more than it would appear on the surface.

Exploring this aspect of Kemetic culture could take an entire lifetime and would fill several volumes. In fact, the Egyptian Yoga Book Series is the fruit of such researches, exploring the essential basis and practice of Kemetic mysticism, and more will come in future years. In this sense it is like no other language. It is a world in and of itself, apart from the spoken verbalizations used to communicate in ordinary human situations. It is a language of the soul and of the cosmos, mystical philosophy and spiritual enlightenment. It is a language designed to take the mind beyond words.

## *New Terms*

This volume will introduce new terminology to describe certain aspects of the writings contained in the *Prt m Hru*. The reason for this is, the terms that have been used by traditional Egyptologist have become outdated, and in order to have a clearer understanding, we must now progress to the use of terms and definitions which more closely approximate the meaning for our modern understanding. This is necessary because many of the terms which have been used are merely conventions devised by Egyptologists to account for Ancient Egyptian words and ideas, which have no direct translation in other languages. Therefore we must begin to study the terms and gain a new understanding and feel for these in their own language.

The pursuit of perfection in life does not come from discovering a grammatically perfect scripture, for there is none. It is gaining understanding from a scripture that speaks to us based on our karmic makeup (personality inclinations) as to the essence of our human existence, the Higher Self. In this sense, all the world's spiritual scriptures are perfectly capable of promoting spiritual enlightenment, for those to whom they appeal, if they are correctly understood and if allowances are made for human frailties. This is why a spiritual preceptor is so important on the spiritual path. That person can steer the mind when it is caught up in the petty issues of spiritual practice. That person is a guide to let the aspirant know how to deal with issues that on the surface seem like insurmountable contradictions or obstacles, which can bring an aspirant's spiritual evolution to a halt, but which are in reality insignificant misunderstandings to be out-stepped.

As stated earlier, in some cases, later versions of the *Prt m Hru* were refined or expanded and sometimes modified by the priests/priestesses or scribes of the later time. An example of this is the refinement of the concept of the neteru or gods and goddesses and their relationship to the initiate. In Utterances 273-274 of the *Pyramid Texts*, the concept of assimilating the neteru is put forth using the metaphor of eating the gods and goddesses and even cooking them as well. In Chapter 27 of the papyrus versions, the concept is refined to direct statements affirming knowledge of the true nature of the neteru and thus, the idea of becoming those same gods and goddesses by self-discovery. This concept is related to the original Kemetic concept of the consecration[30] idea (receiving and consuming the eye of Heru) which is contained in both the earlier texts (*Pyramid Texts*) as well as the later texts (papyrus versions) of the *Prt m Hru*. Where these additions and changes were in harmony with the earlier, original texts and added to the spiritual importance and understanding of the text, they were retained.

---

[30] This is the prototype for the Christian Eucharist ritual of consecrating items such as bread and wine in the Mass Ritual..

## *How To Study The Mystical Teachings Of The* Prt m Hru

The Papyrus of Ani, as it has come to be known, is an excellent example of the *Prt m Hru* text as it existed in the New Kingdom Dynastic period of Ancient Egypt. The hieroglyphic texts of Ancient Egypt, the teachings of Egyptian mystical spirituality are called "Khu" or "Hekau," meaning *utterances* or *words of power,* and are collectively known as "Medtu Neter," Words of The God or Neter Medtu - Divine Speech. Modern Egyptology, the scholarly study of Ancient Egyptian civilization from the early nineteenth century to the present, has labeled these *utterances* as *spells* or *incantations.* In a way this assessment is correct because these utterances are to be understood as words which, when spoken with meaning and feeling, can have a transforming effect on the mind, allowing expansion of consciousness. However, the Hekau should not to be understood in the context of Western magic or witches spells or voodoo, etc. To do so would be a grievous error of intellectual laziness and cultural egoism, trying to make simple correlations to lower forms of spiritual practice. This form of treatment would yield the conclusion that the Ancient Egyptian religion is merely a myriad of conflicting stories and the presumption that Ancient Egyptian spirituality is a conglomerate of idol worshipping and occult nonsense.

In ancient times, Ancient Egyptian spirituality drew followers from all corners of the world. Those who came from far away recognized the greatness of Egypt, which was the fruit of the Temple system of education. The Temple was a formidable power for human mental, physical and spiritual development, healthcare and social government.

Any study of mystical spirituality needs to be carried out from the perspective of the present. This means that the teachings need to be understood in the context of today and how it affects one's life right here and right now. What good would it do to know all about the history of what a Sage, such as Ptahotep, did and taught 5,000 years ago if it is not understood in the context of a teaching which can be used in the present? As the reader, whether or not you believe and practice the teachings or are simply interested in understanding them, you should look upon them from the perspective of something which is alive and viable for today. The following instructions are included for those who wish to seriously integrate the teachings into their lives for the purpose of discovering their deeper meaning and their power to transform the human mind.

Before undertaking this study, we need to establish the parameters by which we will explore the teachings. Many people do not realize that mystical spirituality is like an advanced form of psychotherapy, incorporating not only a keen understanding of psychology, human emotion, and social relationships, but also the relationship between individual human consciousness and Cosmic Consciousness. Unlike the discipline of Western psychotherapy or the psychological treatment of mental, emotional, and nervous disorders, mystical spirituality or psychology is not just concerned with the mentally insane and how to bring them back into the mainstream of society or normal human life. This is because this so called "normal" social structure cannot be so normal if it turns out psychotics or those who suffer from any of a class of serious mental disorders in which the mind cannot function normally and the ability to deal with reality is impaired or lost. These mental illnesses and psychoses include: anger, hatred, greed, lust, envy, jealousy, depression, schizophrenia, sadism, manic depressive psychosis, and paranoia. The structure of modern society is conducive to the development of social stresses, based on passion, greed and lust, as well as both physical and mental disease, due to pollution of the environment and the mind. The ordinary practice of religion does not incorporate a mystical aspect. This shortcoming is the source of strife and dysfunction in family relations, social relations and spiritual relations of in modern culture. Mystical spirituality integrates and develops not only the intellect, but also the emotions to deal with practical life and the will power capacity of the personality, all the while leading the soul to ultimate spiritual self-discovery. It promotes harmony in society, harmony with nature and harmony between humanity and the Divine. Therefore, mystical psycho-spiritual counseling is more powerful than ordinary psychoanalysis.

Mystical teachings should be studied in the context of a transpersonal discipline which not only seeks to promote the ordinary standards of "normalcy," but also to transcend these in order to achieve a supernormal mental, physical and spiritual level of health. This element is what differentiates ordinary thinking in psychology, sociology and medical science from the ideals of mystical teaching. The ordinary discipline seeks to settle for a worldly reward in the form of what is commonly accepted as peace and joy, but which is in reality, limited, ephemeral, fragile and illusory. Mystical psychology seeks to go beyond the ordinary and to discover the that which is to be known and which upon knowing, all is known, the Absolute, which transcends time and space. This idea is extremely important because ordinary human life cannot satisfy the inner need of the heart of a human being since it is transient, ephemeral and unpredictable. So no matter how well integrated ordinary psychology may help a person to become, they will be missing the spiritual dimension wherein lies the abiding fulfillment of the human being.

**Figure 11: Above left: Forms of the God Djehuty (Djehuty)/Djehuty**
The Creator of Hieroglyphic Text and Author of Medu Neter (Divine Words-Speech)

**Figure 12: Above right: Forms of the Goddess Maat/Maati**
The embodiment of truth, justice, regularity and harmony.

She is the bestower of Maak-heru (Spiritual Enlightenment)

## The Elements of the Human Personality

In order to properly understand the perspective of the Pert-m-Heru Egyptian Book of Coming Forth By Day [Enlightenment] it is necessary to have a foundation in the wisdom of the Parts or Elements of the Human Personality. It is important to understand the architecture of the human constitution. The *Prt m Hru* makes a distinction between these because the human personality is a conglomerate or composite of several aspects or levels of existence. These elements are not readily discernible to the ordinary person due to the lack of spiritual sensitivity. Further, one element may not be effective in all planes of existence. For example, the Ka may not be discernible in the Ta or Physical Plane, while the Khat may not be discernible in the Pet or Heavenly Plane. It is necessary to know about these, because in knowing them, one gains greater insight into the higher planes of existence and the teachings of the *Prt m Hru*. This section will concentrate on the subtle human anatomy and the anatomy of all existence. It will discuss the Physical, Astral and Causal planes of existence and their inner workings as they relate to the elements that compose the human personality. First we will review the themes and essential wisdom developed in the book *Egyptian Yoga: The Philosophy of Enlightenment.* Then we will proceed to look into the nature of the subtle spiritual Self with more detail and depth. The Ancient Egyptian concept of the spiritual constitution recognized nine separate but interrelated parts that constitute the personality of every human being.

Thus, the Sage looks on the body as a marionette, created with thoughts by the Self, or as a projection as in a dream. Having awoken from the dream, when the physical body dies, the Sage who has discovered {his/her} oneness with the Self remains as the Self and does not create any more bodies to further incarnate. This is because {he/she} has discovered {his/her} essential nature and there are no more desires for experiences as a human being. Thus, there is no cause for the creation of a new ego-personality. This is the state that Sages experience with respect to the waking world of ordinary human beings. They are no longer caught up in the illusion of the world. This is called Liberation, Salvation, Heruhood, Waking up, Meeting Asar, Resurrection, Nirvana, etc. This is the loftiest goal of human life. "Knowledge derived from the senses is illusory. True knowledge can only come from the understanding of the union of opposites."

–Ancient Egyptian Proverb

If you look at yourself objectively, you will realize that every cell in your body is changing from moment to moment, and that you are never the same as you were a moment ago. Even solid objects are changing and decaying, albeit at a slower rate, but eventually they will decompose into their constituent elements. In much the same way, the human body is changing and constantly moving towards extinction. But is this real? Is this change a quality of your inner Self? Upon closer examination, the real you is not changeable; the real you is Pure Consciousness and one with the Supreme Being who is eternal. Remember the teaching: **"The Great God inside the common folk"** from Chapter 17 of the *"Prt m Hru."* This is what it means. Your inner Self is one with the Divine Self. Initiatic science shows that the real you, the innermost Self, is unchanging.

What is it that is constantly moving, constantly restless from the time you wake up until the time you go to bed again? This is the thinking mind with all of the worries, all of the desires, all the beliefs, all of the ambitions and all of the regrets. These thoughts, worries, desires, beliefs, ambitions and regrets constitute your mental conditioning, your personality, and your ego-self-concept. Through the process of your human experience in the world, your mind has become conditioned to expect to see reality in a certain way and therefore, it perceives life according to its conditioning. This conditioning, your ego, is what is holding you back from being able to realize your innermost Self, which is all encompassing, all-knowing, and all-blissful contentment and peace.

Your ego-personality is like a movie character that emerges at the beginning of a movie and fades away at the end. The movie screen remains in order to receive images from other movies. In the same way your personality emerged out of your mental conditioning at the time of your birth and since then, it has never stopped changing, moving, craving and searching for fulfillment. Egoism is the feeling of separation from the Self and attachment to an illusory personality that arises out of the dream quality of consciousness. It is intensified by the distractions of the mind due to the pursuit of fulfillment of sensual desires. At the time of your death, the gross aspects of your personality (Khat and Ren) will cease to exist, but the impressions created through these in the unconscious will leave you still craving for the unfulfilled desires. This is because the deep unconscious mind with its conditioned impressions of desire, survives death and follows you into the Duat (astral plane) until you finally are born again in the earth plane to once again continue seeking fulfillment.

"Get thyself ready and make the thought in you a stranger to the world-illusion"
–Ancient Egyptian Proverb

The concept of relativity of time is expressed in the hieroglyphic text entitled, *The Songs of The Harper*. In one verse, the relativity of the passage of time is explained as follows:

"The whole period of things done on the earth is but a period of a dream."

This formula of the Harper, when put together with the *Coffin Text* formula given previously about the nature of Atum Ra (*after the millions of years of differentiated creation, the chaos that existed before creation will return; only the primeval god [31] and Asar will remain steadfast-no longer separated in space and time*) form an exceedingly powerful combination which should act as a fuse to ignite the mind's deeper insight into the nature of Self. The "period of millions of years" mentioned in the *Coffin Texts* is in reality the same as the period of a dream, and as you know, a long period of time can be experienced in a dream, but in reality nothing has happened, except that your consciousness has emanated a dream world. But as you also know, the dream world comes to an end and dissolves back into consciousness. In the same manner, God has emanated this world and will someday dissolve it back into the Primeval Ocean of potential consciousness. Consider your dreams. They may seem to occur over a period of hours. You may even experience the passage of years within your dream, and yet upon waking up you realize that the entire time you were in bed asleep for a few hours. In the same way, the entire period of the existence of the universe is nothing but the span of a short dream in the mind of God.

From an advanced perspective, neither time nor space can be said to exist as something that is real, just as time, space, matter or physical objects within a dream cannot be called "real." The entire dream world exists in the mind and does not require real time or space. The phenomenal world, which is experienced in the Waking State of consciousness, is also not real and does not exist except in the mind of God. This teaching is not only confirmed by the *Hymns of Amun*,[32] but it is also a primary teaching of Memphite Theology that is presented in the *Shabaka Inscription*.[33] In reality only eternity is real, and God

---

[31] Referring to the Supreme Being in the form of Atum-Ra
[32] See the book *Egyptian Yoga Volume II* by Dr. Muata Ashby
[33] See also Egyptian Yoga: The Philosophy of Enlightenment (Egyptian Yoga Volume I)

is eternity. Since all matter is in reality constituted of the thought energy of God, and the changes in matter are called time, it must be clearly understood that God is the only reality that exists.

God is eternity itself. The limited perceptions of the unenlightened human mind and senses are what human beings refer to as "time" and "space" awareness. However, the perception of time and space is due to the limitations and conditioning of the human mind and body. If it were possible to perceive the entire universe, then you would discover that there is only oneness, an eternal view that is not restricted to time and space. This is the view that God has towards Creation. The task of the spiritual aspirant is to grow out of the limitations of the mind and body and discover the Cosmic Vision that lies within. When this is accomplished, there is a new perception of the universe. This represents the death of the human being and the birth of the spiritual life in the human being.

God has assumed the form of the neteru or Pauti. These "neteru" are cosmic forces, energies that sustain the universe and which constitute "physical matter." Therefore, this "physical" universe is in reality the body of God and everything in it is Divine, from the smallest atom to the largest celestial bodies in the heavens. It must be emphasized that in this process, *The Universal Ba*[34] itself becomes the individual Ba of every human being, due to its association and identification with the feelings of the emotional body, *Ka,* and the cravings of the Physical body, *Khat.*

By practicing the disciplines of Maat, the initiate is able to curb the wanton desires of the ego and thereby strengthen the will of the intellect. The science of practicing virtue in life will serve to assist the aspirant to purify the heart (mind), to cultivate peace of mind, and thereby to develop insight into the innermost Self. At this stage, the movement or vibration in the Primeval Waters which caused the world to be, subsides. Just as a calm lake reflects a pure image, the purified mind will reflect the clarity of the Cosmic Soul. The waves, caused by movements of the mind, would once again become just as the waves in the Primeval Ocean before creation, silent, at rest, at peace.

Your innermost Self, the Cosmic Soul, is constantly interacting with the world through the mind. If you had yellow sunglasses on, when you look at anything you would see a yellow tinge. In the same way, when you look at the world through your conditioned mind and senses, your vision reflects the tinge of egoism and divergent thoughts, but most of all, ignorance of your true Self which causes body identification. If you were to eradicate your mental conditioning, you would see a different reality. This is the goal of the various disciplines of mystical spirituality, to purify the intellect, **Saa**. By developing your higher intellectual ability to cut through the illusions of life with the ax of wisdom, you purify your subconscious mind from all of the conditioning. It is this purification of Saa which can lead you to awareness of the Higher Self.

The philosophy of the four states of consciousness (waking, dream, dreamless sleep, undifferentiated (transcendental consciousness) is of paramount importance for the spiritual aspirant. A profound understanding of this teaching will lead you to develop subtlety of intellect in discerning the reality of the thoughts in your own mind as well as that which is real around you. In the book *The Cycles of Time*, we explored in depth, the practices of how this teaching is applied in everyday life in order to realize its significance at the deepest levels of the mind through virtuous living, the practice of Maat.

Maat philosophy provides us with a guideline for determining what is real and what is not. This is crucial to the correct operation of the mind because the mind supports whatever reality it believes to be

---

[34] The terms: The Universal, World Ba, Pa Neter, Amun, Nebertcher are to be understood as being synonymous.

true. You experience the world through your mind and senses. You have learned that these are valid criteria to determine the validity of the world and of your inner experience. Everything must be known through your rationalizing mind once it has been perceived by your senses. However, as we showed in the books *Egyptian Yoga: The Philosophy of Enlightenment* and *The Hidden properties of Matter*, what is normally considered to be real and abiding, solid matter, is nothing more than energy in its grosser states of being. It must be clearly understood that mental perceptions are not direct perceptions of matter. Your hand which you use to hold an object is itself a swirling mass of energy which is connected to other masses of energy conduits that lead to the brain. Sensual stimulus is an interaction between different forms of energy that registers in the brain centers in a specific manner. The mind perceives these stimuli by reacting to the centers and then acknowledges a perception. Therefore, perception occurs in the brain itself and not in the hand. Consider for a moment the situation of a paralyzed person or your own experience if a limb has fallen "asleep." In these eventualities, there is still a limb, but there is no perception. Why? Because the perception media, the senses, are incapacitated. Consider the possibility of the paralyzed limb coming into contact with an object. Did any interaction occur? From the standpoint of the observation yes there was some sort of interaction between two objects, but not from the standpoint of the person with the disability.

Now consider the Dream State of consciousness. When you have dreams you perceive various objects, you touch them and you may even feel you own them. They appear to be real and "feel" very solid and true. However, upon waking you realize that they did not exist and never did. They were simply energy forms, which you created out of the subtle astral matter and perceived through the deluded mind. They were fleeting masses of subtle energy that arose out of your own mind and were perceived by your own mind. You developed an illusory triad of consciousness during your Dream State and from this arose an entire world. Your waking ego self-concept dissolved and you became a new subject. This "new" you used the subtle senses to perceive objects which you yourself imagined to exist. This is the triad of *seer, seen and sight*. When you woke up, this triad dissolved into your waking consciousness as if it never existed. However, upon waking up, you did not wake up into a reality, but rather you moved into another form of triad.

The *triad* of human consciousness arises out of your inability to perceive reality without the mind and senses. The mind and senses along with your soul form the three elements of the triad. If you were to transcend the mind and senses, you would perceive reality directly through your soul. Only through direct perception is it possible to know the truth or reality. The teaching of the triad is expressed in the symbolism of the Divine Trinity, which arises out of the Primeval Ocean.

The whole idea here is that the world you perceive as real is illusory. The senses, which you use to perceive the world are illusory, and the mind which you use to perceive the world is also illusory. Therefore, there is only one factor left which qualifies as real. That factor is the *witnessing consciousness* that perceives all of the different states. Through spiritual practices (yoga of wisdom, yoga of action, yoga of devotion and yoga of meditation) you can gradually lead your mind to deeper and deeper levels of perception of the truth until you discover the Absolute Truth beyond all of the illusory layers of the mind.

This essay has been presented so that the practitioner may begin to understand the visualization that is desired by the *Prt m Hru* texts, when it is written that the initiate is to say statements such as the following ones in part tow of this volume as well as understand what part of the personality is being referenced in the ancient text and how that relates to the quest for immortality and enlightenment. They are mystic formulas designed to awaken the innermost memory of one's true and ultimate identity as one with the Divinity who has brought all into existence and who will also dissolve it. This is the ultimate discovery, coveted by all mystics of the world. In other words, the temporary mortal existence is not the ultimate reality.

# Compendium of the Main Religious Traditions and Gods and Goddesses of Ancient Egyptian Spirituality

Ancient Egyptian Religion: The Spiritual Culture and the Purpose of Life: Shetaut Neter

> "Men and women are to become God-like through a life of virtue and the cultivation of the spirit through scientific knowledge, practice and bodily discipline."
>
> -Ancient Egyptian Proverb

The highest forms of Joy, Peace and Contentment are obtained when the meaning of life is discovered. When the human being is in harmony with life, then it is possible to reflect and meditate upon the human condition and realize the limitations of worldly pursuits. When there is peace and harmony in life, a human being can practice any of the varied disciplines designated as Shetaut Neter to promote {his/her} evolution towards the ultimate goal of life, which Spiritual Enlightenment. Spiritual Enlightenment is the awakening of a human being to the awareness of the Transcendental essence which binds the universe and which is eternal and immutable. In this discovery is also the sobering and ecstatic realization that the human being is one with that Transcendental essence. With this realization comes great joy, peace and power to experience the fullness of life and to realize the purpose of life during the time on earth. The lotus is a symbol of Shetaut Neter, meaning the turning towards the light of truth, peace and transcendental harmony.

## Shetaut Neter

We have established that the Ancient Egyptians were African peoples who lived in the north-eastern quadrant of the continent of Africa. They were descendants of the Nubians, who had themselves originated from farther south into the heart of Africa at the Great Lakes region, the sources of the Nile River. They created a vast civilization and culture earlier than any other society in known history and organized a nation that was based on the concepts of balance and order as well as spiritual enlightenment. These ancient African people called their land Kamit, and soon after developing a well-ordered society, they began to realize that the world is full of wonders, but also that life is fleeting, and that there must be something more to human existence. They developed spiritual systems that were designed to allow human beings to understand the nature of this secret being who is the essence of all Creation. They called this spiritual system "Shtaut Ntr (Shetaut Neter)."

*Shetaut* means secret.

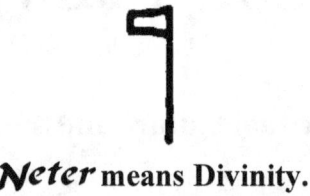

*Neter* means Divinity.

## Who is Neter in Kamitan Religion?

 "Ntr

**The symbol of Neter was described by an Ancient Kamitan priest as:**
**"That which is placed in the coffin"**

The term Ntr ⌒〇𓏏, or Ntjr 𓏏⌒〇, comes from the Ancient Egyptian hieroglyphic language which did not record its vowels. However, the term survives in the Coptic language as *"Nutar."* The same Coptic meaning (divine force or sustaining power) applies in the present as it did in ancient times. It is a symbol composed of a wooden staff that was wrapped with strips of fabric, like a mummy. The strips alternate in color with yellow, green and blue. The mummy in Kamitan spirituality is understood to be the dead but resurrected Divinity. So the Nutar (Ntr) is actually every human being who does not really die, but goes to live on in a different form. Further, the resurrected spirit of every human being is that same Divinity. Phonetically, the term Nutar is related to other terms having the same meaning, such as the latin "Natura," the Spanish Naturalesa, the English "Nature" and "Nutriment", etc. In a real sense, as we will see, Natur means power manifesting as Neteru and the Neteru are the objects of creation, i.e. "nature."

**Sacred Scriptures of Shetaut Neter**

The following scriptures represent the foundational scriptures of Kamitan culture. They may be divided into three categories: *Mythic Scriptures*, *Mystical Philosophy* and *Ritual Scriptures*, and *Wisdom Scriptures* (Didactic Literature).

| MYTHIC SCRIPTURES Literature | Mystical (Ritual) Philosophy Literature | Wisdom Texts Literature |
|---|---|---|
| **SHETAUT ASAR-ASET-HERU**<br><br>The Myth of Asar, Aset and Heru (Asarian Resurrection Theology) - Predynastic<br><br><br>**SHETAUT ATUM-RA**<br><br>Anunian Theology<br><br>Predynastic<br><br><br>Shetaut Net/Aset/Hetheru<br>Saitian Theology – Goddess Spirituality<br><br>Predynastic<br><br><br>**SHETAUT PTAH**<br><br>Memphite Theology<br><br>Predynastic<br><br>Shetaut Amun<br>Theban Theology<br><br>Predynastic | **Coffin Texts**<br><br>(c. 2040 B.C.E.-1786 B.C.E.)<br><br><br>**Papyrus Texts**<br><br>(c. 1580 B.C.E.-Roman Period)[i]<br><br>Books of Coming Forth By Day<br><br><br>Example of famous papyri:<br><br>Papyrus of Any<br><br>Papyrus of Hunefer<br><br>Papyrus of Kenna<br><br>Greenfield Papyrus, Etc. | Wisdom Texts<br>(c. 3,000 B.C.E. – PTOLEMAIC PERIOD)<br><br>Precepts of Ptahotep<br><br>Instructions of Any<br><br>Instructions of Amenemope<br><br>Etc.<br><br><br>**Maat Declarations**<br>Literature<br><br>(All Periods)<br><br><br>**Blind Harpers Songs** |

# Neter and the Neteru

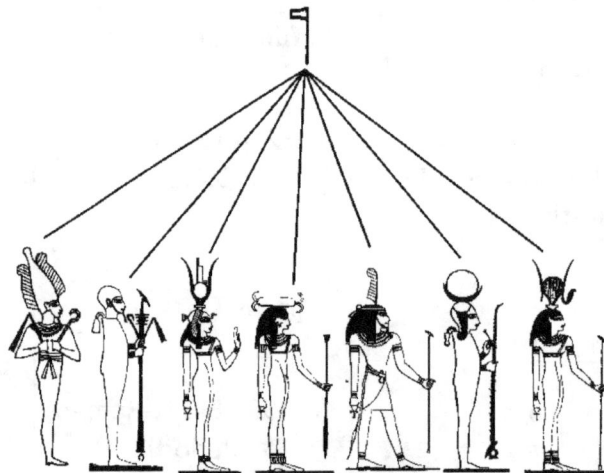

The Neteru (Gods and Goddesses) proceed from the Neter (Supreme Being)

As stated earlier, the concept of Neter and Neteru binds and ties all of the varied forms of Kamitan spirituality into one vision of the gods and goddesses all emerging from the same Supreme Being. Therefore, ultimately, Kamitan spirituality is not polytheistic, nor is it monotheistic, for it holds that the Supreme Being is more than a God or Goddess. The Supreme Being is an all-encompassing Absolute Divinity.

## The Neteru

"Neteru"

The term "Neteru" means "gods and goddesses." This means that from the ultimate and transcendental Supreme Being, "Neter," come the Neteru. There are countless Neteru. So from the one come the many. These Neteru are cosmic forces that pervade the universe. They are the means by which Neter sustains Creation and manifests through it. So Neterianism is a monotheistic polytheism. The one Supreme Being expresses as many gods and goddesses. At the end of time, after their work of sustaining Creation is finished, these gods and goddesses are again absorbed back into the Supreme Being.

All of the spiritual systems of Ancient Egypt (Kamit) have one essential aspect that is common to all; they all hold that there is a Supreme Being (Neter) who manifests in a multiplicity of ways through nature, the Neteru. Like sunrays, the Neteru emanate from the Divine; they are its manifestations. So by studying the Neteru we learn about and are led to discover their source, the Neter, and with this discovery we are enlightened. The Neteru may be depicted anthropomorphically or zoomorphically in accordance with the teaching about Neter that is being conveyed through them.

# The Neteru and Their Temples

**Diagram 1: The Ancient Egyptian Temple Network**

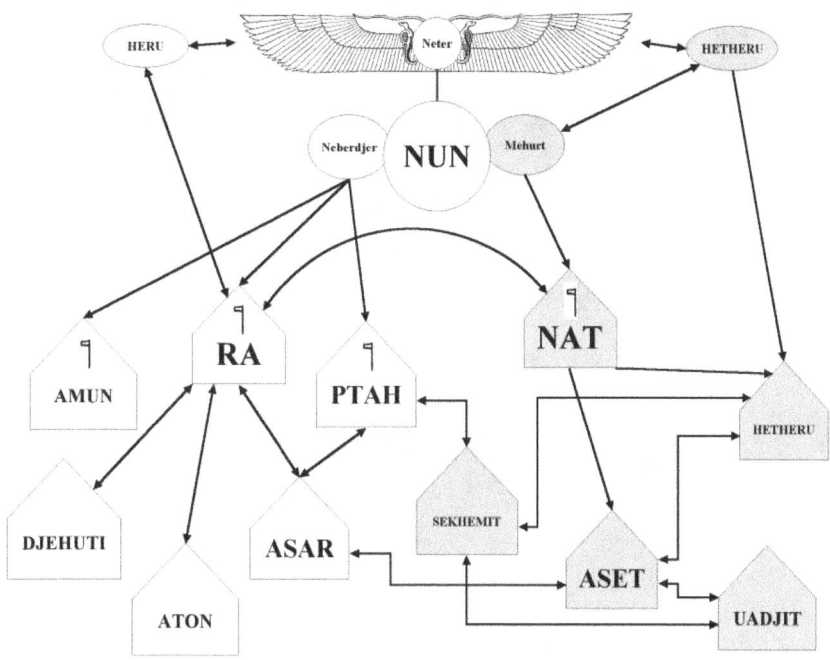

The sages of Kamit instituted a system by which the teachings of spirituality were espoused through a Temple organization. The major divinities were assigned to a particular city. That divinity or group of divinities became the "patron" divinity or divinities of that city. Also, the Priests and Priestesses of that Temple were in charge of seeing to the welfare of the people in that district as well as maintaining the traditions and disciplines of the traditions based on the particular divinity being worshipped. So the original concept of "Neter" became elaborated through the "theologies" of the various traditions. A dynamic expression of the teachings emerged, which though maintaining the integrity of the teachings, expressed nuances of variation in perspective on the teachings to suit the needs of varying kinds of personalities of the people of different locales.

In the diagram above, the primary or main divinities are denoted by the Neter symbol ( ). The house structure represents the Temple for that particular divinity. The interconnections with the other Temples are based on original scriptural statements espoused by the Temples that linked the divinities of their Temple with the other divinities. So this means that the divinities should be viewed not as separate entities operating independently, but rather as family members who are in the same "business" together, i.e. the enlightenment of society, albeit through variations in form of worship, name, form (expression of the Divinity), etc. Ultimately, all the divinities are referred to as Neteru and they are all said to be emanations from the ultimate and Supreme Being. Thus, the teaching from any of the Temples leads to an understanding of the others, and these all lead back to the source, the highest Divinity. Thus, the teaching within any of the Temple systems would lead to the attainment of spiritual enlightenment, the Great Awakening.

## The Neteru and Their Interrelationships
### Diagram : The Primary Kamitan Neteru and their Interrelationships
### Paut Neteru
The Company of Gods and Goddesses of Ancient Egypt

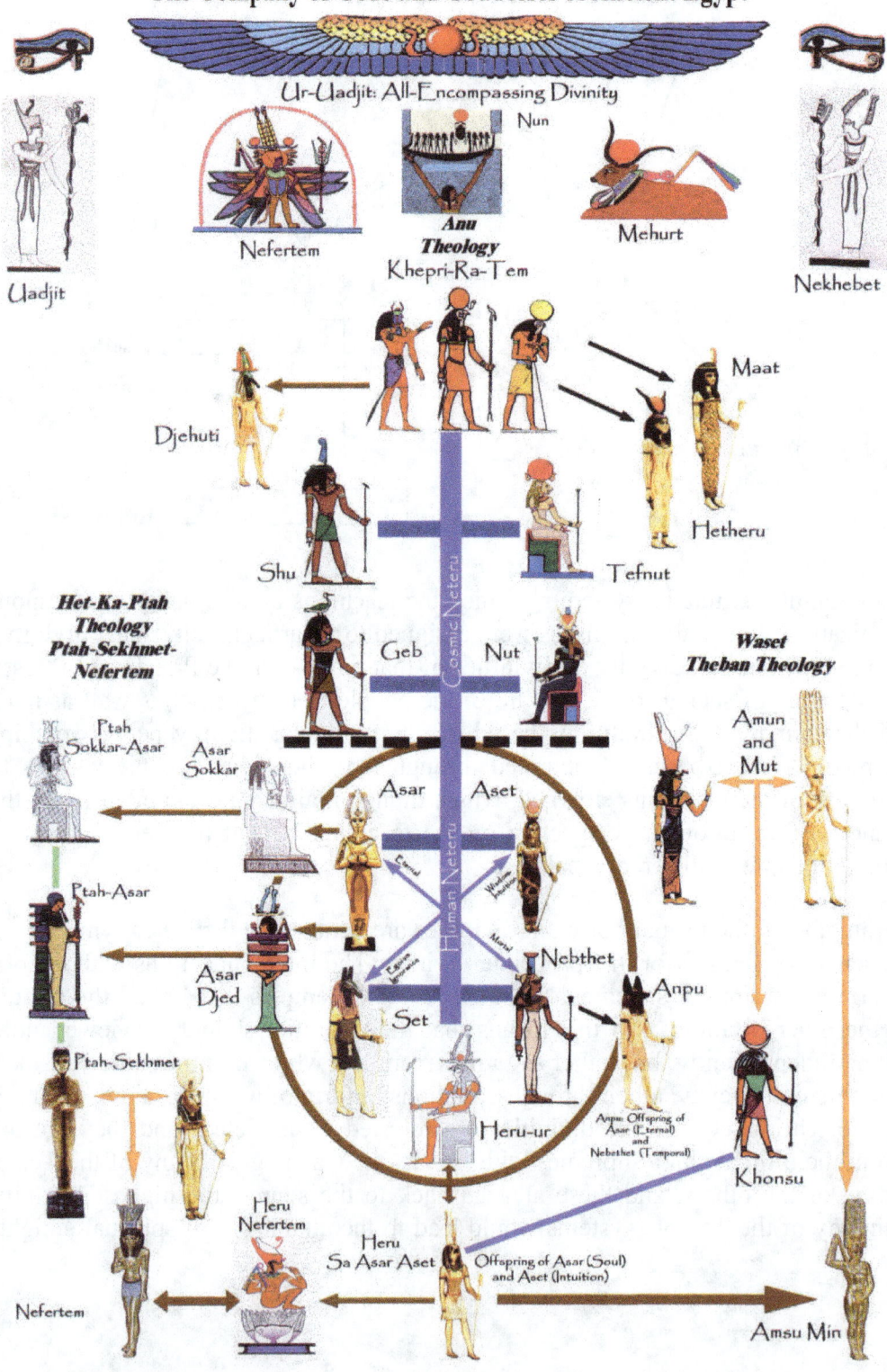

The same Supreme Being, Neter, is the winged all-encompassing transcendental Divinity, the Spirit who, in the early history, is called "Heru." The physical universe in which the Heru lives is called "Hetheru" or the "house of Heru." This divinity (Heru) is also the Nun or primeval substratum from which all matter is composed. The various divinities and the material universe are composed from this primeval substratum. Neter is actually androgynous and Heru, the Spirit, is related as a male aspect of that androgyny. However, Heru in the androgynous aspect, gives rise to the solar principle and this is seen in both the male and female divinities.

The image above provides an idea of the relationships between the divinities of the three main Neterian spiritual systems (traditions): Anunian Theology, Wasetian (Theban) Theology and Het-Ka-Ptah (Memphite) Theology. The traditions are composed of companies or groups of gods and goddesses. Their actions, teachings and interactions with each other and with human beings provide insight into their nature as well as that of human existence and Creation itself. The lines indicate direct scriptural relationships and the labels also indicate that some divinities from one system are the same in others, with only a name change. Again, this is attested to by the scriptures themselves in direct statements, like those found in the *Prt m Hru* text Chapter 4 (17).[ii]

## Listening to the Teachings

*"Mestchert"*

"Listening, to fill the ears, listen attentively-"

What should the ears be filled with?

The sages of Shetaut Neter enjoined that a Shemsu Neter (follower of Neter, an initiate or aspirant) should listen to the WISDOM of the Neterian Traditions. These are the myth related to the gods and goddesses containing the basic understanding of who they are, what they represent, how they relate human beings and to the Supreme Being. The myths allow us to be connected to the Divine.

An aspirant may choose any one of the 5 main Neterian Traditions.

- Shetaut Anu     – Teachings of the Ra Tradition
- Shetaut Menefer – Teachings of the Ptah Tradition
- Shetaut Waset   – Teachings of the Amun Tradition
- Shetaut Netrit  – Teachings of the Goddess Tradition
- Shetaut Asar    – Teachings of the Asarian Tradition
- Shetaut Aton    – Teachings of the Aton Tradition

# The Anunian Tradition

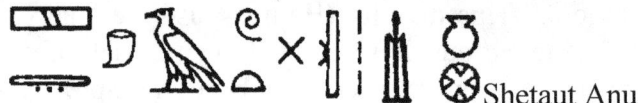Shetaut Anu

Below: The Heliopolitan Cosmogony.   The city of Anu (Amun-Ra)

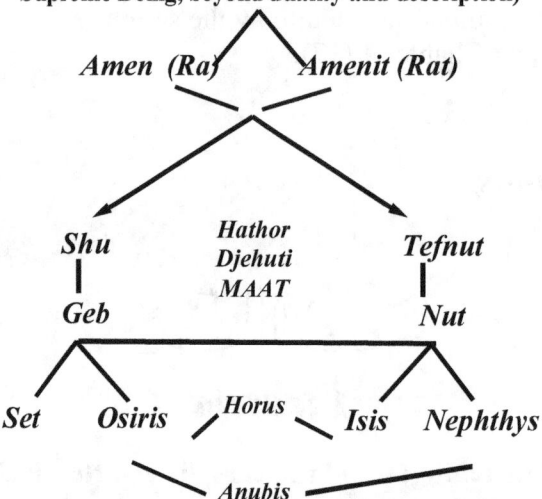

The Neters of Creation -
The Company of the Gods and Goddesses.
*Neter Neteru*
*Nebertcher - Amun* (unseen, hidden, ever present, Supreme Being, beyond duality and description)

The Mystery Teachings of the Anunian Tradition are related to the Divinity Ra and his company of Gods and Goddesses.( See the Book Anunian Theology by Muata Ashby) This Temple and its related Temples espouse the teachings of Creation, human origins and the path to spiritual enlightenment by means of the Supreme Being in the form of the god Ra. It tells of how Ra emerged from a primeval ocean and how human beings were created from his tears. The gods and goddesses, who are his children, go to form the elements of nature and the cosmic forces that maintain nature.

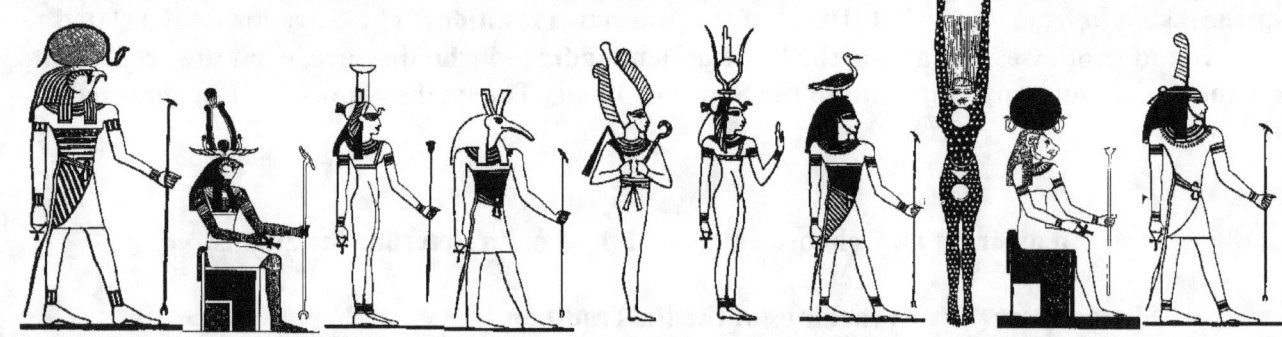

Top: Ra. From left to right, starting at the bottom level- The Gods and Goddesses of Anunian Theology: Shu, Tefnut, Nut, Geb, Aset, Asar, Set, Nebthet and Heru-Ur

# The Memphite Tradition

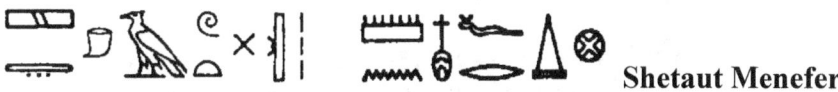 **Shetaut Menefer**

Below: The Memphite Cosmogony.

The city of Hetkaptah (Ptah)

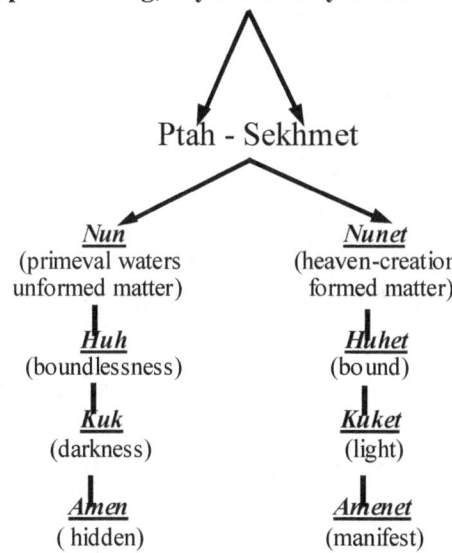

The Neters of Creation -
The Company of the Gods and Goddesses.
*Neter Neteru*
*Nebertcher - Amun* (unseen, hidden, ever present,
Supreme Being, beyond duality and description)

Ptah - Sekhmet

*Nun* (primeval waters unformed matter) — *Nunet* (heaven-creation formed matter)

*Huh* (boundlessness) — *Huhet* (bound)

*Kuk* (darkness) — *Kuket* (light)

*Amen* (hidden) — *Amenet* (manifest)

The Mystery Teachings of the Menefer (Memphite) Tradition are related to the Neterus known as Ptah, Sekhmit, Nefertem. The myths and philosophy of these divinities constitutes Memphite Theology.[iii] This temple and its related temples espoused the teachings of Creation, human origins and the path to spiritual enlightenment by means of the Supreme Being in the form of the god Ptah and his family, who compose the Memphite Trinity. It tells of how Ptah emerged from a primeval ocean and how he created the universe by his will and the power of thought (mind). The gods and goddesses who are his thoughts, go to form the elements of nature and the cosmic forces that maintain nature. His spouse, Sekhmit has a powerful temple system of her own that is related to the Memphite teaching. The same is true for his son Nefertem.

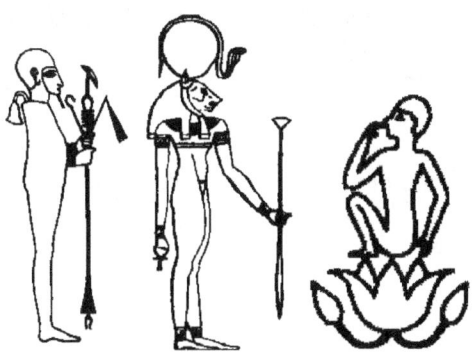

Ptah, Sekhmit and Nefertem

# The Theban Tradition

 **Shetaut Amun**

The Mystery Teachings of the Wasetian Tradition are related to the Neterus known as Amun, Mut Khonsu. This temple and its related temples espoused the teachings of Creation, human origins and the path to spiritual enlightenment by means of the Supreme Being in the form of the god Amun or Amun-Ra. It tells of how Amun and his family, the Trinity of Amun, Mut and Khonsu, manage the Universe along with his Company of Gods and Goddesses. This Temple became very important in the early part of the New Kingdom Era.

Below: The Trinity of Amun and the Company of Gods and Goddesses of Amun

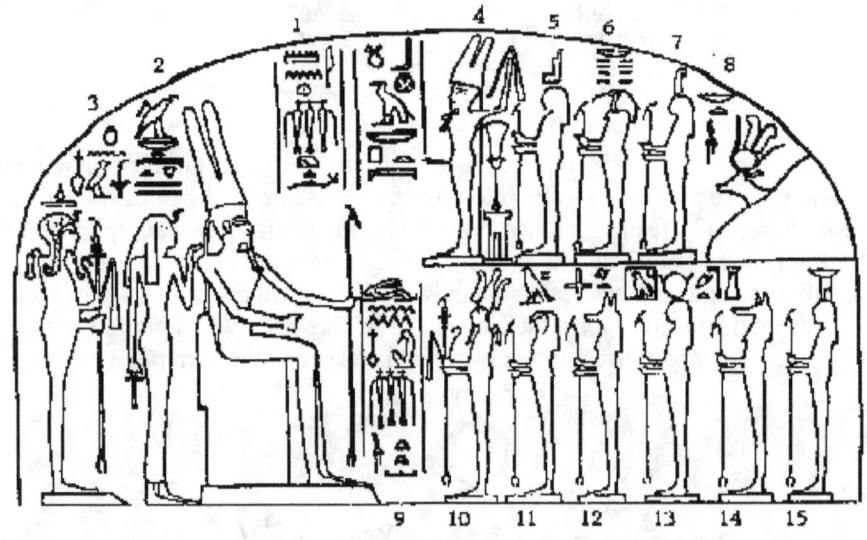

See the Book *Egyptian Yoga Vol. 2* for more on Amun, Mut and Khonsu by Muata Ashby

# The Goddess Tradition
## Shetaut Netrit

"Arat"

The hieroglyphic sign Arat means "Goddess." General, throughout ancient Kamit, the Mystery Teachings of the Goddess Tradition are related to the Divinity in the form of the Goddess. The Goddess was an integral part of all the Neterian traditions but special temples also developed around the worship of certain particular Goddesses who were also regarded as Supreme Beings in their own right. Thus as in other African religions, the goddess as well as the female gender were respected and elevated as the male divinities. The Goddess was also the author of Creation, giving birth to it as a great Cow. The following are the most important forms of the goddess.[iv]

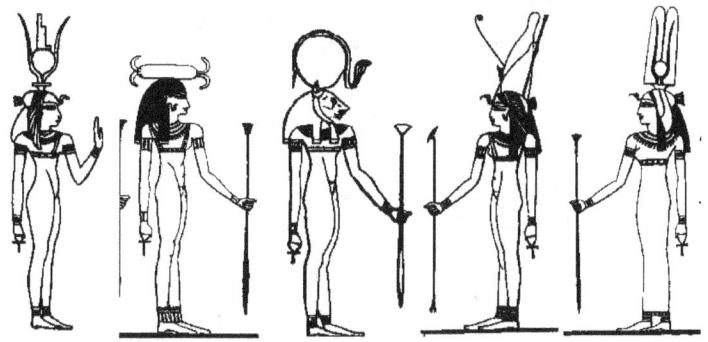

Aset, Net, Sekhmit, Mut, Hetheru

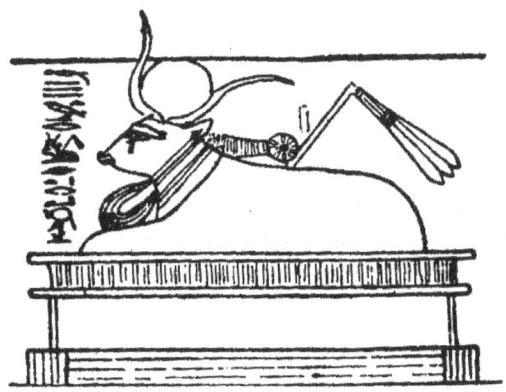

# Mehurt ("The Mighty Full One")

# The Asarian Tradition

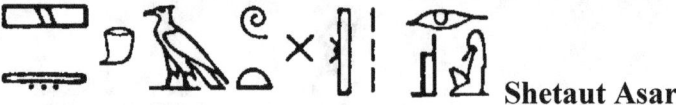 **Shetaut Asar**

    This temple and its related temples espoused the teachings of Creation, human origins and the path to spiritual enlightenment by means of the Supreme Being in the form of the god Asar. It tells of how Asar and his family, the Trinity of Asar, Aset and Heru, manage the Universe and lead human beings to spiritual enlightenment and the resurrection of the soul. This Temple and its teaching were very important from the Pre-Dynastic era down to the Christian period. The Mystery Teachings of the Asarian Tradition are related to the Neterus known as: Asar, Aset, Heru (Osiris, Isis and **Heru (Horus)**)

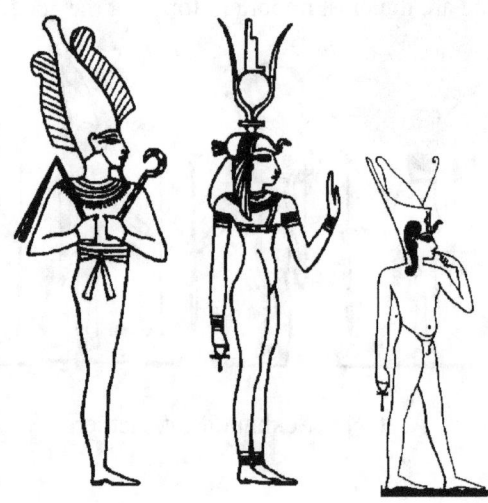

The tradition of Asar, Aset and Heru was practiced generally throughout the land of ancient Kamit. The centers of this tradition were the city of Abdu containing the Great Temple of Asar, the city of Pilak containing the Great Temple of Aset[v] and Edfu containing the Ggreat Temple of Heru.

# The Aton Tradition

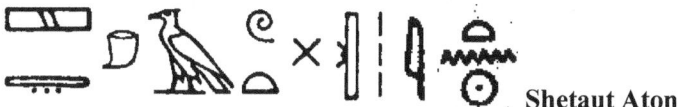 Shetaut Aton

This temple and its related temples espoused the teachings of Creation, human origins and the path to spiritual enlightenment by means of the Supreme Being in the form of the god Aton. It tells of how Aton with its dynamic life force created and sustains Creation. By recognizing Aton as the very substratum of all existence, human beings engage in devotional exercises and rituals and the study of the Hymns containing the wisdom teachings of Aton explaining that Aton manages the Universe and leads human beings to spiritual enlightenment and eternal life for the soul. This Temple and its teaching were very important in the middle New Kingdom Period. The Mystery Teachings of the Aton Tradition are related to the Neter Aton and its main exponent was the Sage King Akhnaton, who is depicted below with his family adoring the sundisk, symbol of the Aton.

## Akhnaton, Nefertiti and Daughters

For more on Atonism and the Aton Theology see the Essence of Atonism Lecture Series by Sebai Muata Ashby ©2001

# The Mystical Creation Myth

Ra-Tem
⇩
Hathor
Djehuti
Maat
⇩
Shu ⇔ Tefnut
⇩
Geb ⇔ Nut
↙     ⇩     ↘
Set — Nebthet   Asar ⇔ Aset   Asar ⇔ Nebthet
⇩            ⇩
Heru (Horus)      Anubis

The diagram above shows that the *Psedjet* (Ennead), the creative principles that are embodied in the primordial neteru (Gods and Goddesses) of creation, emanated from the Supreme Being. Ra or Ra-Tem arose out of the *Nu*, the Primeval Ocean, the hidden essence, and began sailing the *"Boat of Millions of Years"* which included the Company of Gods and Goddesses. On his boat emerged the neteru, the Gods and Goddesses who symbolize the cosmic principles of Creation. The neteru of the Ennead are Ra-Atum, Shu, Tefnut, Geb, Nut, Asar, Aset, Set, and Nebthet. Hathor, Djehuti (dehuti) and Maat represent attributes of the Supreme Being as the very *stuff* or *substratum* which makes up creation. Shu, Tefnut, Geb, Nut, Asar, Aset, Set, and Nebthet represent the principles upon which creation manifests. Anubis is not part of the Ennead. He represents the feature of intellectual discrimination in the Ausarian myth. "Sailing" signifies the beginning of motion in creation. Motion implies that events occur in the realm of time and space, thus, the phenomenal universe comes into existence as a mass of moving essence we call the elements. Prior to this motion, there was the primeval state of being without any form and without existence in time or space.

Above: The Creation: Ra emerges from the Nu (primeval waters) along with the Company of Gods and Goddesses.

God rises out of the primeval waters and His continuous motion through the cosmos sustains the universe. This same barque is constantly attacked by the evil forces headed by the serpent Apep. Apep represents the fetters of the soul. It is the task of the initiate to eradicate the obstructions (Apep) from the path of spiritual progress. Sublimating the Setian forces, the lower self, represented by Set, can do this.

Above: The Great Trinity of Ancient Egypt including both male and female principles. A-Amun and Amenit or Amunet (Mut), B- Ra and Rai, C- Ptah and Sekhmet.

The Mysteries of Anu are considered to be the oldest exposition of the teachings of Creation and they formed a foundation for the unfoldment of the teachings of mystical spirituality which followed in the mysteries of the city of *Hetkaptah* through the Divinity in the name Ptah, and the Mysteries of *Newt (Waset or Thebes)*, through the Divinity in the name Amun. With each succeeding exposition, the teaching becomes more and more refined until it reaches its quintessence in the *Hymns of Amun*. Thus, while each of the divinities in the Ancient Egyptian Trinity (Amun-Ra-Ptah) are related, in their own tutelary way they assume the form of the *High Divinity* or *Supreme Being* with name and form. However, as we have seen, they are only representations or symbols (representation with name and form) of the transcendental androgynous Divinity which is without name or form who is referred to as Neberdjer. This understanding holds vast implications for the comprehension of Ancient Egyptian Religion and its message in reference to the human soul because the human soul is related to Neberdjer just as the Trinity is related to Neberdjer. How is this possible? This is the teaching of the Hymns of Amun.

This work represents an introduction to the sacred scriptures from one segment of the Ancient Egyptian Trinity. It is provided for those who would like to begin their studies of Theban Theology and to practice the teachings contained therein. These sacred scriptures encompassed in the Hymns-Hessu are to be used for praying, chanting, memorizing and repeating, and should be studied ardently. When they are propitiated-Amma, in this manner, they bestow spiritual wisdom-Såa, mental calm and spiritual upliftment.

# Prominent Ancient Egyptian Gods and Goddesses

The Main Ancient Egyptian Gods and Goddesses

Forms of Amun-Ra – Creator | Ra – Creator | Ptah – Creator | Atum – Demiurge

Khepri, the morning sun. | Rā, the noon-day sun. | Temu (Atem), the setting sun.

Rā, the god One or Only god, in his three chief aspects.

Shu – Air – Ether | Tefnut – Water | Geb – Earth | Nut – heavens | Djehuti – Intellect – Writing, words

Asar – Soul | Aset – Wisdom | Heru – Kingship, Spiritual Victory | Apuat – Discernment | Asar – King of the Dead

## The Main Ancient Egyptian Gods and Goddesses Cont.

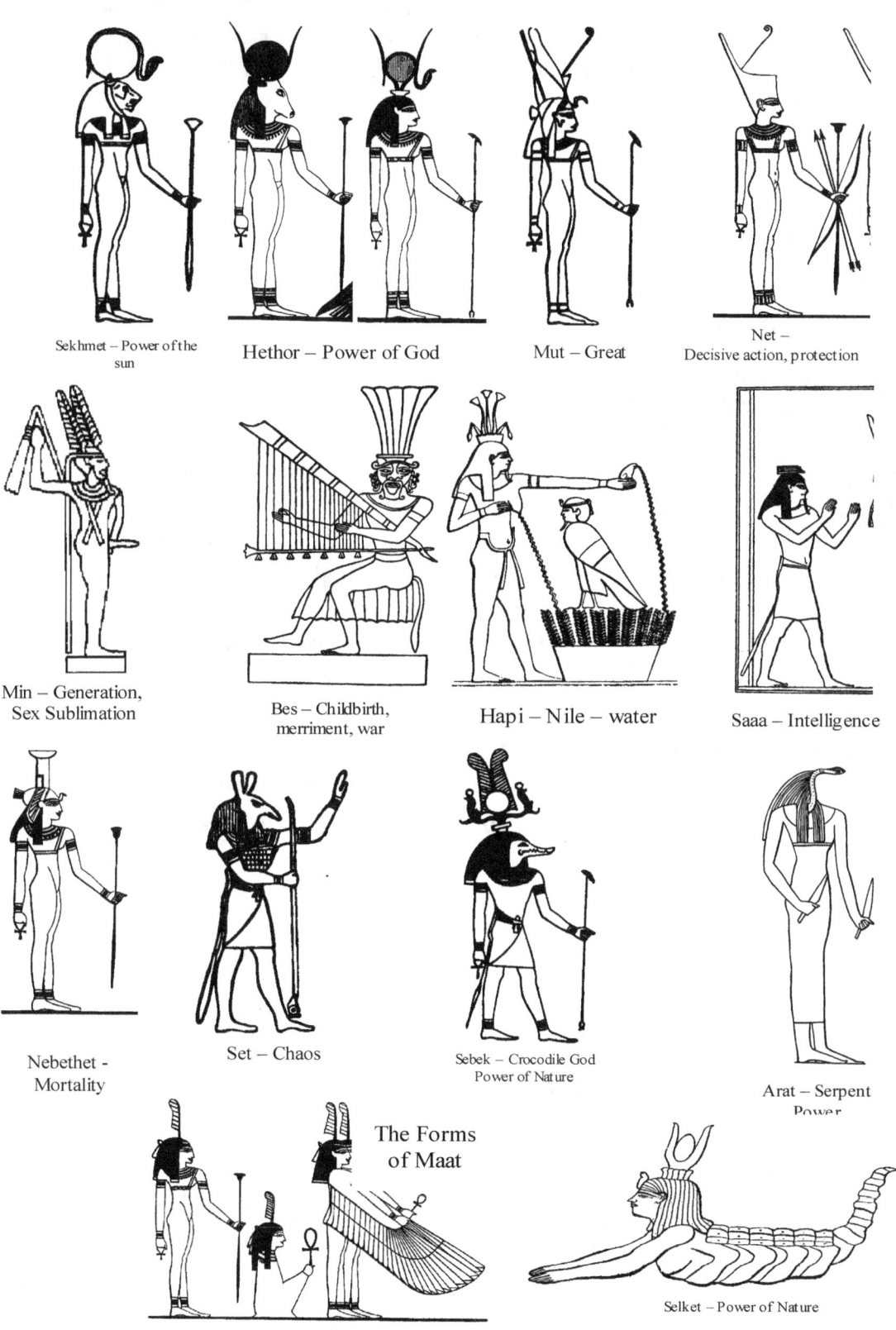

# The Forces of Entropy

In Neterian religion, there is no concept of "evil" as is conceptualized in Western Culture. Rather, it is understood that the forces of entropy are constantly working in nature to bring that which has been constructed by human hands to their original natural state. The serpent Apep (Apophis), who daily tries to stop Ra's boat of creation, is the symbol of entropy. This concept of entropy has been referred to as "chaos" by Western Egyptologists.

Apep

**Above: Set protecting the boat of Ra from the forces of entropy (symbolized by the serpent Apep).**

As expressed previously, in Neterian religion there is also no concept of a "devil" or "demon" as is conceived in the Judeo-Christian or Islamic traditions. Rather, it is understood that manifestations of detrimental situations and adversities arise as a result of unrighteous actions. These unrighteous actions are due to the "Setian" qualities in a human being. Set is the Neteru of egoism and the negative qualities which arise from egoism. Egoism is the idea of individuality based on identification with the body and mind only as being who one is. One has no deeper awareness of their deeper spiritual essence, and thus no understanding of their connectedness to all other objects (includes persons) in creation and the Divine Self. When the ego is under the control of the higher nature, it fights the forces of entropy (as above). However, when beset with ignorance, it leads to the degraded states of human existence. The vices (egoism, selfishness, extraverted ness, wonton sexuality (lust), jealousy, envy, greed, gluttony) are a result.

Set

**Set and the Set animal**

# The Great Awakening of Neterian Religion

"Nehast"

Nehast means to "wake up," to Awaken to the higher existence. In the Prt m Hru Text it is said:

*Nuk pa Neter aah Neter Ɓah asha ren*[vi]

**"I am that same God, the Supreme One, who has myriad of mysterious names."**

The goal of all the Neterian disciplines is to discover the meaning of "Who am I?," to unravel the mysteries of life and to fathom the depths of eternity and infinity. This is the task of all human beings and it is to be accomplished in this very lifetime.

This can be done by learning the ways of the Neteru, emulating them and finally becoming like them, Akhus, (enlightened beings), walking the earth as giants and accomplishing great deeds such as the creation of the universe!

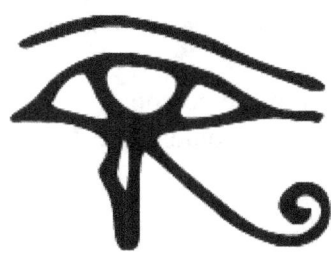

Udjat

The Eye of Heru is a quintessential symbol of awakening to

Divine Consciousness, representing the concept of Nehast.

# The Human Personality and its Relationship to the Gods and Goddesses

**Figure 13: A two dimensional depiction of the elements of the personality.**

The diagram above shows the Kemetic concept of the elements of the personality (bodies) with the grossest (human body) at the center, and the subtlest (Spirit, God) at the outer edge.

The human personality has aspects or elements or parts that are derived from a source. Each element derives from a universal source lime a drop from an ocean. That source is the Divine Self or Universal God/Goddess. The following illustration provides a visual representation of this Ancient Egyptian concept. Therefore, the Individual derives from and remains supported by and connected to the Universal.

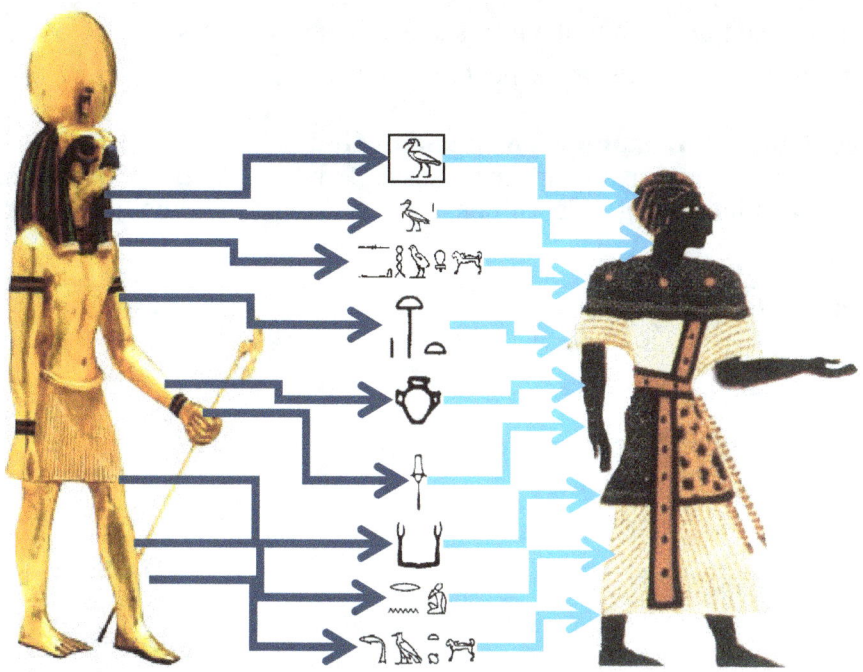

**Figure 14: The elements of the Individual human personality are derived from the Universal God Ra**

## The Mystical and Cosmic Implications of the Elements of the Personality

This section will provide a more detailed classification of the human being in an attempt to understand the underlying origin and cause of human existence. Also, it will seek to bring forth a deeper understanding of how the Cosmic Forces operate through the human constitution at gross and subtle levels.

As discussed earlier, the Universal Soul, God, Pure Consciousness, emanates Creation and all that is within it, all that is. The human being is like a ray of that emanation which refracts into several parts composing all of the levels of existence. Human consciousness may be compared to a reflection of the sun in a pool of water. Human consciousness is a reflection of divine consciousness in the pool of the mind which operates through the brain and nervous system. This idea is also reflected in the relationship between the parts of the spirit called BA and AB.

**BA ⇔ AB**

The Ab is the heart or seat of the mind, and it is in the mind where the soul, Ba, reflects. So the mind has no independent existence without the soul's sustaining life force and consciousness, and the individual human soul has no independent existence without the Universal Soul.

**Universal Ba ⇨ Individual Ba ⇨ Individual Ab[35]**

---

[35] Human heart and mind.

These levels of existence transfer into the four states of consciousness and various levels of psycho-spiritual psychology related to the Uraeus-Serpent Power system.[36]

**Table 5: The Three Bodies of Men and Women and of God**
The three basic parts of the human being are the Causal Body, the Astral Body and the Physical Body. They may be viewed in an increasing order of density as follows. These bodies also relate to the bodies of the universe:

| Neberdjer (Universal Self) | Universal Self |
|---|---|
| ↓ | ↓ |
| Heaven (Ament)[37] | Causal Body |
| ↓ | ↓ |
| Duat | Astral Body |
| ↓ | ↓ |
| Earth | Physical Body |

The Universal Ba or Soul, or in other words, the consciousness of the Supreme Being, emanates and sustains each individual human being through the various parts of the human spirit. There are three basic parts to the human being. These are further broken down into more specific parts.

Sages of ancient times who were able to discern, through their intuitional vision (spiritual eye), the different levels of vibration and psychology within all human beings, have set forth this teaching about the constitution of the human being. An important point to note is that each of the lower three states involves duality while the highest state involves non-duality. The human soul is a projection of the divine into the realm of duality (causal -astral- physical planes). The human soul forgets its divine origin and believes itself to be a creature among other creatures; hence, the idea of duality arises. The ignorant human being is not aware that {he/she} is at all times most intimately connected to the Universal Self, as are all objects and all other human beings. Just as each wave in the ocean is essentially the same as the ocean, each wave-like human personality and all the objects in Creation are essentially the Primeval Ocean, the Self. Ignorance of this then gives rise to the various egoistic feelings. The ignorant human being, not aware of {his/her} storehouse of innate potential to experience fullness and peace within, goes on seeking for fulfillment in the worlds of duality instead of seeking to know and experience the only source of true fulfillment, the Universal Self, which encompasses all other realms. Non-duality is experienced as absolute oneness and interconnectedness with all that exists. There is no feeling of you and me, here and there, male or female; there is no desire for objects because all objects are one with the Self. There is only the experience of awareness of the Self. Human words and concepts are not capable of describing the actual experience of oneness with the Self, therefore, all mystical descriptions are transcended in the actual experience. They are like a map, but you must take the journey and arrive at

---
[36] See the book *The Serpent Power* by Dr. Muata Ashby
[37] In Kemetic Philosophy there are two heavens, a lower physical heaven wherein the lower aspects of the personality (Khat, Ren, Sekhem, Ab) reside and a higher heaven wherein the higher aspects of the personality such as the Akhu, Sahu, and Ba reside.

These levels of existence transfer into the four states of consciousness and various levels of psycho-spiritual psychology related to the Uraeus-Serpent Power system.[36]

**Table 5: The Three Bodies of Men and Women and of God**
The three basic parts of the human being are the Causal Body, the Astral Body and the Physical Body. They may be viewed in an increasing order of density as follows. These bodies also relate to the bodies of the universe:

| Neberdjer (Universal Self) | Universal Self |
|---|---|
| ↓ | ↓ |
| Heaven (Ament)[37] | Causal Body |
| ↓ | ↓ |
| Duat | Astral Body |
| ↓ | ↓ |
| Earth | Physical Body |

The Universal Ba or Soul, or in other words, the consciousness of the Supreme Being, emanates and sustains each individual human being through the various parts of the human spirit. There are three basic parts to the human being. These are further broken down into more specific parts.

Sages of ancient times who were able to discern, through their intuitional vision (spiritual eye), the different levels of vibration and psychology within all human beings, have set forth this teaching about the constitution of the human being. An important point to note is that each of the lower three states involves duality while the highest state involves non-duality. The human soul is a projection of the divine into the realm of duality (causal -astral- physical planes). The human soul forgets its divine origin and believes itself to be a creature among other creatures; hence, the idea of duality arises. The ignorant human being is not aware that {he/she} is at all times most intimately connected to the Universal Self, as are all objects and all other human beings. Just as each wave in the ocean is essentially the same as the ocean, each wave-like human personality and all the objects in Creation are essentially the Primeval Ocean, the Self. Ignorance of this then gives rise to the various egoistic feelings. The ignorant human being, not aware of {his/her} storehouse of innate potential to experience fullness and peace within, goes on seeking for fulfillment in the worlds of duality instead of seeking to know and experience the only source of true fulfillment, the Universal Self, which encompasses all other realms. Non-duality is experienced as absolute oneness and interconnectedness with all that exists. There is no feeling of you and me, here and there, male or female; there is no desire for objects because all objects are one with the Self. There is only the experience of awareness of the Self. Human words and concepts are not capable of describing the actual experience of oneness with the Self, therefore, all mystical descriptions are transcended in the actual experience. They are like a map, but you must take the journey and arrive at

---
[36] See the book *The Serpent Power* by Dr. Muata Ashby
[37] In Kemetic Philosophy there are two heavens, a lower physical heaven wherein the lower aspects of the personality (Khat, Ren, Sekhem, Ab) reside and a higher heaven wherein the higher aspects of the personality such as the Akhu, Sahu, and Ba reside.

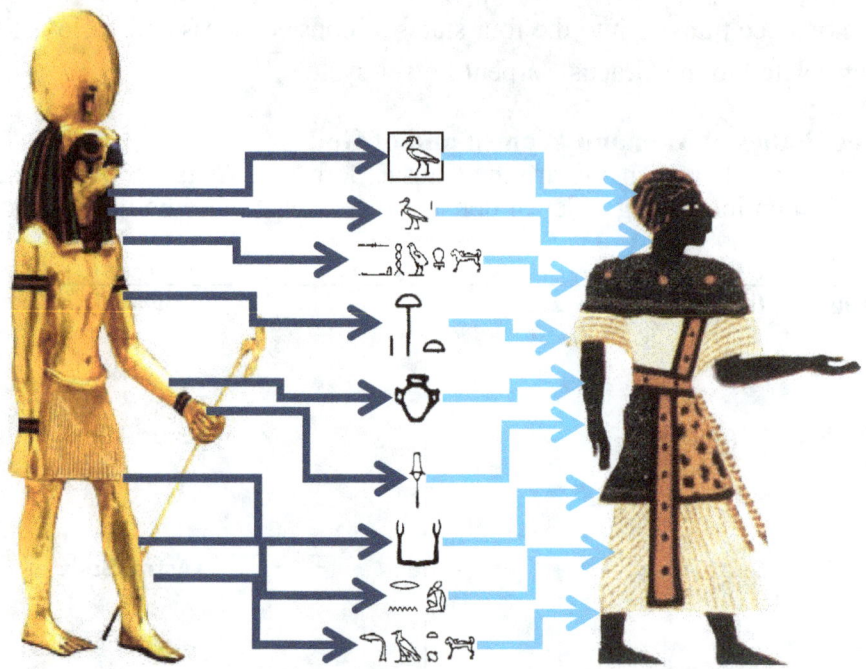

**Figure 14: The elements of the Individual human personality are derived from the Universal God Ra**

## The Mystical and Cosmic Implications of the Elements of the Personality

This section will provide a more detailed classification of the human being in an attempt to understand the underlying origin and cause of human existence. Also, it will seek to bring forth a deeper understanding of how the Cosmic Forces operate through the human constitution at gross and subtle levels.

As discussed earlier, the Universal Soul, God, Pure Consciousness, emanates Creation and all that is within it, all that is. The human being is like a ray of that emanation which refracts into several parts composing all of the levels of existence. Human consciousness may be compared to a reflection of the sun in a pool of water. Human consciousness is a reflection of divine consciousness in the pool of the mind which operates through the brain and nervous system. This idea is also reflected in the relationship between the parts of the spirit called BA and AB.

**BA ⇔ AB**

The Ab is the heart or seat of the mind, and it is in the mind where the soul, Ba, reflects. So the mind has no independent existence without the soul's sustaining life force and consciousness, and the individual human soul has no independent existence without the Universal Soul.

**Universal Ba ⇨ Individual Ba ⇨ Individual Ab[35]**

---

[35] Human heart and mind.

the destination by your own will and self-effort. Thus, they serve as guides, to lead the mind toward the understanding of yogic philosophy. --

The nine major elements or parts of the human personality espoused by the Ancient Egyptian Sages may be classified as follows within the three basic bodies for the purpose of study and understanding, as illustrated below. God is also understood to have three bodies: Universal Causal Body, Universal Astral Body, Universal Physical Body, the three aspects of universe or planes of existence. Within these bodies are the constituent elements, totaling nine in number. God also has nine elements. However, unlike those of the human being which are limited and characterized by their individuality, the divine elements are universal and all-pervading in their respective level of existence. Thus we are told in the Ancient Egyptian scriptures that God has a Universal Ba, a Universal Sahu, a Universal Khu (Akhu), a Universal Khaibit, a Universal Ka, a Universal Sekhem, a Universal Ab, a Universal Khat, and a Universal Ren. Thus, the individual elements that compose the personality of each individual human being emanate from the same Supreme Being.

**Table 6: The Nine Aspects of the Human personality and of God.**

| Human Constitution | Universal Self |
|---|---|
| ↓ | ↓ |
| Causal Body | Causal Body |
| Khu (Akhu) | Universal Khu (Akhu) |
| Ba | Universal Individual – Ba |
| Sahu | Universal Sahu |
| Khaibit | Universal Khaibit |
| ↓ | ↓ |
| Astral Body | Astral Body |
| Ab | Universal Ka |
| Sekhem | Universal Sekhem |
| Ka | Universal Ab |
| ↓ | ↓ |
| Physical Body | Physical Body |
| Ren | Universal Khat |
| Khat | Universal Ren |

Ren = Name

Khat = Form

(Name and form are the basis of physical existence on the earth plane.)

It should be noted that while the gross elements of the ego-personality are evident at the level of the physical body, the original cause of the existence of the individual and {his/her} separation from the Divine occurs at the level of the Causal Body. Many people erroneously think of their soul as existing within their physical body. However, the opposite is true. The soul emanates from the Self. It in turn creates the other parts of the personality. All of this creation occurs within the Divine Self and not the body. The Causal Body is where the slightest tendency towards thought and desire occurs. It is here where the deep unconscious impressions cause the other parts of the body to emerge. When the physical body of an un-enlightened person dies, the gross elements of the ego (name and personality used in a particular lifetime) also die. The Astral and Causal bodies survive with the unconscious impressions collected from that lifetime. Through these bodies the soul continues the pursuit of fulfillment of desire (unconscious impressions lodged in the Astral-Causal mental subtle matter). The pursuit of fulfillment of desires may continue in the Astral plane (Duat-Netherworld) for a time, where the individual experiences of pain or pleasure (heaven or hell) according to {his/her} Meskhenet (karmic basis composed of impressions gathered from feelings, actions and desires of many lifetimes).

The task of an aspirant is to cleanse the Physical, Astral and Causal planes of the mind so as to regain conscious perception of the Universal Self. Since the Universal Self is non-dual, immortal, eternal and the source of all planes and all objects within those planes, the union with the Universal Self bestows omniscience and a boundless vision of infinity, immortality and a feeling of non-duality and connectedness to all things great and small. The correct practice of the various yogic disciplines are designed to accomplish this cleansing process. If successful, the soul comes into communion with the Self (Universal Ba, Asar, Ra, Aset, etc.) while still alive, and after death the soul of the enlightened person dissolves in the ocean of pure consciousness from whence it came originally. This is the meaning behind the teaching of *merging with the maker* presented in the Ancient Egyptian story known as *The Story of Sinuhe*.[38]

Earlier we discussed the fact that in the process of embodiment, the Universal Ba itself becomes the individual Ba of every human being due to its association and identification with the feelings of the emotional body, *Ka,* and the cravings of the physical body, *Khat.* If this is true, then how is it possible that the Universal Self (*Ba*) is also non-dual, meaning without a second, one and alone, all-encompassing as well as transcendental? At this more advanced level you must understand that all of the parts of the body are merely emanations from that same divine Self, just as you emanate a dream in your sleep or an idea in your Waking State, out of the depths of your consciousness.

In the same way this entire universe and everything in it is nothing but the emanation of God's consciousness. All that exists is ethereal, subtle matter, the Self. The process of thought has the effect of coagulating matter in a form as directed by the thought. In this way you have created your body and mind along with all of the other parts of your individual existence. In reality these parts are nothing more than subtle energy held together by your thoughts and ultimately, every one of those parts are not yours, but are parts of the Self. Thus, nothing exists outside of the Self, God. Therefore, even though there appears to be many objects, colors and differences in creation, the underlying essence of it all is the Self. Think about it. If there was something other than the Self, then the Self could not be all-pervasive, all-encompassing and all-powerful. Its movements would be restricted. The idea that there is a devil or some evil being who is the nemesis of God is erroneous because there can be no other being outside of the Self. The Self is the soul or substratum of all that is.

---

[38] See Egyptian Yoga: The Philosophy of Enlightenment (Egyptian Yoga Volume I)

The idea of a "devil" who is a counterpart or nemesis of God who is "all good" was a development out a dualistic way of understanding life and mythology. This dualistic view is contrary to the teachings of mystical spirituality. It is the basis for egoism and misunderstanding in the practice of true religion. True religion means that you look for a connection, a oneness between yourself and God. For this to be possible you need to discover that your ego-personality is only a superficial expression of your deeper reality which is God. When you discover the depths of your own being, you realize that you are not an individual, separate from the universe and God. You discover that underneath the apparent separation there is oneness. A dualistic view looks for differences and affirms that there is a separation between God, creation and humankind. Thus, a practitioner of dualism prays to God, looks to God for salvation and believes he exists as an individual while the non-dualist practices the teachings that lead to the understanding that the innermost reality in the heart is God. God is in all things everywhere, and nothing exists besides God.

If you were to let go of your thoughts related to your body consciousness, you would discover that you are separate from your body. In the advanced stages, you could dematerialize and materialize it at will as well as perform other feats that are considered as miracles or psychic powers. The parts of the spiritual body are in reality like layers of clothing on your true Self. Therefore, in the *Gospel of Thomas*, Jesus exhorts his disciples to strip without being ashamed and on that day they will see him (Christhood, Enlightenment).

42. His disciples say to him: "On what day wilt thou appear to us, and what day shall we see thee?" Jesus says: "When you strip yourselves without being ashamed, when you take off your clothes and lay them at your feet like little children and trample them! Then {you will become} children of Him who is living, and you will have no more fear."

All of the elements of the personality come together and create a conglomerate which collectively makes up likes and dislikes, opinions, feelings, thoughts, and desires of an individual. All of them constitute a conditioning[39] of the individual consciousness. This conditioning is referred to as egoism. The ego must be dismantled and stripped from the mind. When this occurs you will discover that what seemed so real and concrete (astral body, physical body) is nothing more than condensed thoughts. This discovery will free you from them as a bird is freed from a cage. When you take them off, what is left is the true Absolute you. All Creation has that same Absolute Self at its core. Therefore, you must seek to transcend all of the layers of ethereal matter so as to discover your true Self. This is accomplished by the practice of all of the disciplines of yoga presented here and in the Egyptian Yoga Book Series.

When we speak of "conditioning" we are referring to the conditioning of consciousness into the forms of the parts of the spirit in the same way that consciousness becomes conditioned into various forms (subjects, objects and interactions) in a dream. What is holding it all together? Desire born of ignorance of the Higher Self, which is transcendental and independent of concepts, and is whole, or free from fragmentation. The subtlest parts of the body: *Khaibit, Individual - Ba, Sahu,* and *Khu or Akhu,* are the deepest levels of the unconscious mind. Contained in them is the cause of separation between the individual soul and God. This individuation principle is called *ignorance*. Therefore, ignorance, based in the causal body, is the primary "cause" of the astral and physical bodies (ego) coming into being. This is why it is called the causal body. It causes the other bodies to come into existence. When this ignorance

---

[39] See also Egyptian Yoga: The Philosophy of Enlightenment (Egyptian Yoga Volume I)

is removed, all of the bodies become as if transparent, as when you wake up in a dream even when you are still asleep. The dream continues, but you "know" it is a dream, so you witness it as a dream and not as reality. Upon waking from a dream you discover that even while things seemed to be so real, they were not. You were not even moving; you were placidly lying on the bed. In the same way, a Sage discovers that the Self is not moving; only the thoughts, senses and body controlled by those thoughts can be said to be moving. Does a dream move? No. In the same way, the real you is not located in the body and is not moving. Therefore, you are the "Unmoved Mover." You are Atum, the creator who causes movement but itself does not move.

Thus, the Sage looks on the body as a marionette, created with thoughts by the Self, or as a projection as in a dream. Having awoken from the dream, when the physical body dies, the Sage who has discovered {his/her} oneness with the Self remains as the Self and does not create any more bodies to further incarnate. This is because {he/she} has discovered {his/her} essential nature and there are no more desires for experiences as a human being. Thus, there is no cause for the creation of a new ego-personality. This is the state that Sages experience with respect to the waking world of ordinary human beings. They are no longer caught up in the illusion of the world. This is called Liberation, Salvation, Heruhood, Waking up, Meeting Asar, Resurrection, Nirvana, etc. This is the loftiest goal of human life.

> "Knowledge derived from the senses is illusory. True knowledge can only come from the understanding of the union of opposites."
>
> –Ancient Egyptian Proverb

If you look at yourself objectively, you will realize that every cell in your body is changing from moment to moment, and that you are never the same as you were a moment ago. Even solid objects are changing and decaying, albeit at a slower rate, but eventually they will decompose into their constituent elements. In much the same way, the human body is changing and constantly moving towards extinction. But is this real? Is this change a quality of your inner Self? Upon closer examination, the real you is not changeable; the real you is Pure Consciousness and one with the Supreme Being who is eternal. Remember the teaching: **"The Great God inside the common folk"** from Chapter 17 of the *"Prt m Hru."* This is what it means. Your inner Self is one with the Divine Self. Initiatic science shows that the real you, the innermost Self, is unchanging.

What is it that is constantly moving, constantly restless from the time you wake up until the time you go to bed again? This is the thinking mind with all of the worries, all of the desires, all the beliefs, all of the ambitions and all of the regrets. These thoughts, worries, desires, beliefs, ambitions and regrets constitute your mental conditioning, your personality, and your ego-self-concept. Through the process of your human experience in the world, your mind has become conditioned to expect to see reality in a certain way and therefore, it perceives life according to its conditioning. This conditioning, your ego, is what is holding you back from being able to realize your innermost Self, which is all encompassing, all-knowing, and all-blissful contentment and peace.

Your ego-personality is like a movie character that emerges at the beginning of a movie and fades away at the end. The movie screen remains in order to receive images from other movies. In the same way your personality emerged out of your mental conditioning at the time of your birth and since then, it has never stopped changing, moving, craving and searching for fulfillment. Egoism is the feeling of separation from the Self and attachment to an illusory personality that arises out of the dream quality of consciousness. It is intensified by the distractions of the mind due to the pursuit of fulfillment of sensual desires. At the time of your death, the gross aspects of your personality (Khat and Ren) will cease to exist, but the impressions created through these in the unconscious will leave you still craving for the unfulfilled desires. This is because the deep unconscious mind with its conditioned impressions of desire, survives death and follows you into the Duat (astral plane) until you finally are born again in the earth plane to once again continue seeking fulfillment.

> "Get thyself ready and make the thought in you a stranger to the world-illusion"
> –Ancient Egyptian Proverb

The concept of relativity of time is expressed in the hieroglyphic text entitled, *The Songs of The Harper*. In one verse, the relativity of the passage of time is explained as follows:

> "The whole period of things done on the earth is but a period of a dream."

This formula of the Harper, when put together with the *Coffin Text* formula given previously about the nature of Atum Ra (*after the millions of years of differentiated creation, the chaos that existed before creation will return; only the primeval god [40] and Asar will remain steadfast-no longer separated in space and time*) form an exceedingly powerful combination which should act as a fuse to ignite the mind's deeper insight into the nature of Self. The "period of millions of years" mentioned in the *Coffin Texts* is in reality the same as the period of a dream, and as you know, a long period of time can be experienced in a dream, but in reality nothing has happened, except that your consciousness has emanated a dream world. But as you also know, the dream world comes to an end and dissolves back into consciousness. In the same manner, God has emanated this world and will someday dissolve it back into the Primeval Ocean of potential consciousness. Consider your dreams. They may seem to occur over a period of hours. You may even experience the passage of years within your dream, and yet upon waking up you realize that the entire time you were in bed asleep for a few hours. In the same way, the entire period of the existence of the universe is nothing but the span of a short dream in the mind of God.

From an advanced perspective, neither time nor space can be said to exist as something that is real, just as time, space, matter or physical objects within a dream cannot be called "real." The entire dream world exists in the mind and does not require real time or space. The phenomenal world, which is experienced in the Waking State of consciousness, is also not real and does not exist except in the mind of God. This teaching is not only confirmed by the *Hymns of Amun*,[41] but it is also a primary teaching of Memphite Theology that is presented in the *Shabaka Inscription*.[42] In reality only eternity is real, and God is eternity. Since all matter is in reality constituted of the thought energy of God, and the changes in matter are called time, it must be clearly understood that God is the only reality that exists.

God is eternity itself. The limited perceptions of the unenlightened human mind and senses are what human beings refer to as "time" and "space" awareness. However, the perception of time and space is due to the limitations and conditioning of the human mind and body. If it were possible to perceive the entire universe, then you would discover that there is only oneness, an eternal view that is not restricted to time and space. This is the view that God has towards Creation. The task of the spiritual aspirant is to grow out of the limitations of the mind and body and discover the Cosmic Vision that lies within. When this is accomplished, there is a new perception of the universe. This represents the death of the human being and the birth of the spiritual life in the human being.

God has assumed the form of the neteru or Pautti. These "neteru" are cosmic forces, energies that sustain the universe and which constitute "physical matter." Therefore, this "physical" universe is in reality the body of God and everything in it is Divine, from the smallest atom to the largest celestial

---

[40] Referring to the Supreme Being in the form of Atum-Ra
[41] See the book *Egyptian Yoga Volume II* by Dr. Muata Ashby
[42] See also Egyptian Yoga: The Philosophy of Enlightenment (Egyptian Yoga Volume I)

bodies in the heavens. It must be emphasized that in this process, *The Universal Ba*[43] itself becomes the individual Ba of every human being, due to its association and identification with the feelings of the emotional body, *Ka,* and the cravings of the Physical body, *Khat.*

By practicing the disciplines of Maat, the initiate is able to curb the wanton desires of the ego and thereby strengthen the will of the intellect. The science of practicing virtue in life will serve to assist the aspirant to purify the heart (mind), to cultivate peace of mind, and thereby to develop insight into the innermost Self. At this stage, the movement or vibration in the Primeval Waters which caused the world to be, subsides. Just as a calm lake reflects a pure image, the purified mind will reflect the clarity of the Cosmic Soul. The waves, caused by movements of the mind, would once again become just as the waves in the Primeval Ocean before creation, silent, at rest, at peace.

Your innermost Self, the Cosmic Soul, is constantly interacting with the world through the mind. If you had yellow sunglasses on, when you look at anything you would see a yellow tinge. In the same way, when you look at the world through your conditioned mind and senses, your vision reflects the tinge of egoism and divergent thoughts, but most of all, ignorance of your true Self which causes body identification. If you were to eradicate your mental conditioning, you would see a different reality. This is the goal of the various disciplines of mystical spirituality, to purify the intellect, **Saa**. By developing your higher intellectual ability to cut through the illusions of life with the ax of wisdom, you purify your subconscious mind from all of the conditioning. It is this purification of Saa which can lead you to awareness of the Higher Self.

The philosophy of the four states of consciousness (waking, dream, dreamless sleep, undifferentiated (transcendental consciousness) is of paramount importance for the spiritual aspirant. A profound understanding of this teaching will lead you to develop subtlety of intellect in discerning the reality of the thoughts in your own mind as well as that which is real around you. In the book *The Cycles of Time*, we explored in depth, the practices of how this teaching is applied in everyday life in order to realize its significance at the deepest levels of the mind through virtuous living, the practice of Maat.

Maat philosophy provides us with a guideline for determining what is real and what is not. This is crucial to the correct operation of the mind because the mind supports whatever reality it believes to be true. You experience the world through your mind and senses. You have learned that these are valid criteria to determine the validity of the world and of your inner experience. Everything must be known through your rationalizing mind once it has been perceived by your senses. However, as we showed in the books *Egyptian Yoga: The Philosophy of Enlightenment* and *The Hidden properties of Matter*, what is normally considered to be real and abiding, solid matter, is nothing more than energy in its grosser states of being. It must be clearly understood that mental perceptions are not direct perceptions of matter. Your hand which you use to hold an object is itself a swirling mass of energy which is connected to other masses of energy conduits that lead to the brain. Sensual stimulus is an interaction between different forms of energy that registers in the brain centers in a specific manner. The mind perceives these stimuli by reacting to the centers and then acknowledges a perception. Therefore, perception occurs in the brain itself and not in the hand. Consider for a moment the situation of a paralyzed person or your own experience if a limb has fallen "asleep." In these eventualities, there is still a limb, but there is no perception. Why? Because the perception media, the senses, are incapacitated. Consider the possibility of the paralyzed limb coming into contact with an object. Did any interaction occur? From the standpoint of the observation yes there was some sort of interaction between two objects, but not from the standpoint of the person with the disability.

Now consider the Dream State of consciousness. When you have dreams you perceive various objects, you touch them and you may even feel you own them. They appear to be real and "feel" very solid and true. However, upon waking you realize that they did not exist and never did. They were simply energy forms, which you created out of the subtle astral matter and perceived through the

---

[43] The terms: The Universal, World Ba, Pa Neter, Amun, Nebertcher are to be understood as being synonymous.

deluded mind. They were fleeting masses of subtle energy that arose out of your own mind and were perceived by your own mind. You developed an illusory triad of consciousness during your Dream State and from this arose an entire world. Your waking ego self-concept dissolved and you became a new subject. This "new" you used the subtle senses to perceive objects which you yourself imagined to exist. This is the triad of *seer, seen and sight*. When you woke up, this triad dissolved into your waking consciousness as if it never existed. However, upon waking up, you did not wake up into a reality, but rather you moved into another form of triad.

The *triad* of human consciousness arises out of your inability to perceive reality without the mind and senses. The mind and senses along with your soul form the three elements of the triad. If you were to transcend the mind and senses, you would perceive reality directly through your soul. Only through direct perception is it possible to know the truth or reality. The teaching of the triad is expressed in the symbolism of the Divine Trinity, which arises out of the Primeval Ocean.

The whole idea here is that the world you perceive as real is illusory. The senses, which you use to perceive the world are illusory, and the mind which you use to perceive the world is also illusory. Therefore, there is only one factor left which qualifies as real. That factor is the *witnessing consciousness* that perceives all of the different states. Through spiritual practices (yoga of wisdom, yoga of action, yoga of devotion and yoga of meditation) you can gradually lead your mind to deeper and deeper levels of perception of the truth until you discover the Absolute Truth beyond all of the illusory layers of the mind.

This essay has been presented so that the practitioner may begin to understand the visualization that is desired by the *Prt m Hru* texts, when it is written that the initiate is to say statements such as the following ones below. They are mystic formulas designed to awaken the innermost memory of one's true and ultimate identity as one with the Divinity who has brought all into existence and who will also dissolve it. This is the ultimate discovery, coveted by all mystics of the world. In other words, the temporary mortal existence is not the ultimate reality.

# TRANSLATION FORMATS USED FOR PRESENTING THE TRANSLATIONS WITH THE TRILINEAR METHOD

## Conventional Interlinear Format

The conventional or regular interlinear format of translating Ancient Egyptian hieroglyphic texts presents a phonetic transliteration of the Ancient Egyptian hieroglyphs and transposes the hieroglyphs into the characters of the language they are being translated into. The second line presents a word for word translation. This level of translation can sometimes result in a limited, choppy and less intelligible presentation of the original intent of the script. When the translation is between languages of dissimilar structure and cultural references such as the difference between the Ancient Egyptian language, which is rich in metaphor and iconographical implied wisdom versus the European languages which are based on a stricter alphabetic matrix, the structural differences along with differences of culture mean that a strict word for word translation can be insufficient to convey a full understanding of the intended meaning. So, while the conventional interlinear format is useful to a certain extent, a more comprehensive translation matrix is needed to gain the deeper richness of the meaning and import of the original hieroglyphic text.

**Example of the Regular Interlinear Format:**

Verse 1.    ORIGINAL TEXT
    1.1.    Transliteration into the phonetic letters of the language of the reader
    1.2.    Translation in to the words of the language of the reader

Ex:

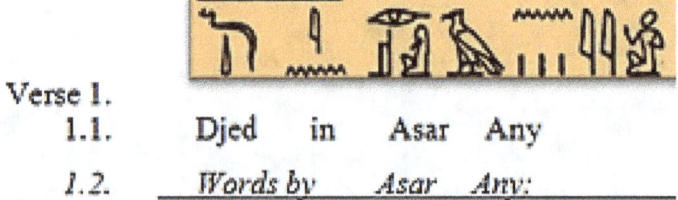

Verse 1.
    1.1.    Djed    in    Asar    Any
    1.2.    Words by    Asar    Any:

# Trilinear Contextual Format

The Trilinear Format for translating the Ancient Egyptian writing is a method as well as, to some degree, also a decipherment protocol that allows a layout for viewing the meaning from its source through layers of meaning extraction to the final rendition. The term "decipherment" is used because to the modern mind, whose concerns are often far removed from the world and philosophy of the Ancient Egyptians, the contexts and philosophy of the ancients is akin to more than a mystery, but also as an scarcely fathomable idea that is like a code or formula to be discovered so as to unlock the secrets of life, death and the afterlife. Over the years, Dr. Muata Ashby has developed a format of translating Ancient Egyptian hieroglyphs into the native language of the reader that incorporates three levels of translation instead of the two levels of the ordinary conventional interlinear format. In a few cases the conventional interlinear format is used in this volume. However, in most other cases a Ternary System will be used. The Ternary System devised by Dr. Muata Ashby adds a third layer of translation to the work that includes a contextual translation beyond the word for word translation. This added layer of translation may be termed "Contextual Translation" and all together constitutes the ***Trilinear Contextual format***.

The Trilinear Form (which is a ternary system) of translations is a format developed by Dr. Muata Ashby for translating the Ancient Egyptian Hieroglyphic texts. It contains a *tripartite* arrangement composed of three translation sections or layers/levels. The <u>first level</u> is a phonetic transliteration. The <u>second level</u> is a direct word for word translation from hieroglyphic to the native language of the reader. These two levels generally constitute the "Conventional Interlinear Format" of translation. The Trilinear Format adds a new level of translation. The <u>third level</u> of translation is a contextual translation bringing out the meaning in an informal colloquial context in prose style incorporating: A- the Ancient Egyptian Sebait (philosophical) tenets along with B- the Ancient Egyptian Matnu (mythic) references and Ancient Egyptian "Maut" (morals or takeaways of the myth to which the text appertains) contained in the text in order to better reveal the intended meaning for the reader's language and culture.

C- In this volume a new feature has been added to the trilinear system; the last translated verse will also include, where possible, a summary making contextual sense of the wisdom presented throughout the text, with particular focus on the beginning verse so as to clarify the takeaway by recalling the status of the spiritual aspirant at the beginning, then the transformation experiences throughout the text in its key hieroglyphic expressions and concluding with the outcome expressed in the final verse.

<u>**Example of the Trilinear Format:**</u>

*Verse 1.*   ORIGINAL TEXT
- 1.1.   Transliteration into the phonetic letters of the language of the reader
- 1.2.   Translation in to the words of the of the language of the reader
- 1.3.   Translation with contextual insights which may include philosophical and or mythological and/or historical background insights with colloquial references.

Ex:

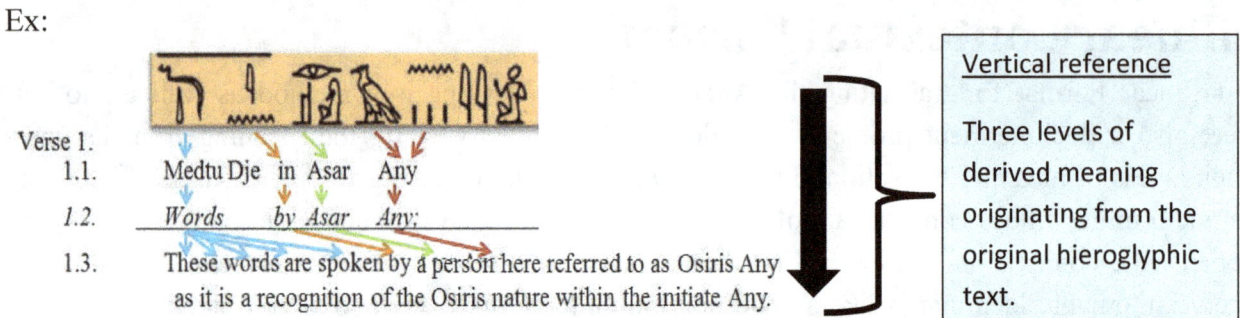

NOTE: Each level of translation is designed to be both a reference to the other levels (vertically) but also to the previous and next statement in each level; so for example: Verse translation Level 2.1 relates to 2.2 and 2.3 (vertical) but 2.2 also relates to 1.2 and 3.2 (horizontal). Therefore, if all the Level 2 translations are read by themselves or Level 3 translations are read by themselves one after the other, there will be a continuous and coherent rendering of the text

**Example**

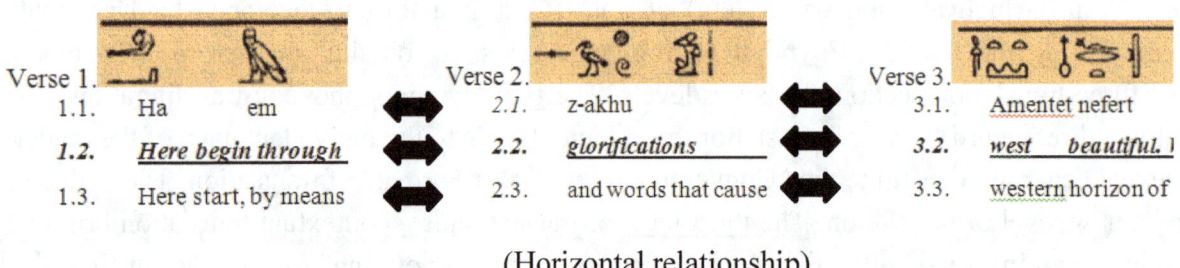

(Horizontal relationship)

In this way, the readings of Verse 1.2 followed by Verse 2.2, followed by Verse 3.2, translations, one after the other (ignoring .1 and .3 levels), horizontally, provide a continuous and coherent word for word narative of the translation.

Also, the readings of Verse 1.3 followed by Verse 2.3, followed by Verse 3.3, translations, one after the other (ignoring .1 and .2 levels), horizontally, provide a continuous and coherent prose narative of the translation.

Note: When some text appears in red it is because the original hieroglyphic text was written in the same way. This was done to highlight certain parts of the text or to highlight the chapter titles of the text. See example below.

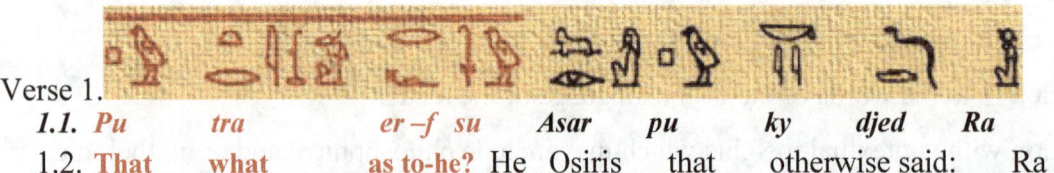

Verse 1.
  1.1. *Pu        tra        er –f  su    Asar    pu    ky    djed    Ra*
  1.2. That      what      as to-he? He  Osiris  that  otherwise said:  Ra
  1.3. What is that personality that is being talked about? That personality is Osiris. Another way of thinking about it is that Osiris is also Ra…

# Reading the Philosophy Embedded in Ancient Egyptian Hieroglyphic Writings

Here I will provide two examples, using two of the most important hieroglyphs to demonstrate why and how the philosophy of the Ancient Egyptian Mysteries is determined in the texts to be read. As stated earlier, reading the Ancient Egyptian texts in a literal way, ascribing meanings that relate to the culture of the reader is a disservice to the ancient culture and also it is a distortion of the meaning of the texts and the legacy of the original priests and priestesses who created them.

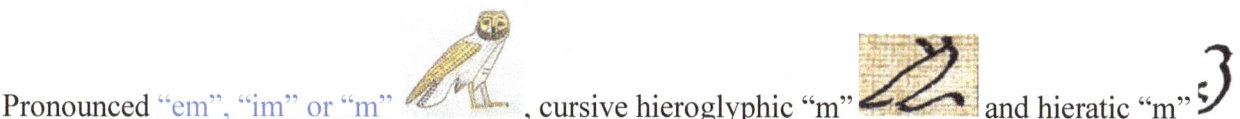

Pronounced "em", "im" or "m" , cursive hieroglyphic "m" and hieratic "m" .

The first glyph is the owl. Perhaps one of the most important glyphs, unlike determinatives, which do not convey phonetic aspects to the word, the owl has phonetic and philosophical meaning. Whenever the owl appears the meaning can range from "in, within, inside, though, as, in the form of. This means that it is a pivotal term especially when it relates the person for whom the text has been created to any particular or general Divinity [god or goddess]. It therefore means that such a person is being identified with that divinity or with an aspect of divinity or they are being recognized as "becoming, or appearing or manifesting as". This of course signifies a movement of transformation either in progress or already attained. This glyph is seldom interpreted in such a manner and thus the overall outcomes of such neglectful translations will render a mundane and or erroneous insight into the Ancient Egyptian hieroglyphic writings.

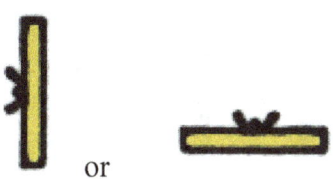

**Another important glyph is the scroll.**

Generally, the Ancient Egyptian language is composed of phonetic, ideographic and determinative glyphs. The determinative glyphs do not contribute a phonetic aspect to the word but rather contributes a reference and or philosophical implication to be inferred by the reader. The scroll is a determinative glyph that, when appears, forces the application of a perspective abstractness that allows a vision of a meaning that transcends a strictly mundane or specific application. This is a reading that incorporates a philosophical and or conceptual basis to the meaning of the particular word. An example of how to apply the scroll in reading a word or sentence or passage is that its conceptual abstractness is to be applied to the regular meaning of the world; and the abstractness relates to the Ancient Egyptian philosophy of the spiritual mysteries that affirms a transcendental nature of life that goes beyond physical reality.

As a group, determinatives provide a similar function and constitute an integral and essential means of understanding the deeper wisdom and intent of the Ancient Egyptian written language. Below are some of the most important determinatives.

For more on the Ancient Egyptian Hieroglyphic Writing see the book *Ancient Egyptian Hieroglyphs for Beginners* by Muata Ashby

# SECTION 2

# ANCIENT EGYPTIAN BOOK OF THE DEAD HIEROGLYPH TRANSLATIONS OF SELECTED CHAPTERS AND ASSOCIATED TEXTS

# PART 1: CREATION MYTH & THE ORIGIN OF MIND, THE FIELD OF HUMAN EXISTENCE & *EXPERIENCE*

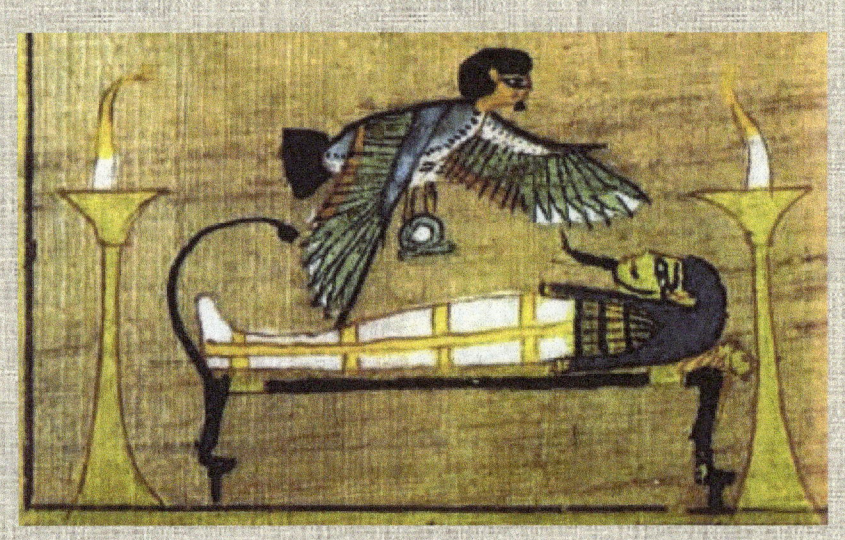

# SELECTIONS FROM ANUNIAN CREATION MYTH A.
# Book of Knowing the forms of the Creator and defeating the principle of chaos/degradation/decay

TRANSLATION BY Dr. Muata Ashby

Creation Papyrus

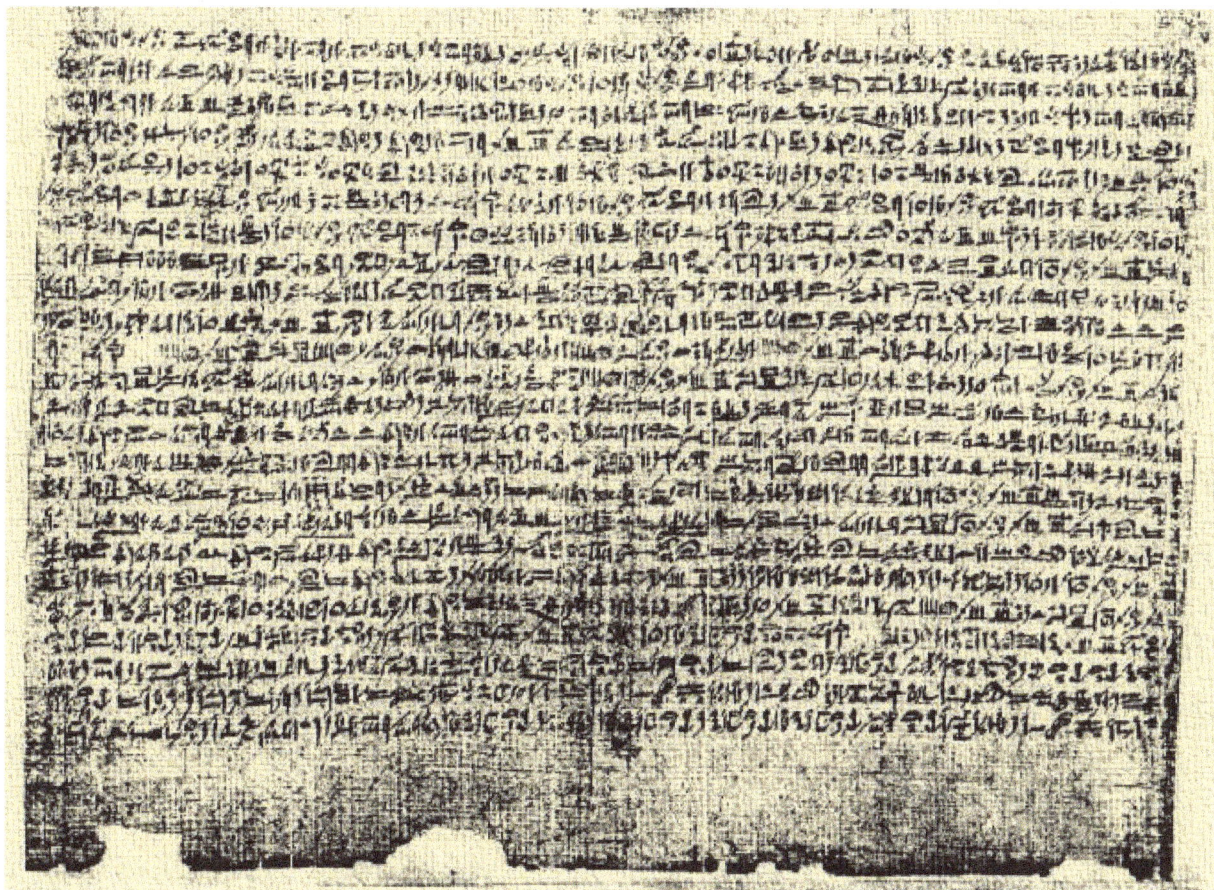

**Verse 1.**

1.1. *shat     nty     rech     kheperu     nu     Ra*
1.2. book     of     knowing     forms/images/representations     of     Creator
1.3. This book contains the wisdom about understanding forms/images/representations of Ra, the creator of Creation…

**Verse 2.**

2.1. *Secher     Apep     djedu     Neberdjer     Djed - f*
2.2. defeating     Apophis     Words said     All-encompassing Divinity     speech- his
2.3. …and for defeating Apophis, the force that counters Ra in relation to his creative work. The following words were spoken by Neberdjer, the all-encompassing Divine Self that gave rise to Ra.

**Verse 3.**

3.1. *mchet     Kheper - f     nuk     a     pu     Kheper     a*
3.2. After     creating - self     am     I     the     Creator     I
3.3. After creating himself he, Neberdjer now in the form of the Creator, said "I am the Creator";

**Verse 4.**

4.1. *m     Khepera     kheper - na     kheper     kheperu*
4.2. as     The Creator     creating - me     creating     creations
4.3. …and as The Creator, I created myself (the Creator) and the things (creations) that were created through my creative work.

## Verse 5.

**5.1.** *kheper            kheperu            neb        m       chet        kheper        asha*

5.2. <u>creation             creations           all       following       created       multitude</u>

5.3. Additionally, the things that were created by my creations, followed by my creating those creations, all of those things, the multiplicity of created things,

## Verse 6.

**6.1.** *Kheperu                      m       pert       m       ra       a       an*

6.2. <u>forms/images/representations      as  coming forth   through       mouth mine    not</u>

6.3. …those forms/images/representations all came forth through the sound vibrations of my mouth, when I spoke them into existence. Before that time there was not…

## Verse 7.

**7.1.** *kheper – pet         an       kheper – ta       an       qemam*

7.2. <u>created – heavens/sky   not     created - earth     not     fashioned/created</u>

7.3. …a heavens/sky that had been created yet and neither was there an earth yet. Also, I had not yet made…

## Verse 8.

**8.1.** *satatu             djeftu              m       bet       puy*

8.2. <u>earthly life forms     crawling life forms     in     places     those</u>

8.3. …any of the earthly creatures, the animals or plants or even the reptilian creatures and none of them had been placed in their proper habitats.

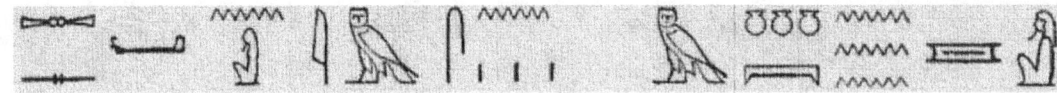

**Verse 9.**
    *9.1.*    *Tjez    - n-a    im    senu    m    Nunu    {Net}*
    9.2.    Knitted    - of – I    in    them    in    primeval waters  {Divine}
    9.3.    Also I had not yet interweaved, interlocked, linked or put them together in myself yet, within the undifferentiated consciousness, the primordial substratum of Creation, my body, from which all solid matter is composed, which at that time was…

**Verse 10.**
    *10.1.*    *m    nenu    an    gem    - na    bet    aha    n-a*
    10.2.    in    inactivity.    Not    found    - for I    place    stand    for-I
    10.3.    …in a state of inactivity, inertness, with no movement and on no forms. In the beginning there was only the primeval undifferentiated consciousness and nowhere for myself to stand, therefore there was no solid matter yet since I had not created it yet.

**Verse 11.**
    *11.1.*    *imy    akht {mdj - na    m    abt*
    11.2.    within    creative Spirit energy – to me    in    heart body part
    11.3.    Withiness { scroll signifies abstract concept}, in an internal dimension, I used creative intent on myself, in my heart {mind}, the place of deep mind contained in my own body. This caused motion in the primeval undifferentiated consciousness and brought forms into appearance.

**<u>NOTE:</u>** Below are highlighted key terms used in this verse with the realization that the heart of Ra that he applied the creative spirit energy on, is actually his cosmic mind.

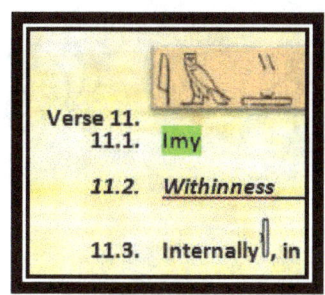
**Highlight 1**

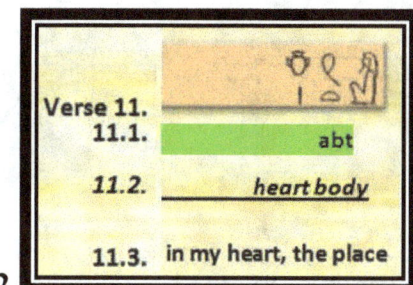
**Highlight 2**

"Ab n Ra"

The term "Imy", along with the use of the scroll in the term "Imy", denoting what is abstract, and the term "abt" are interrelated in the context that we are told that Ra created Creation by acting or applying Khu spirit fire of life energy on his own heart. The term abt relates to a physical heart which means it is his body and not a mythic conceptual idea. In other words it is God's actual body and elsewhere we learn that the heart of Ra has a formal name, the term "Ab n Ra" or "The Heart of Ra". Additionally, we also learn that this title applies to the God Djehuty (Thoth/Hermes). In Ancient Egyptian psychomythology, Lord Djehuty (image left) is the scribe of Ra and in essence his cosmic mind. Therefore, Creation occurs in the cosmic mind of God and is to be thought of as a projection of mind on the body of God not unlike the world created when a person goes to sleep and creates a dream world.

**Verse 12.**

12.1. *Zenty - na        m      Shu      ari      n-a        aru            nebt*

12.2. Foundation - of me    in    Shu    made   of-self   forms/images   all[fem]

12.3. So a foundation for the universe was setup on my body and through the cosmic force, the God Shu, my son, my ethereal light, who brought into existence air and space, which I made, out of myself. Thus, the forms/images/representations, ALL of them were made by me and are composed of me. Thus, I the Spirit behind Creation created Creation which is itself my female half.

Verse 22.

| | | | |
|---|---|---|---|
| **22.1.** | *per* | *n-a* | *m* | *oabu* |
| 22.2. | coming forth | the I | as | plants |

22.3. Thus I came forth in the form of vegetation.

Verse 23.

| | | | | | |
|---|---|---|---|---|---|
| **23.1.** | *djd-ft* | *nebt* | *khepr* | *nebt* | *im* | *sen* |
| 23.2. | crawling | all | creations | all | as | those |

23.3. All the crawling animals, I manifest as those as well.

Verse 24.

| | | | | | | | |
|---|---|---|---|---|---|---|---|
| **24.1.** | *mesu* | *in* | *Shu* | *di-f* | *Tfnut* | *hna* | *Nut* | *mesu* | *in* |
| 24.2. | birth | by | Shu | gives-he | Tefnut | and | Nut | birth gives by |

24.3. I gave birth to the God Shu (air, ether, light) and the Goddess Tefnut (moisture and life force) and they gave birth to the Goddess Nut (sky and heavens) and…

Verse 25.

| | | | | | | |
|---|---|---|---|---|---|---|
| **25.1.** | Geb | Nut | Asar | Her Khent an maa | Setep | Aset |
| 25.2. | Geb | Nut | Osiris | Horus foremost blind | Set | Isis |

25.3. Geb (earth) and Nut (sky and heavens) gave birth to Osiris (the soul), Horus the foremost blind (the potential spiritual aspiration for redemption of the soul) one along with Set (ego) and Isis (intuitional wisdom)…

## Verse 26.

| | | | | | | | | |
|---|---|---|---|---|---|---|---|---|
| **26.1.** | Nebthet | m | chat | ua | m | sa | ua | im | sen |
| 26.2. | Nephthys | through | body | one | by | after | one | through | them |
| 26.3. | …and Nephthys (physicality), they came one by one through my body and through their bodies came… | | | | | | | | |

## Verse 27.

| | | | | | | | |
|---|---|---|---|---|---|---|---|
| **27.1.** | mesu | senu | ashatu | sen | m | ta | pn |
| 27.2. | …birth | theirs | many | those | forms | earth | that |
| 27.3. | …the births of all the many things that came into being on the earth planet. In this way, I am the source of all that came into being through the gods and goddesses as I created them of myself and thus anything they create is also using parts of my body; thus all their creations are also mine. | | | | | | |

# Scripture of the Creation Version B-Book of Knowing the forms of the Creator and defeating the principle of chaos/degradation/decay

**Trans. by Muata Ashby**

Verse 1.

1.1. shat        nty        rech        kheperu              nu      Ra
1.2. book       the        knowing     forms/creations      of      Ra
1.3. This is the book containing the teachings about the Creation of the universe, that is to say, the forms of objects created by the god Ra.

Verse 2.

2.1. se-cher          Apep       djedu           Neb-er-djer         djed    f
2.2. causing downfall Apophis    words to speak  Lord-of-utmost limit says   he
2.3. The knowledge herein causes there to be a downfall of the divinity Apophis, the cosmic force of dissolution and disintegration. The following words are spoken by the transcendental Divine, the underlying source from whence Ra arose: Neberdjer, the All-Encompassing-Divinity speaks thus:

Verse 3.

3.1. Khepera       kheper      kheperu     kheperu     kua        im
3.2. Creator God   created     forms       created     myself     as
3.3. In the form of the Creator god Khepera, the forms of Creation were created by me, myself as…

Verse 4.

4.1. kheperu       en        Khepera       kheper      im       zep-tpy
4.2. forms         of/by     Creator God   created     in       beginning
4.3. …those forms that were created by the Creator God Khepera in the beginning of time.

Verse 5.

**5.1.** *kheper-kua*     *im*     *kheperu*     *en*     *Khepera*     *kheper*     *a*

5.2. created-myself    form of    forms    of    Creator God    created    I

5.3. Therefore, I created myself as the forms that were created by the creator god Khepera. I created…

Verse 6.

6.1. *kheper*     *kheperu*     *pu*     *en*     *pa*     *n-a*

6.2. creation    forms    those    of    that    of-I

6.3. …those forms/ objects that are in Creation are composed of me.

Verse 7.

**7.1.** *iu*     *pautetu*     *suht*     *n-a*     *pa*     *n-a*     *im*

7.2. it is    primeval material/matter    egg    of-I    that    of-I    form of

7.3. It is composed of the primeval undifferentiated material. Creation emerged out of an egg that came out of me…

Verse 8.

**8.1.** *Pa*     *ren*     *-a*     *Ausarz*     *pautet*     *pautu*

8.2. through the    name-mine    Osiris    primeval substratum    Primeval material

8.3. [Summary of the previous text up to this point: Neberdjer has said It (Neberdjer) is manifesting as the god Khepera and created Creation at the beginning of time, and as Khepera brought forth Creation from himself, through primeval undifferentiated matter in the primeval ocean.] Now, in this final verse of the History of the Creation Version B, Khepera is stating…

… {I Neberdjer say} that name of mine, when thinking of me in time and space, is actually Osiris. Being *Neberdjer* I am the substratum of the entire Creation. As *Asar* (Osiris), I am the substratum of the primeval ocean, which is my subtle sustaining aspect in time and space. As Asar, I am the substratum of souls, whose bodies emanate from the primeval ocean and whose soul consciousness, is Asar (which ultimately are all me). As *Khepera,* I am the dynamic Creator of Creation and as Asar, I am the inactive Spirit substratum, soul identity, of Neberdjer, supporting and individuating principle in the primeval ocean, which Creation has emerged from and is a coagulated part, and which was given form to by Khepera, and all souls in it. Thus, I am the foremost soul of all souls and all gods and goddesses.

Verse 9.
- **9.1.** ary a mertu a nebet
- 9.2. do I desire I all
- 9.3. I am able to do any and all Creative actions in accord with my will…

Verse 10.
- **10.1.** im ta pen usech n-a im –f
- 10.2. in earth, this encompassing of –myself within he
- 10.3. …within and on this earth and also as this Creation is within myself I encompass all the Creation and all my Creative work within myself.

Verse 20.
- **20.1.** Ary a kheperu a
- 20.2. Did I creations/forms myself
- 20.3. Thus, it was I who created the forms which are reflections of myself in time and space…

Verse 21.
- **21.1.** imy im Ba a puy tjez n-a
- 21.2. within through soul mine these binding of-me
- 21.3. …that actually has all come to exists through the existence of my individuating principle, my soul, to which I have attached connected joined combined trussed, varied parts of the primeval matter, that I caused to take the form of elements, in varied combinations…

Verse 22.
- **22.1.** imy im nunu im nen an
- 22.2. within through Primeval Waters Divinity manifesting inert/still not
- 22.3. … I have done this through the being of the Primeval Ocean Divinity, who was initially inert still immobile inactive but part of which I caused to become active dynamic operational. I did the actions of creating because I could not…

Verse 23.

**23.1.** gemy n-a bet aha n-a imy Akhut n-a
23.2. finding for-I place stand for-I inside spirit of-me
23.3. … find any solid place to stand on, as it was like an ocean where you have no land or island to set foot down on solid firm ground. So I activated some of the Spirit-will power of my own Spirit Being…

Verse 24.

**24.1.** im ab – a zenty n-a im her-a ary n-a aryu
24.2. within heart-mine foundation for-I in personality-I action to-I actions
24.3. …within my own heart, which is the unconscious potential of the mind of my own personality and acted, applied that energy-force on myself causing more Creation within myself to occur just as when the personality goes to sleep and a dream emerges from part of the person's own mind. The actions of mine, in the form of the creations I made out of myself and which are part of me…

Verse 25.

**25.1.** nebt uau k{ua} zenty n-a im ab-a qemam n-a
25.2. all one me founded of-I/me within heart-mine Creation of-I
25.3. … all of them are actually one in me and not many, i.e. since I created Creation out of myself and within my own mind there is no separate reality like Creator and Created, it is all me; I am the one reality, the one existence. The foundation for Creation is in my heart, which is my mind and intellect.

Verse 26.

**26.1.** Ky kheperu ashat kheperu nu Khepera a
26.2. Other creations manifold creations of Khepera I
26.3. The varieties of other things that may appear in Creation were also created by me, the Creator of what was created.

Verse 27.
- **27.1.** *Kheper   in   mesu   senu   im   Kheperu   nu   mesu   senu*
- 27.2. Creation   by offspring   they   within   creations   of   offspring   theirs
- 27.3. The creation by and within the things that I created, and their offspring are also my Creations and part of the oneness of me, the original Creator who created everything in the beginning out of my self and through the primeval ocean of consciousness with my mind, by acting one with it with creative intent energy to cause parts of the primeval matter of the primeval ocean to take the forms that caused them to take and thus appear as many objects in Creation, though in reality all the objects are formed from the same primeval matter and they are all parts of me.

# Ancient Egyptian Creation Myth B Continued: Origin of Feelings: Remy is the name of Ra source of vegetation, animals and people (endowed with sentiment (feelings). Sentiments give rise to  {emotions})

Verse 43.
- **43.1.** *oabu*
- 43.2. vegetation
- 43.3. Flora/ plant life…

Verse 44.
- **44.1.** *hefyu   im   Remy   im   remty*
- 44.2. reptiles   within   Ra the crier   in   weeping
- 44.3. and reptiles were within the tears of the eyes of Ra's form as the Crier Divinity. In the tears

Verse 45.
- **45.1.** *er   a   ka   en   arit [ra]   a   kheper   remteju*
- 45.2. from   I   behold   of   eyes [solar]   I   created   people
- 45.3. …from me, know this now, men and women were created from the shining of my eye. Thus, the life and feelings in plants and reptiles came into being from my life and feelings through my tears that shone forth, falling to earth, from my eye [the sun] that are the rays of the sun containing the moisture and shining life force from my very own consciousness.

# Invoke name of Ra and conquer Apep

Verse 51.
- **51.1.** Shenut      sen       ren {Neter}   secher   sen
- 51.2. Invoking   they      name {divine}  defeats   the
- 51.3. The practice of invoking Gods Name defeats…

Verse 52.
- **52.1.** Cheftu    sen     qemam        senu       hekau        en
- 52.2. Nemeses   those   creating     they       words of power   of
- 52.3. Inimical forces. It has the effect of creating, by those who do it, words of power for…

Verse 53.
- **53.1.** se-cher          Apep        auf         hersaau
- 53.2. causing overthrow  Apophis    body        person tied up
- 53.3. … causing those inimical forces, primary among them being Apophis, the divinity of chaos and disintegration, to be as if bound, tied up and overpowered.

**NOTE:** The following Ancient Egyptian Proverbs, based on the later Hermetic period writings, are presented as parallel philosophical concepts of using vibrations such as those that arise from speech, along with the energies behind the speech, cultivated by the study of Ancient Egyptian philosophy, to change the states of matter and mood (feelings) so as to promote a conducive psychological and energetic environment for overcoming negative feelings, desires and thoughts.

"To change your mood or mental state, change your vibration."

"To destroy an undesirable rate of mental vibration, concentrate on the opposite vibration to the one to be suppressed."

-Kybalion

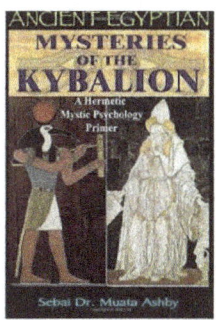

A book by Dr. Muata Ashby

**53-Ancient Egyptian Mysteries of The Kybalion: A Hermetic Mystic Psychology Primer Paperback – November 28, 2014**

# Ancient Egyptian Creation Myth B Continued: CREATION OF THE GODS AND GODDESSES THAT COMPOSE THE ELEMENTS OF NATURE AND THE COMPONENTS OF THE HUMAN PSYCHE

Verse 54.
54.1.   Mes   en   Shu   di-f   Tefnut   Nut   Asar   Heru Khenty an Maa
54.2.   Birth   of   Shu   given-he   Tefnut   Nut   [Geb]   Osiris   Horus foremost blind
54.3.   Have given birth to the god Shu, the god of air, light, and conscience, ether; to Tefnut, the goddess of moisture and life-force; to Osiris, the god of the Soul and Horus the foremost blind and innocence of life aspiration…

Verse 55.
55.1.   Setep   Aset   Nebethet   in   mesu - senu
55.2.   Set   Isis   Nephthys   by   birthing - they
55.3.   …as well as Set, the god of the personality (ego); to Isis, the goddess of wisdom and immortality; and to Nephthys, the goddess of physicality and mortality. Behold! They give birth…

Verse 56.
56.1.   Qemam   senu   kheperu   ashatu   im   ta
56.2.   create   they   creations   many   on   earth
56.3.   …they create their creations, their many offspring, on the earth planet.

Verse 57.
57.1.   Pen   em   kheperu   nu   mesu   em   kheperu   nu mesu senu
57.2.   These   through   creations   the   children   through   creations   the children theirs.
57.3.   These successive generations occur through the creations of their own children and the generation of their children's children etc. (i.e. from their children's children) This, all the generations from the generations all originate in my, the original and only Creator and that creator form originated and is rooted in my transcendental all-expansive and encompassing being.

# TREE OF LIFE OF ANUNIAN CREATION THEURGY
## Based on the Creation Myth Scripture

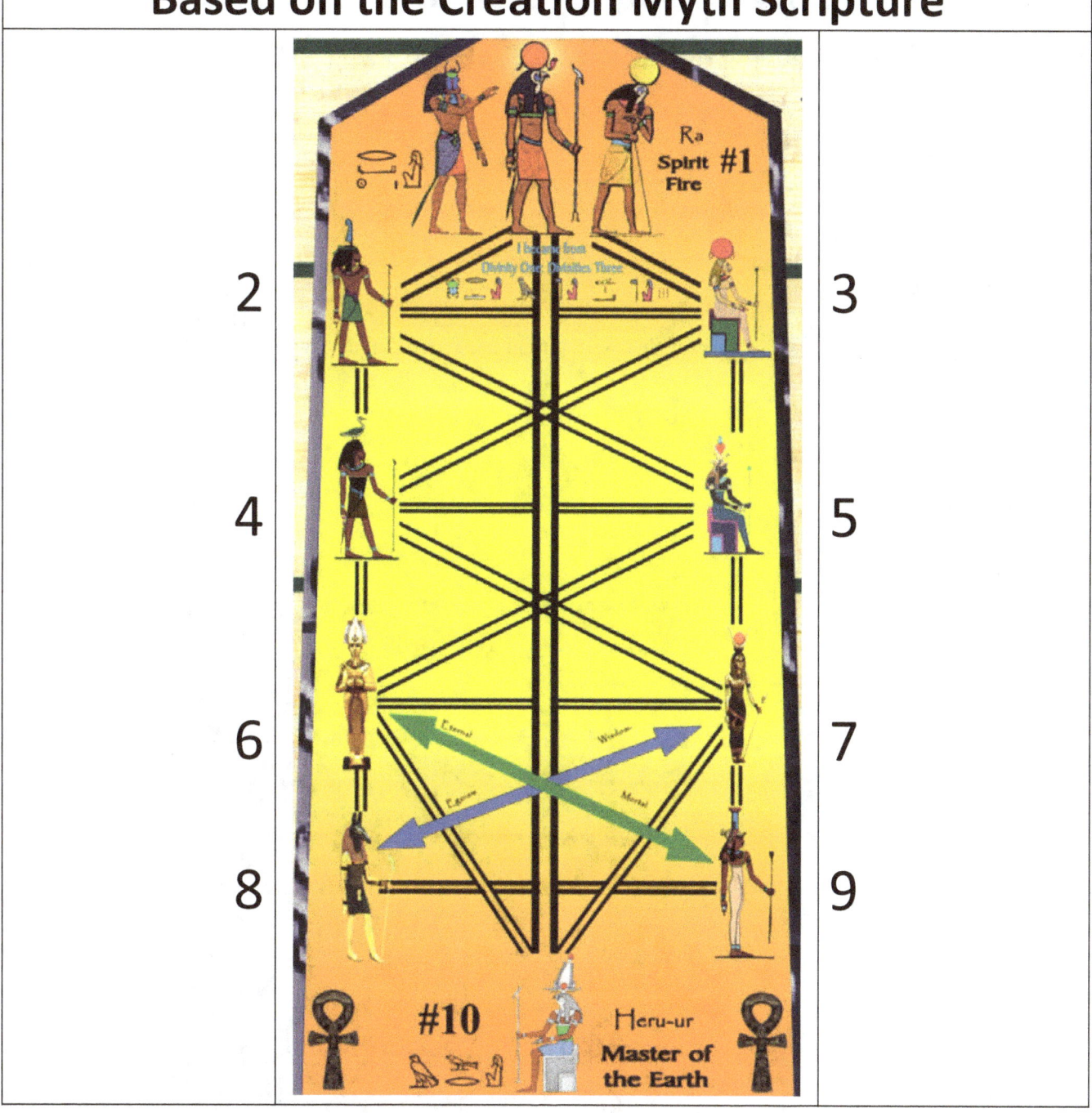

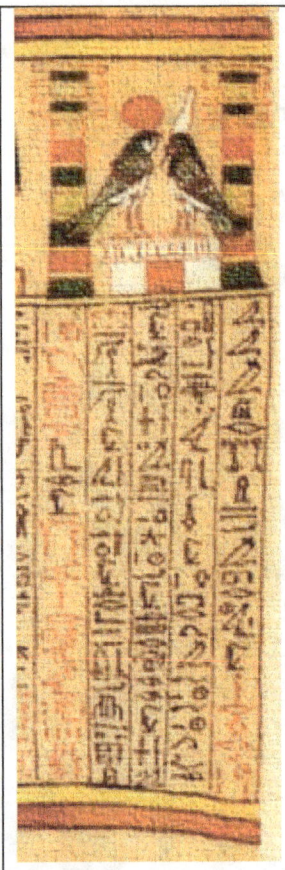

# Egyptian Book of the Dead: The relationship of the Soul of Ra and Osiris: Papyrus Ani-The Souls of Osiris and Ra meet in the netherworld.

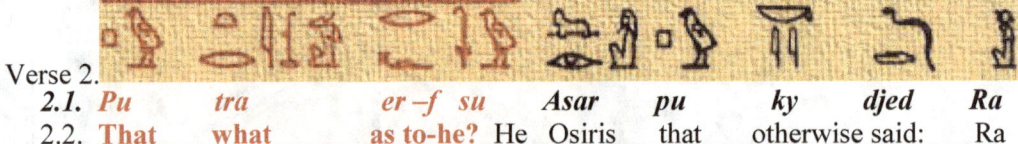

Verse 2.
- 2.1. *Pu    tra    er –f    su    Asar    pu    ky    djed    Ra*
- 2.2. That    what    as to-he?    He    Osiris    that    otherwise said:    Ra
- 2.3. **What is that personality that is being talked about?** That personality is Osiris. Another way of thinking about it is that Osiris is also Ra…

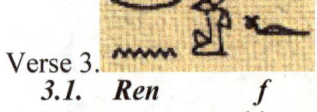

Verse 3.
- 3.1. *Ren    f*
- 3.2. name    his
- 3.3. …therefore, Ra is another name of Osiris and vice versa.

**Trans. by Muata Ashby**

# PART 3: Body Conscience and Mental Complexes

# Selections from Papyrus Petersburg 1116A: Instruction for Mery-ka-ra

## ABOUT THE MISERABLE ASIATIC
**Trans. by Muata Ashby**

Verse 1.

| 1.1. | Djed | suten | na | ger | en | pedjty |
|---|---|---|---|---|---|---|
| 1.2. | Words | royal | those | about | the | foreigners |

1.3. The following words are about the foreigners, the same ones who have military forces composed of bowmen.

Verse 2.

| 2.1. | As | aamu | khazy | kesn | pu | en | bu | ent-f | im |
|---|---|---|---|---|---|---|---|---|---|
| 2.2. | Behold, | Asiatics | miserable | irksome | they | of | place | of-he | within |

2.3. Consider that the Asiatic personality is a miserable character with negative temperament. The Asiatic personality is annoying, trying, vexing, and even exasperating. The Asiatic personality is within a place that...

Verse 3.

| 3.1. | ahu | mu | shetau | [mdj] | im | chet | ashau |
|---|---|---|---|---|---|---|---|
| 3.2. | troublemaker | water | hidden | [abs] | in | wood | abundance |

3.3. produces a rabble-rouser, agitator, and menace for society. This happens because their water is hidden from them under the parched dessert lands, they have an abundance of wood but...

**Verse 4.**

4.1. *watu    ary    kesn    ma    djuu*
4.2. paths    make (way)    irksome    behold    mountains
4.3. ...the paths through their lands are rough and that is before we even consider their many mountains that are hard to traverse!

**Verse 5.**

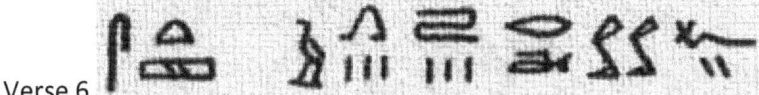

5.1. *an    in    f    im    aset-per    uat*
5.2. not    hastening    he    into    abode    one
5.3. The Asiatic personality does not hasten to a single abode, one place to consider as his home where he can be stable.

**Verse 6.**

6.1. *setesh    usten    peher    red    fy*
6.2. Set    stepping    circles    feet    theirs
6.3. The Setian, egoistic, self-centered barbarous consciousness pushes and drives his steps as they wander the land in circles, on foot.

**Verse 7.**

7.1. *Iu    f    her    aha    djer    er – k hau    Heru*
7.2. It is    he    personality    warlike    since    to-thee time    Horus
7.3. It is he who is a warlike, combative, aggressive personality and he has been that way since the time of Horus, from ancient times.

**Verse 8.**

8.1. *an    qen    n -    f    an    ger    qentu    f*
8.2. not    conquer    of-    he    not    also    conquerable    he
8.3. he is not able to conquer us and conversely, he is not conquerable; so the conflict goes on in an never-ending stalemate.

# Selections from Papyrus Petersburg 1116A: Instruction for Mery-ka-ra -continued

*ABOUT HOW THE ACTIONS OF A PERSON ARE JUDGED EVEN AFTER THEY ARE DEAD AND THE CONCEPT OF ARYU OR KARMA*

**Trans. by Muata Ashby**

Verse 1.

    1.1.     Maa     senu     aha   {ra}     im     unut     {ra}
    1.2.     Look/view     they     lifetime {consc} as     moment     {consc.}
    1.3.     The gods and goddesses who judge the dead view a human lifetime {time of being conscious (as opposed to being unconscious as in being dead)} as if it occurred in a moment.

Verse 2.

    2.1.     zepp     senu     im     necht     menat     {mut}
    2.2.     Persisting     they     in strength locomotion bandages     {death}
    2.3.     However, even after a person is dead and they are wrapped in mummy bandages, there is a part of them that persists after {death} and has the capacity for movement even when the physical body is wrapped up tight and immobile.

Verse 3.

    3.1.     Rau     zepu     f     er-gs     f     im     ahau     {mdj}
    3.2.     Establish remains over     he     as to-side his form as lifetime judged
    3.3.     That part that remains over, after death of the body, establishes itself on one side of the person in the form of witnesses as the gods and goddesses judge {abstract[44]} that person's actions during their lifetime[45].

---

[44] {the presence of a scroll means that the concept being discussed should be regarded with an abstract ideal; thus it is not to be considered as an concrete tally but rather as summary or sum total effect of a person's actions on their character through their actions, thoughts, feelings and experiences that they engendered and became unconscious impressions that survive the death of the body and the conscious mind.}

[45] The deeper meaning of the terms "aha (with a sundisk symbol)" and "ahau" (lifetime judgment) relates to time of waking experiences, in other words, time of being alive, which applies to the current life that just ended but also applies to the previous lives or times of waking conscious experiences where actions were performed that led to previous thoughts, feelings and experiences, etc.

### Verse 4.

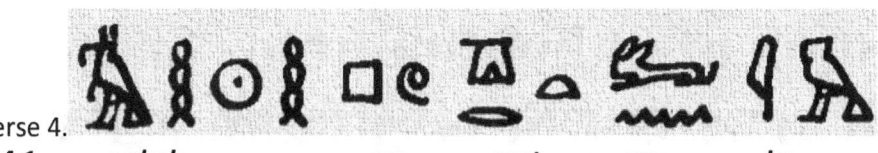

| 4.1. | nheh | pu | gert | un | im |
|---|---|---|---|---|---|
| 4.2. | Eternity | this | though | existing | within |

4.3. Nevertheless, there is existence for eternity within.

### Verse 5.

| 5.1. | ucha | pu | ari | tjez | {det} {det} | set |
|---|---|---|---|---|---|---|
| 5.2. | Ignorant fool unrighteous that | | doing | knot | {rise} {fight} | it |

5.3. The ignorant fool is one who by doing actions binds him or herself to that heap of unconscious impressions that remained over after death, the impressions from past life actions and their thoughts, feelings and the experiences derived from those that produced a sum total effect on the character of the personality and then fights about it; i.e. there is no use in {raising objections} or {fighting} about the unconscious impressions one has allowed oneself to bind oneself to, as if one's possessions, and it was an ignorant foolish thing to do in the first place and later raise objections about it.

### Verse 6.

| 6.1. | ar | peh | set | an | arit | iu | {ndj} |
|---|---|---|---|---|---|---|---|
| 6.2. | about | arrival | it | not | vision | fault/ iniquity | {bereft} |

6.3. Now, in reference to those who arrive at the judgment hall where all must face the judgment whereby the heap of past actions, thoughts, feelings and experiences established themselves on the side of the person, as their witnesses, the place where those are accounted for, and appear there, in the judgment hall, without fault or taint in their character, i.e. not being {bereft of virtue}...

### Verse 7.

| 7.1. | un | n–f | im | mi | Neter | {Her} |
|---|---|---|---|---|---|---|
| 7.2. | being | to-he | within | like | God | {Horus on Standard} |

7.3. ...it means arriving there and being regarded as one who, though despite appearing as a human soul, nevertheless, internally, they are recognized as being God, a {Horus being}.

# Pert-M-Heru. Book of Enlightenment- Chapter of the Heart of Carnelian. Souls do the will of the Mind and experience its experiences as if they were its own

**Trans. by Muata Ashby**

"Tumbled" – Processed, polished Carnelian Stone

Natural Carnelian Stone

# Pert-M-Heru. Book of Enlightenment- Chapter of the Heart of Carnelian. Souls do the will of the Mind and experience its experiences as if they were its own

**Trans. by Muata Ashby**

"Tumbled" – Processed, polished Carnelian Stone

Natural Carnelian Stone

Verse 4.

| 4.1. | nheh | pu | gert | un | im |
|---|---|---|---|---|---|
| 4.2. | Eternity | this | though | existing | within |

4.3. Nevertheless, there is existence for eternity within.

Verse 5.

| 5.1. | ucha | pu | ari | tjez | {det} {det} | set |
|---|---|---|---|---|---|---|
| 5.2. | Ignorant fool unrighteous | that | doing | knot | {rise} {fight} | it |

5.3. The ignorant fool is one who by doing actions binds him or herself to that heap of unconscious impressions that remained over after death, the impressions from past life actions and their thoughts, feelings and the experiences derived from those that produced a sum total effect on the character of the personality and then fights about it; i.e. there is no use in {raising objections} or {fighting} about the unconscious impressions one has allowed oneself to bind oneself to, as if one's possessions, and it was an ignorant foolish thing to do in the first place and later raise objections about it.

Verse 6.

| 6.1. | ar | peh | set | an | arit | iu | {ndj} |
|---|---|---|---|---|---|---|---|
| 6.2. | about | arrival | it | not | vision | fault/ iniquity | {bereft} |

6.3. Now, in reference to those who arrive at the judgment hall where all must face the judgment whereby the heap of past actions, thoughts, feelings and experiences established themselves on the side of the person, as their witnesses, the place where those are accounted for, and appear there, in the judgment hall, without fault or taint in their character, i.e. not being {bereft of virtue}…

Verse 7.

| 7.1. | un | n – f | im | mi | Neter | {Her} |
|---|---|---|---|---|---|---|
| 7.2. | being | to-he | within | like | God | {Horus on Standard} |

7.3. …it means arriving there and being regarded as one who, though despite appearing as a human soul, nevertheless, internally, they are recognized as being God, a {Horus being}.

**Verse 1.**

1.1. *Ra   en   ab   en   zeheru medtu-dje in   Asar Any   maa-kheru nuk-a*

1.2. Chapter of heart of carnelian words spoken by Osiris Any spiritual victory: I am

1.3. **This is the chapter of the Book of Enlightenment that has to do with the heart amulet that is composed of red carnelian stone. These are the words to be spoken by** the Spiritually Victorious initiate by the name Osiris Any: "I am…

**Verse 2.**

2.1. **Bennu   Ba   en   Ra   zehem   neteru   er   duat   pert   zenu**

2.2. Phoenix   soul   of   Creator Spirit   guiding   gods and goddesses   as to netherworld   going forth/out they

2.3. …the Phoenix, the soul of Ra, the Creator Spirit, guiding the gods and goddesses as to the paths of the Netherworld. They go forth/out…

**Verse 3.**

3.1. **Bau   tep   ta   er   arit   meretu   Kau   zenu   pert   Ba   en   Asar**

3.2. Souls   top   earth   as to   actions   loved   minds   theirs. Go forth/out   soul   of   Osiris

3.3. …the souls on the surface of the earth planet, to do the actions that are desired by their minds. In the same way, the soul will go forth, that is, the soul of this Osiris…

**Verse 4.**

4.1. *Any   merr   Ka   f*

4.2. Initiate Any   love   mind   his

4.3. …initiate, known by the name Any, also does/follows the dictates of his mind.

Above: Images of the Bennu and the Ba of Ra

## The wisdom of pregnancy – BAKA vs. KABA

Verse 1.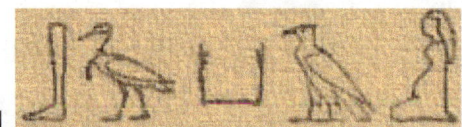

***Verse 2. Baka***

Verse 3. <u>Soul into mind</u>

Verse 4. Pregnancy {alt. soul residing in the mind)

**Below: Image of the boat of Osiris-from the temple of Hathor at Dendera depicting how the soul is going "along for the ride" and the other divinities are leading it along set course.**

Verse 1.
**1.1. Ka imy khat**
1.2. Mind within physical body
1.3. The mental and emotional astral body residing within the physical body

| Ba | → | Ka | → | Khat |
|---|---|---|---|---|
| Soul | Residing within | Mind | Residing within | Body |
| | (Metaphor) | | (Metaphor) | |
| **Important points:** | | | | |
| Non-local if enlightened | Attuned to | Mind has locomotion. Ex. Extends from head through eyes  Can have astral projection experiences | Attuned to | Local and bound to Ta or earth plane |

Verse 1.
1.1. Ba ar pet shat ar ta
1.2. Soul is to heaven body is to earth
1.3. The soul belongs to heaven and the body belongs to the earth

From the Prt m Hru of the Pyramid Texts (3,200-2,575 B.C.E.)

"The body becomes what the foods are, as the spirit becomes what the thoughts are."

# Chap 17-The Wisdom of Body and Excrement
**Trans. by Muata Ashby**

Verse A.

| A.1. | *tra* | *er-f* | *su* | *Heru* | *puy* | *en* | *aba* | *Heru* | *im* | *f* |
|---|---|---|---|---|---|---|---|---|---|---|
| A.2. | time | about-him | he | Horus | that | of | fighting | Horus | in | he |

A.3. **This is about that time, remember as it is told in our ancient myth when the god** Horus was involved in a struggle within himself…

Verse B.

| B.1. | *hena* | *zetep* | *im* | *ud* | *setau* | *im* | *her* | *Heru* |
|---|---|---|---|---|---|---|---|---|
| B.2. | with | Set | in | thrusting | excrement | in | person/face | Horus |

B.3. …and the god Set when Set had killed Osiris, his own brother, and Horus' father, and then started fighting with Horus over who would be king of Egypt. At one point in the struggle Set injured Horus by thrusting excrement in his face and temporarily blinded him.

Verse G.

| G.1. | *khat* | *f* | *pu* | *ky* | *djed* | *er* | *setatu* | *f* |
|---|---|---|---|---|---|---|---|---|
| G.2. | physical body | his | that | otherwise said | | about | excrements | his |

G.3. in reference to his (of the initiate aspirant) physical body, **another way to think** about it is that it (body) is his excrement.

The events related above recall the episode in the Myth of the Osirian Resurrection where the god Set threw excrement in the face of Horus, temporarily blinding him. This myth is recounted in the books AFRICAN RELIGION VOLUME 4: Asarian Theology and THE STORY OF ASAR ASET AND HERU by Dr. Muata Ashby

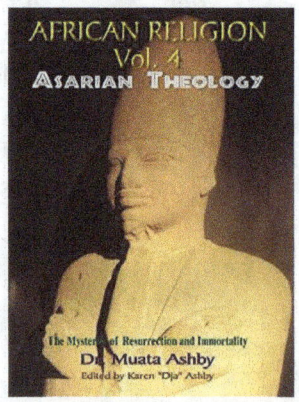

# PART 4: WISDOM OF HARMONIZATION of the Human Personality and Overcoming Mental Complexes from the Pert-em-Heru

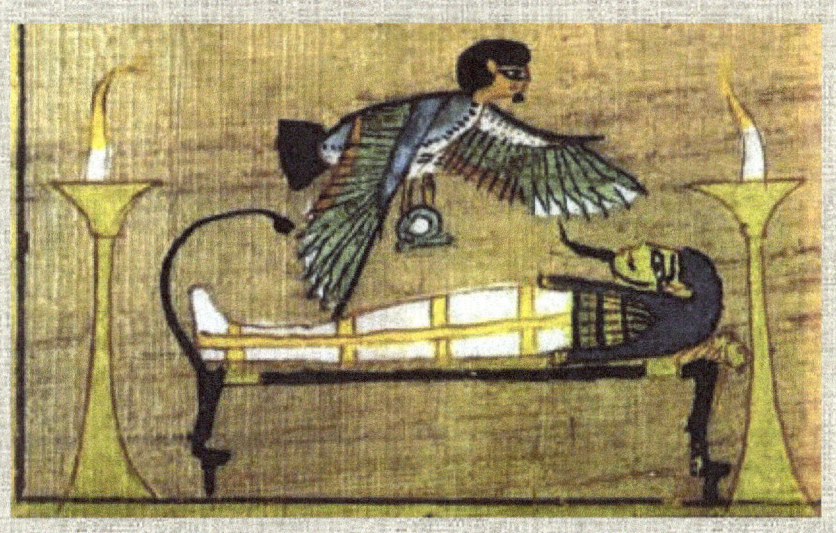

# Introduction to the Ka (mind), purity and the perpetual existence with waking conscience, from the Pyramid Texts of Pepi

**Trans. by Muata Ashby**

Verse 1.

1.1.　Aay　　　　su　　　　Ka　-k　　　hems　　　　Ka - k
1.2.　cleansed　　the　　　mind - thine　relaxed　　mind-thine
1.3.　Now that your mind has been cleansed from the aryu of previous living in accord with unrighteous thoughts, feelings and desires and the memories of those past experiences, now your mind can rest…

Verse 2.

2.1.　Unema- f　　ta　　　hena　　　k　　ant　urdu　en　　djet　　djeta
2.2.　eats　-he　bread　　with　　　thee　not　swooning of　body　forever…
2.3.　…it even eats with you and is your companion without mental fluctuations; thereby you have centered mind and inner peace as your mind is in harmony with you and no longer wayward, sometimes with you and at other times against you, in conflict and disarray.

Verse 3.

3.1.　aha　　　　　uab　　　　k　　　　uab　　　　ka　k
3.2.　standing　　purity　　　thine　　purity　　　mind thine
3.3.　…and that forever existence will be vertical and upright, alert and alive and not horizontal and dead. This is owed to thy purity, the purity of your mind…

Verse 4.

4.1.　uab　　　　Ba　　k　　　uab　　　　sekhem　　　k
4.2.　pure　　　soul　thine　pure　　　vital body　　thine
4.3.　…the purity of your soul and the purity of your vital body.

# Chapter 156-Chapter of buckle of carnelian: Provisioning with Creative Power From the Feminine Divine

**Trans. by Muata Ashby**

Verse 1.

*1.1.* *Ra   en   tyet   im   achenem   medtu-dje in* **Asar   Any   maa-kheru**

1.2. Chapter of buckle of carnelian stone words to speak by Osiris Initiate Spiritual Victory

1.3. This is the chapter about the buckle amulet. It is made of carnelian stone. These are the words to be spoken by the Osiris initiate in order to generate Spiritual Victory.

Verse 2.

*2.1.* *zenefu   en   Aset   hekau   en   Aset   akhu   en   Aset*

2.2. Blood of Isis   words of power   of   Isis   Shining Spirit   of   Isis

2.3. The blood of Isis, which is the seat of her life power; this is the words of power of Isis, this is the instrument of her power; this is the Shining Spirit Divinity of Isis, the essence of her Divinity.

Verse 3.

3.1. Udjat　　　　　　ser　pen　sa　er　betau　　　　　f　pu
3.2. Eye of Horus　　　elder　that　protection　from　iniquity　　his　that.
3.3. The eye of Horus the elder, the mature, the sovereign king of the personality, that eye is the protection of the personality, from wrongdoing or from inimical forces that may befall the initiate.

Verse 4.

4.1. Djedtu　　ra　pen　her　tyet　ent　chenm　mezta　　　im　moo　nu
4.2. Speaking　words　these　person　buckle　of　carnelian/red jasper　decoction　in　water　of
4.3. The words of this chapter are to be spoken along with the presence of a buckle composed of red jasper for a person. There is to be prepared a decoction containing water of…

Verse 5.

5.1. ankh-amyu　　mench-ta　her　khaty　ent　nehet　erdi-ta　er　cheche　en
5.2. living flowers　carved　upon　body　of　sycamore　deposit　onto　neck　of
5.3. …living flowers. The buckle amulet is to be placed into a carved [chiseled] section of sycamore weed. When that is done the carved section of wood with the buckle embedded in it are to be paced on the throat of…

Verse 6.

6.1. Akhu Shemsu pen ar　arytu　n-f　shat　ten　unenz　khutu　en　Aset
6.2. Spiritualized/ that as to doing this for-him chapter this　being　Shining Spirit power of  Isis…
Venerable/
Holy Person
6.3. That person who is considered as being a Venerable, Holy person. If this chapter is understood and performed for such a person then it means that the Shining Spirit Power of the goddess Isis…

Verse 3.

3.1. Udjat        ser      pen     sa      er      betau          f      pu
3.2. Eye of Horus  elder   that   protection  from  iniquity      his   that.
3.3. The eye of Horus the elder, the mature, the sovereign king of the personality, that eye is the protection of the personality, from wrongdoing or from inimical forces that may befall the initiate.

Verse 4.

4.1. Djedtu      ra      pen     her    tyet    ent    chenm      mezta       im    moo   nu
4.2. Speaking   words   these   person  buckle  of   carnelian/red jasper  decoction in  water  of
4.3. The words of this chapter are to be spoken along with the presence of a buckle composed of red jasper for a person. There is to be prepared a decoction containing water of…

Verse 5.

5.1. ankh-amyu        mench-ta      her    khaty  ent   nehet     erdi-ta     er    cheche    en
5.2. living flowers    carved      upon    body   of   sycamore   deposit    onto    neck     of
5.3. …living flowers. The buckle amulet is to be placed into a carved [chiseled] section of sycamore weed. When that is done the carved section of wood with the buckle embedded in it are to be paced on the throat of…

Verse 6.

6.1. Akhu Shemsu pen ar   arytu     n-f    shat    ten    unenz      khutu     en    Aset
6.2. Spiritualized/ that as to doing this for-him chapter this    being   Shining Spirit power of Isis…
     Venerable/
     Holy Person
6.3. That person who is considered as being a Venerable, Holy person. If this chapter is understood and performed for such a person then it means that the Shining Spirit Power of the goddess Isis…

# Chapter 156-Chapter of buckle of carnelian: Provisioning with Creative Power From the Feminine Divine

**Trans. by Muata Ashby**

Verse 1.

**1.1.** *Ra    en    tyet    im    achenem    medtu-dje in* Asar   Any    maa-kheru

1.2. Chapter of   buckle   of  carnelian stone words to speak by Osiris Initiate Spiritual Victory

1.3. **This is the chapter about the buckle amulet. It is made of carnelian stone. These are the words to be spoken by** the Osiris initiate in order to generate Spiritual Victory.

Verse 2.

**2.1.** *zenefu       en     Aset     hekau      en    Aset    akhu     en    Aset*

2.2. Blood    of    Isis    words of power   of   Isis   Shining Spirit  of   Isis

2.3. The blood of Isis, which is the seat of her life power; this is the words of power of Isis, this is the instrument of her power; this is the Shining Spirit Divinity of Isis, the essence of her Divinity.

> **NOTE:** The ![akhu] *Akhu* (Shining Spirit) has ![khut] *Khut* (Spiritual Power) that comes from the Shining Spirit Being of the Divine.

Verse 7.

| 7.1. | im | sau | f | haa | Heru | sa | Aset | maa | f | su | an | djera |
|---|---|---|---|---|---|---|---|---|---|---|---|---|
| 7.2. | form | protection | he | praises! | Horus | son | Isis | seeing | he | him | not | obstructed |

7.3. ...will manifest in the form of spiritual protection for that person. Horus, the son of Isis, extols utterances of Praises/Adorations/Glorifications upon seeing that this venerable person is not obstructed on their spiritual path!

Verse 8.

| 8.1. | en | wat | nebt | er-f | a | -f | er | pet | a | -f | er | ta | shesu | tep |
|---|---|---|---|---|---|---|---|---|---|---|---|---|---|---|
| 8.2. | to | path | any | as to | –his | hand | –his | as to | heaven | hand | –his | as to | earth | concern | boss |

8.3. …on any path of his that he may choose to act in, be it in heaven or on earth alike; concerning this issue, he is the boss, the captain over his capacities and will to act in accord with his will on these planes of existence.

# Egyptian Book of the Dead Chapter 89. Chapter of Causing the Soul to come into Harmony with the Physical Body to Produce a Glorious Body

**Trans. by Muata Ashby**

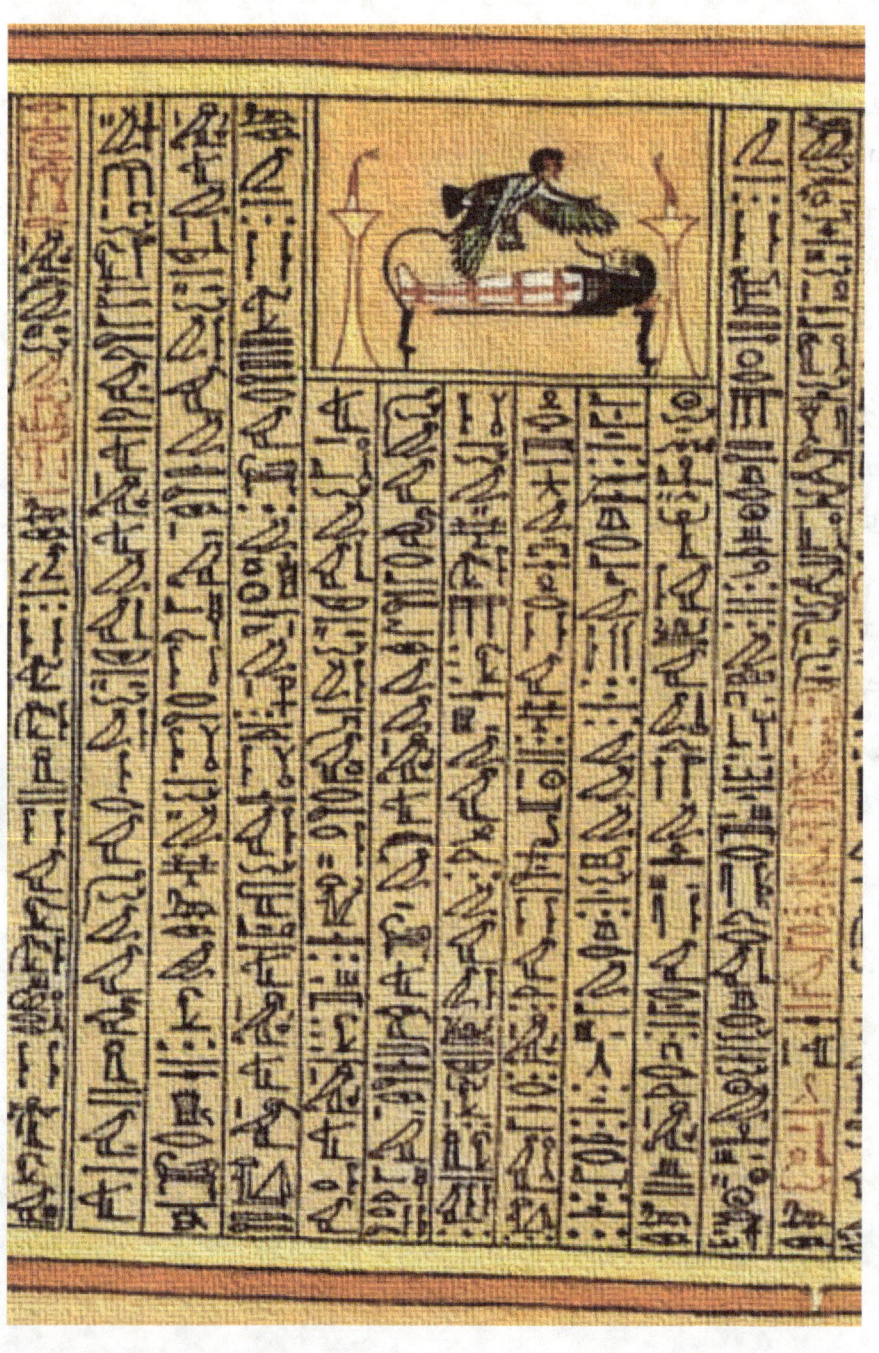

**Verse 1.**
**1.1.** *Ra*    *en*    *erta*    *dma*    Ba    khat    f    im    Neterchert    *medtu-dje*   *in*
**1.2.** Chapter of giving harmonization Soul body his in cemetery speech by
**1.3.** **This is the chapter for causing the soul of a person to approach their body and harmonize** with it while the body of the person is in the cemetery, the lower part of heaven, so as to allow the further journey, of the soul, to continue. **These following words are being spoken by:**

**Verse 2.**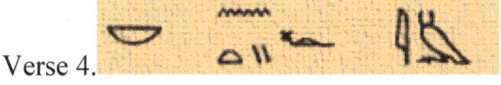
**2.1.** Asar    Any
2.2. Osiris    Any
2.3. …is spoken by the Osiris initiate by the name Any.

**Verse 3.**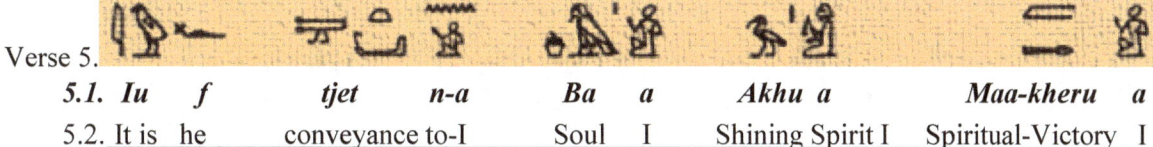
**3.1.** Neter-aah    di    k    tu    n-a    Ba    a    im    bu
3.2. Divinity great give thee come to-I Soul mine in place
3.3. Oh Great divinity! Grant to me that my soul may come to me from whatever place,

**Verse 4.**
**4.1.** neb    enty    f    im
4.2. every existing he/it in
4.3. Any place that it might be in.

**Verse 5.**
**5.1.** Iu    f    tjet    n-a    Ba    a    Akhu   a    Maa-kheru   a
5.2. It is he conveyance to-I Soul I Shining Spirit I Spiritual-Victory I
5.3. In finding, taking custody of, and carrying my Soul back to me, my Shining Spirit can attain the coveted goal of spiritual enlightenment…

**Verse 6.**
**6.1.** hena    f    im    bu    neb    enty    f    im
6.2. with him in place every existing he in.
6.3. With him in every place where he might be located in so that just as my Soul non-local and thus may be existing in every place where he might find it, my victory will also be in every place that my Soul may be found. And just as he is enlightened and able to find my soul everywhere that it might be, so too I will be enlightened as he is.

Verse 7.

7.1. Erda    n-k        maa            Ba    a    khat        a
7.2. Grant  of-thee  seeing          Soul  I    physical body  I
7.3. Oh Great Divinity! Grant my soul the opportunity to return to the burial chamber and gaze upon my physical body.

Verse 8.

8.1. Aa      neteru      zetau        im    uia        en      neb    hehu
8.2. Hail    divinities  slaughterers in    boat       of      Lord   millions
8.3. Hail to you, gods who take care of slaughtering unworthy souls, you who reside in the boat of the lord of Millions and Millions of years…

Verse 9.

9.1. Z-tekenyu            Bau      er    Zahu          aui tenu      meh      cher
9.2. cause togetherness   souls    to    Glorious Body arms theirs   filled   possessing
9.3. …who cause souls to harmonize with their Glorious Body, whose arms are pervaded…

Verse 10.

10.1. aqau          tenu … deru      ten    cheft
10.2. …peak         theirs … destroy them   demoniac
10.3. …to the utmost … oh! I ask you to destroy those mischievous fiends who are the enemies of spiritual victory, enlightenment.

Verse 11.

11.1. Asu      erta    tenu    per    Ba    pen    en    Asar    Any      Maa-Kheru  kher neteru [MK]
11.2. Consider grant  you all  going forth Soul this of Osiris Aspirant  Spiritual Victory  presence
                                                                                              Gods and Goddesses
                                                                                              Spiritual Victory
11.3. Behold, grant what I ask; allow this Soul of the Osiris, the Aspirant by the name of Any, to have Spiritual Victory, to attain Spiritual Enlightenment in the presence of the Gods and Goddesses.

Verse 7.

7.1. Erda n-k maa Ba a khat a
7.2. Grant of-thee seeing Soul I physical body I
7.3. Oh Great Divinity! Grant my soul the opportunity to return to the burial chamber and gaze upon my physical body.

Verse 8.

8.1. Aa neteru zetau im uia en neb hehu
8.2. Hail divinities slaughterers in boat of Lord millions
8.3. Hail to you, gods who take care of slaughtering unworthy souls, you who reside in the boat of the lord of Millions and Millions of years…

Verse 9.

9.1. Z-tekenyu Bau er Zahu aui tenu meh cher
9.2. cause togetherness souls to Glorious Body arms theirs filled possessing
9.3. …who cause souls to harmonize with their Glorious Body, whose arms are pervaded…

Verse 10.

10.1. aqau tenu … deru ten cheft
10.2. …peak theirs … destroy them demoniac
10.3. …to the utmost … oh! I ask you to destroy those mischievous fiends who are the enemies of spiritual victory, enlightenment.

Verse 11.

11.1. Asu erta tenu per Ba pen en Asar Any Maa-Kheru kher neteru [MK]
11.2. Consider grant you all going forth Soul this of Osiris Aspirant Spiritual Victory presence
Gods and Goddesses
Spiritual Victory
11.3. Behold, grant what I ask; allow this Soul of the Osiris, the Aspirant by the name of Any, to have Spiritual Victory, to attain Spiritual Enlightenment in the presence of the Gods and Goddesses.

Verse 1.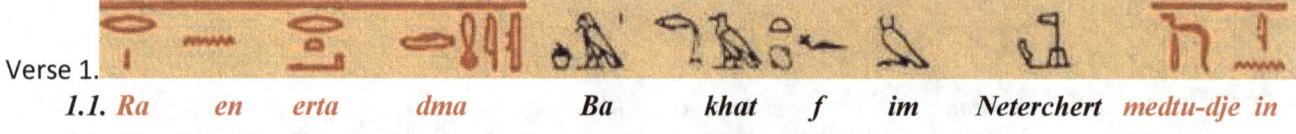
- 1.1. *Ra   en   erta   dma   Ba   khat   f   im   Neterchert   medtu-dje in*
- 1.2. Chapter of   giving   harmonization Soul   body   his   in   cemetery   speech   by
- 1.3. **This is the chapter for causing the soul of a person to approach their body and harmonize** with it while the body of the person is in the cemetery, the lower part of heaven, so as to allow the further journey, of the soul, to continue. **These following words are being spoken by:**

Verse 2.
- 2.1. *Asar   Any*
- 2.2. Osiris   Any
- 2.3. …is spoken by the Osiris initiate by the name Any.

Verse 3.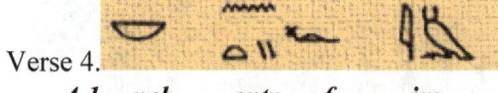
- 3.1. *Neter-aah   di   k   tu   n-a   Ba   a   im   bu*
- 3.2. Divinity great   give   thee   come   to-I   Soul   mine   in   place
- 3.3. Oh Great divinity! Grant to me that my soul may come to me from whatever place,

Verse 4.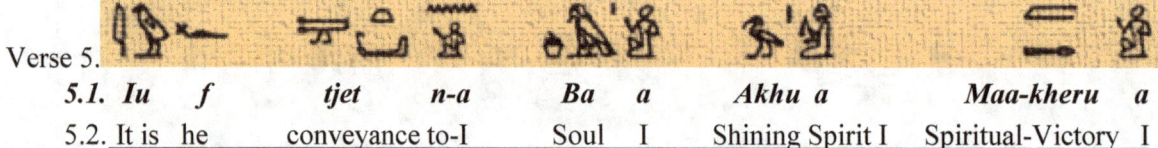
- 4.1. *neb   enty   f   im*
- 4.2. every   existing   he/it   in
- 4.3. Any place that it might be in.

Verse 5.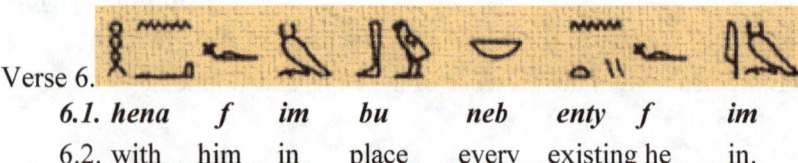
- 5.1. *Iu   f   tjet   n-a   Ba   a   Akhu   a   Maa-kheru   a*
- 5.2. It is   he   conveyance to-I   Soul   I   Shining Spirit   I   Spiritual-Victory   I
- 5.3. In finding, taking custody of, and carrying my Soul back to me, my Shining Spirit can attain the coveted goal of spiritual enlightenment…

Verse 6.
- 6.1. *hena   f   im   bu   neb   enty   f   im*
- 6.2. with   him   in   place   every   existing   he   in.
- 6.3. With him in every place where he might be located in so that just as my Soul non-local and thus may be existing in every place where he might find it, my victory will also be in every place that my Soul may be found. And just as he is enlightened and able to find my soul everywhere that it might be, so too I will be enlightened as he is.

## Verse 12.

12.1. maa        f      khat    f     hetep  f     her         zahu          f
12.2. Seeing    he     body   his   peace  he  personality glorious body his

12.3. May he be able to see his body and may this occur in the contentment of supreme peace, as an integrated personality with his glorious body.

## Verse 13.

13.1. An   sek    f    an    hetem   f    en   djet    en    djeta
13.2. Not diminish he  not  fragment he   of   body   for   forever

13.3. Do not allow any diminution or any fragmentation of him, of his body, forever.

## Verse 14.

14.1. Medtu dje fedu her   Ba    en    nubu    meh    im    aatu    rau    en
14.2. Words spoken four over Soul of  golden  full    in    stone  establishing to

14.3. These words are to be said in multiples of four. They are to be said over the amulet of soul figure that is made of gold and embedded in stone. Then it is to be placed/established…

## Verse 15.

15.1. se- a       shenbet     f      Asar
15.2. the person  neck       his   the Osiris

15.3. …on the neck of the person's mummy, that is to say, the neck of the Osiris person for whom this ritual has been performed.

Above: The *khat* - physical body is visited by the soul. It encounters the "idealized image" by looking at the mask and then its attention turns to that idealized image as its higher abode and the *zahu* or higher expression of the lower, perishable physical form.

# Egyptian Book of the Dead Chapter XCI. "The Chapter of not letting the soul of a person be captive in " Neter-khert." (See pp. 114, 319, and pi. 17.)

**Trans. by Muata Ashby**

Verse 1.
- **1.1.** *Ra    en    temt    erda    chenatu    Ba    z - a    im    neterchert*
- 1.2. **Chapter of disallow giving imprisonment** Soul cause- person in cemetery
- 1.3. **This is the chapter of the Book of Enlightenment that has to do with not allowing, to be held captive,** the soul of a person, after they exit the surface of the earth, which is the land of the living, **in the** cemetery, which is the lower part of heaven and a weigh station before proceeding on the spiritual journey. If the soul is held captive in the cemetery it cannot progress into the netherworld in order to discover heavenly existence and spiritual enlightenment.

Verse 2.
- **2.1.** *Medtu-dje in Asar    Any    Aa    aq    duau    f    tu    ur*
- 2.2. **These words spoken by** Osiris Any    Hail    praises adorations    he    you    great
- 2.3. **The following words are being spoken by** the Osiris initiate who is known as Any. Hail to you, praises and my solemn adorations on to you, oh great one…

Verse 3.
- **3.1.** *Bau    Ba    aah {mdj} shefsheftu    didi    neru    f    en    neteru    cha*
- 3.2. of souls,    soul    great    beneficent power    giving    victorious    he    of    gods(desses)    crowned
- 3.3. …great Soul of souls, who is the magnanimous and great power who is also beneficent and loving as well as victorious over all the gods and goddesses. He is the crowned…

Verse 4.
- 4.1. *her    nest    f    urt    ari - f    wat    en    akh    en    Ba    en*
- 4.2. person throne his    great    action-his    path    of    Shining Spirit    to    Soul    of
- 4.3. …as a person on his throne. This is a great action of his, to have followed a path that has led to the Shining Spirit coming to the soul of…

**Verse 1.**

1.1. *Ra    en    temt    erda    chenatu    Ba    z-a    im    neterchert*

1.2. <u>Chapter of disallow giving imprisonment</u> Soul cause- person in cemetery

1.3. **This is the chapter of the Book of Enlightenment that has to do with not allowing, to be held captive,** the soul of a person, after they exit the surface of the earth, which is the land of the living, **in the** cemetery, which is the lower part of heaven and a weigh station before proceeding on the spiritual journey. If the soul is held captive in the cemetery it cannot progress into the netherworld in order to discover heavenly existence and spiritual enlightenment.

**Verse 2.**

2.1. *Medtu-dje in* Asar    Any    Aa    aq    duau    f    tu    ur

2.2. <u>These words spoken by</u> Osiris Any    Hail    praises  adorations    he    you    great

2.3. **The following words are being spoken by** the Osiris initiate who is known as Any. Hail to you, praises and my solemn adorations on to you, oh great one…

**Verse 3.**

3.1. *Bau    Ba    aah {mdj}  shefsheftu    didi    neru    f    en    neteru    cha*

3.2. <u>of souls,   soul   great     beneficent power giving victorious  he  of  gods(desses)  crowned</u>

3.3. …great Soul of souls, who is the magnanimous and great power who is also beneficent and loving as well as victorious over all the gods and goddesses. He is the crowned…

**Verse 4.**

4.1. *her    nest    f    urt    ari-f    wat    en    akh    en    Ba    en*

4.2. <u>person  throne his  great    action-his   path   of   Shining Spirit   to   Soul   of</u>

4.3. …as a person on his throne. This is a great action of his, to have followed a path that has led to the Shining Spirit coming to the soul of…

# Egyptian Book of the Dead Chapter XCI. "The Chapter of not letting the soul of a person be captive in " Neter-khert." (See pp. 114, 319, and pi. 17.)

**Trans. by Muata Ashby**

Verse 5.

5.1. Asar    Any         iu   a   aper   k   nuk   a   akhu Sheps   aper      ari   n-a
5.2. Osiris  Any         It is I  provisioned thine. I am Shining Spirit Noble provisioned  deed to-I
5.3. …the Osiris aspirant by the name Any. This means that Osiris Any is provisioned by his Shining Spirit. Thus, Osiris Any can say "I am a Noble Shining Spirit, an enlightened being, due to the deed of spiritual provisioning, for this mystic journey, that was done to me…

Verse 6.

6.1. wat   er   bu   enty   Ra   HetHeru   im   *ar   rech   ra   pen*
6.2. Path  as to  place     exist Creator Spirit Creation within *as to knowledge chapter this*
6.3. …on the path concerning reaching the place where the goddess Hathor, who represents Creation is and where Ra, the Creator Spirit is within that Creation. **Concerning the knowledge about this.**

Verse 7.

*7.1.  Iu    f   kheper-f   im   akh sheps   aper im   neterchert   an chena      tu-f*
7.2.  It is  he creating-he in Shining Spirit Noble **provisioned in** cemetery **not imprisoned to-he**
**7.3. The knowledge of the wisdom contained in this chapter is the knowing of how to create the personality into the form as** Noble (enlightened) Shining Spirit; that is, a person having conscious knowledge of one's Shining Spirit Being, knowing oneself as only being human and mortal but being Spirit, immortal and eternal. Having followed this path of creating one's own enlightenment means **having provisioned oneself with the knowledge of self-knowledge** so as not to be held up in the cemetery, **not being blocked from progressing on the spiritual path to discover the ultimate Divine.**

Verse 8.

*8.1.  Her sba   neb   en  Amuntet   im      aq         pert       nu-pet*
8.2.  Person hall all   of   West      within  go in       come out    of-heaven
**8.3. This means being a person who can have entry into all the halls of the final Western Abode of all righteous and provisioned souls. Further, it means being able to go into any and all regions of that coveted Beautiful Western Abode, in the heavenly plane, and being able to come out of there at will; thus it means being a free Soul, unencumbered by human ignorance, whose Spirit has been able to come to liberate and unencumber it.**

# Pert-Im-Heru Chapter XCII. "The Chapter of opening the tomb to the soul and the" shadow, of coming forth by day, and of getting power over the legs." (See pp. 115, 319, and pi. 17.)

**Trans. by Muata Ashby**

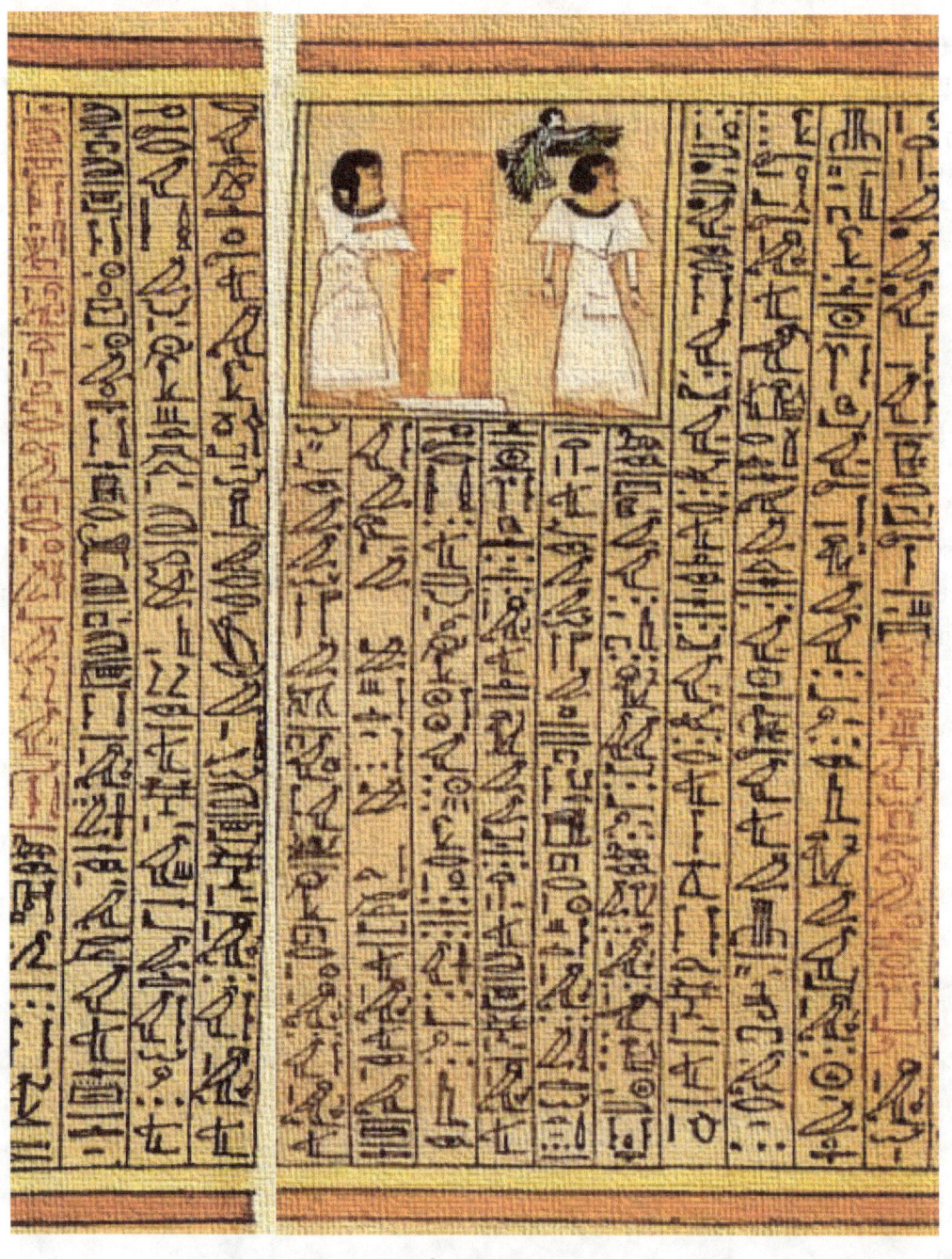

Verse 1.
1.1. *Ra   en   un   ashy   en   Ba   en   Khaibit   pert   im*
1.2. Chapter of opening tomb   of  Soul   of  Shadow   going forth/out into
1.3. This is a chapter of the Ancient Egyptian Book of Enlightenment concerning the opening of the tomb so that the Soul of a person and the Shadow of a person that related to their soul may be able to go forth/out into…

Verse 2.
2.1. *heru   Sekhem   im   redyu   medtu-dje in **Asar**   sesh   Any*
2.2. day   vital-power   in   legs   Words-speech by **Osiris**   scribe   Any
2.3. …the daylight, that is to say, enlightenment with vitality in the legs, the capacity to move; **These are the words that the Osiris initiate, known as the scribe Any, is to speak:**

Verse 3.
3.1. *maa-kheru   unt   unti   chet   chetemti   z-djer*
3.2. Spiritual victory   shrine   opened   sealed   (sealed)-treasure   sleep/death
3.3. I am spiritually victorious as the shrine of the divine has been opened for me. It was sealed and the treasure that was locked away in the sleep of death…

Verse 4.
4.1. *unt   unti   en   Ba   imy   -z   arit   Heru*
4.2. shrine   opened   to   Soul   within   -it   eye   Horus
4.3. …in the shrine has been opened to the soul that was within it. The Eye of Horus…

Verse 5.
5.1. *Shedu   a   ze-ment   kakeru   wept   Ra   ped*
5.2. plot-of-land I   cause-establish   ornaments/jewels   brow   Creator Spirit   hastening
5.3. is on the plot of land that I have caused to be established, as a jeweled ornament, on the forehead of Ra, the Creator Spirit. Now, after opening the shrine and causing to be placed the ornament of the Eye of Heru on the brow, I hasten…

Verse 6.
6.1. *nemmat   uny   masety   ari   n-a   wat   pu   aaah   {mdj}   aufu   a*
6.2. striding away getting up running thighs   action of-I   path   the   greeaatt   {abs}   body parts   I
6.3. …I even start striding, and even more, I am running on the greeaaatt spiritual path and I have the energy to run as my body parts…

Verse 7.

| | | | | | | |
|---|---|---|---|---|---|---|
| *7.1.* | *rud* | *nuk* | *a* | *Heru* | *netedjnu* | *tef* *[f]* |
| 7.2. | vitality | I am | | Horus | redeemer | father [his] |

7.3. …have vitality. I am Horus, the redeemer/protector of his father, Osiris.

# PART 5: SPECIAL DESCRIPTIONS OF SHEDY SPIRITUAL PRACTICES AS A PROCESS FOR RISING ABOVE COMPLEXES: PRIMER ON KEMETIC PSYCHOLOGY OF WELL-ADJUSTED (INTEGRATED) PERSONALITY TO PROMOTE SPIRITUAL ENLIGHTENMENT

# Ancient Egyptian Book of the Dead Chapter 78 – Transforming into a Hawk

**Trans. by Muata Ashby**

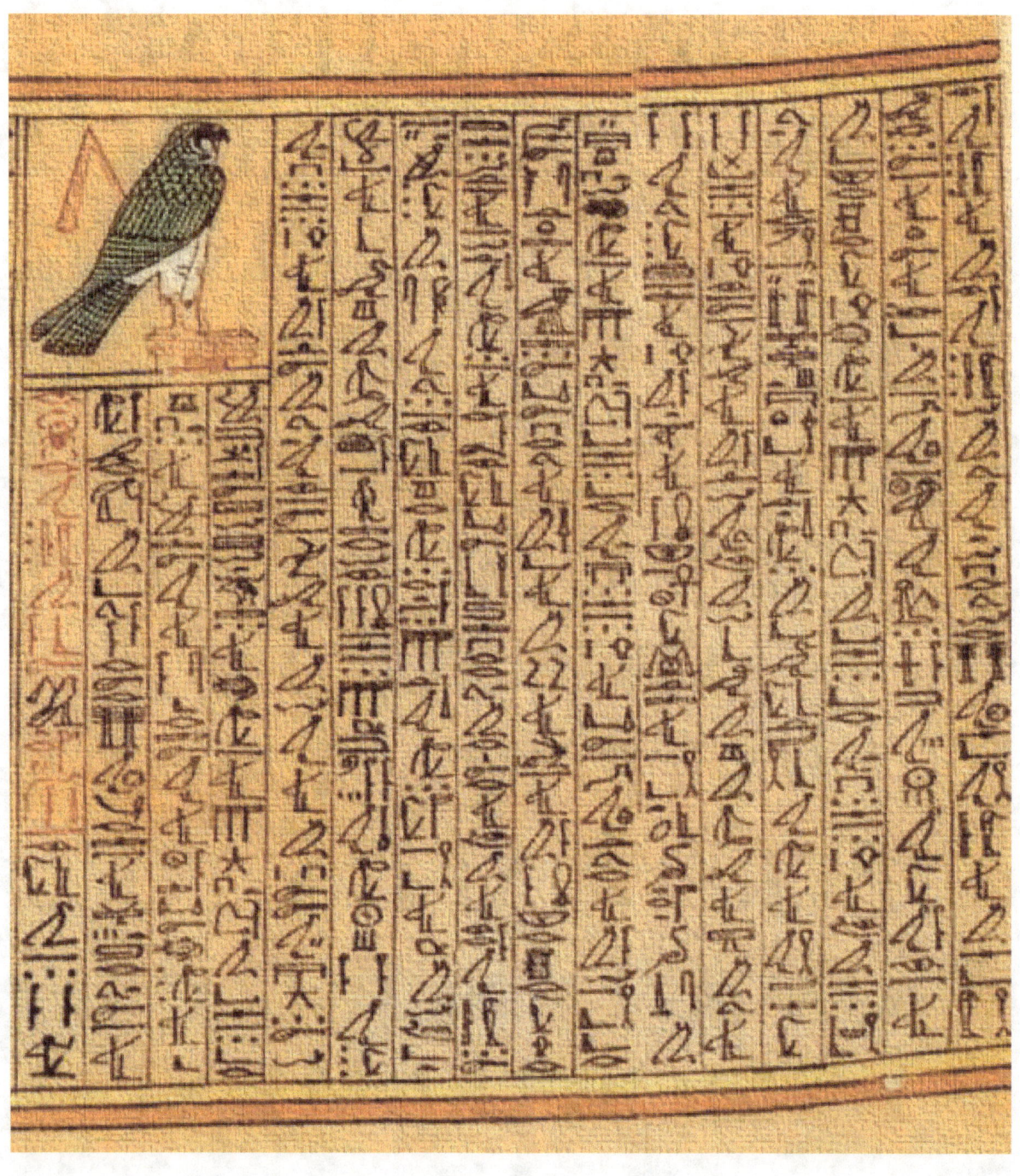

# Ancient Egyptian Book of the Dead Chapter 78 – Transforming into a Hawk Verses-1, 22-24, 27-30

Verse 1.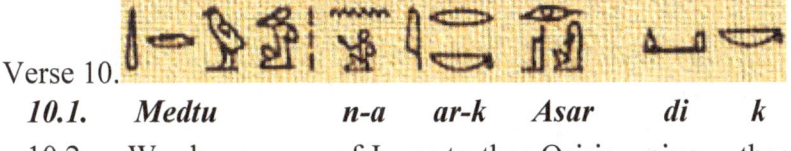
1.1.   *arit*    *kheperu*    *em*    *Bak*    *{Heru}*    *Netery*
1.2.   act    creating/becoming    form as    Hawk    {Horus}    Divine
1.3.   **This is the chapter that has to do with the actions that are necessary for a person/initiate of the temple, to become a Divine** Hawk. This metaphor means transforming consciousness into that of Horus, the redeemer of the soul.

# Egyptian Book of the Dead Chapter 78 – Transforming into a Hawk verses 10-13

**Trans. by Muata Ashby**

Verse 10.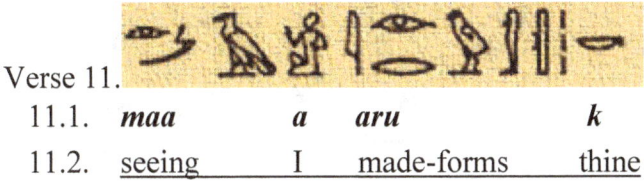
10.1.   *Medtu*    *n-a*    *ar-k*    *Asar*    *di*    *k*
10.2.   Words    of-I    as to-thee    Osiris    give    thee
10.3.   These words are from me to thee, Osiris: I ask you to please give…

Verse 11.
11.1.   *maa*    *a*    *aru*    *k*
11.2.   seeing    I    made-forms    thine
11.3.   …to me the capacity to see your forms…

Verse 12.
12.1.   *Djez-k*    *seqednu*    *a*    *Baiu*    *k*    *di*    *k*    *pert*    *a*    *sekhem*    *a*
12.2.   thine-own    disposed    I    Souls    thine    give    thee    going forth/out    I    vital energy    I
12.3.   …your own forms, as you manifest in the life of all creatures and as the very soul of Creation itself. Oh Osiris: I ask you to please give me the capacity of going forth/out, when going into the temple for spiritual evolution and coming out transformed; grant to me the capacity of going forth/out with life force vital energy…

|  | Verse 13. | | | | | | | | | | | |
|---|---|---|---|---|---|---|---|---|---|---|---|---|
| 13.1. | | im | red | a | un | a | im | mi | Neberdjer | heri | nest | f |
| 13.2. | | in | legs | I | being | I | within | like | Lord-All-Encompass | personality heavenly | throne | his |

13.3. …for my legs, so that I may move on the spiritual path as is necessary for successful spiritual evolution, leading to being like the Lord-All-Encompassing-Divinity, whose throne extends to the limits of existence.

# Egyptian Book of the Dead Chapter 78 – Transforming into a Hawk verses 22-24

**Highlight: Affirmation of being one of the Akhu living on light and worthy through God's worth–**

|  | Verse 22. | | | | | | | | | | |
|---|---|---|---|---|---|---|---|---|---|---|---|
| 22.1. | | Nuk | a | ua | im | nenu | en | akhu shepsu | imemu | akhu | iu | ari n-a |
| 22.2. | | I am | | one | in | those | of | Noble Shining Spirits | within Divinities | illumined | It is | deed to-I |

22.3. I declare that I am, indeed, one of the Enlightened beings among the enlightened beings illumined by the Divine. It is what has been done to me by the Divine…

|  | Verse 23. | | | | | | | | |
|---|---|---|---|---|---|---|---|---|---|
| 23.1. | | aru | a | im | aru | f | im | iut | f | pert | f |
| 23.2. | | forms | I | in | forms | his | in | coming | he | going forth/out | his |

23.3. …that I am a Shining Spirit Being since my Shining Spirit Being is within, and an expression of, the Shining Spirit Being of he who is the Supreme Shining Spirit. Going forth, coming out of…

| | | | | | | | | | |
|---|---|---|---|---|---|---|---|---|---|
| Verse 13. | | | | | | | | | |
| 13.1. | im | red | a | un | a | im | mi Neberdjer | heri | nest f |
| 13.2. | in | legs | I | being | I | within | like Lord-All-Encompass | personality heavenly | throne his |

13.3. …for my legs, so that I may move on the spiritual path as is necessary for successful spiritual evolution, leading to being like the Lord-All-Encompassing-Divinity, whose throne extends to the limits of existence.

# Egyptian Book of the Dead Chapter 78 – Transforming into a Hawk verses 22-24

**Highlight: Affirmation of being one of the Akhu living on light and worthy through God's worth–**

| | | | | | | | | | |
|---|---|---|---|---|---|---|---|---|---|
| Verse 22. | | | | | | | | | |
| 22.1. | Nuk | a | ua | im | nenu | en | akhu shepsu imemu | akhu | iu ari n-a |
| 22.2. | I am | | one | in | those | | of Noble Shining Spirits within Divinities | illumined | It is deed to-I |

22.3. I declare that I am, indeed, one of the Enlightened beings among the enlightened beings illumined by the Divine. It is what has been done to me by the Divine…

| | | | | | | | |
|---|---|---|---|---|---|---|---|
| Verse 23. | | | | | | | |
| 23.1. | aru | a | im | aru | f | im | iut f | pert f |
| 23.2. | forms | I | in | forms | his | in | coming he | going forth/out his |

23.3. …that I am a Shining Spirit Being since my Shining Spirit Being is within, and an expression of, the Shining Spirit Being of he who is the Supreme Shining Spirit. Going forth, coming out of…

# Ancient Egyptian Book of the Dead Chapter 78 – Transforming into a Hawk Verses-1, 22-24, 27-30

Verse 1.
1.1.    *arit        kheperu               em      Bak       {Heru}    Netery*
1.2.    act        creating/becoming    form as   Hawk    {Horus}   Divine
1.3.    **This is the chapter that has to do with the actions that are necessary for a person/initiate of the temple, to become a Divine** Hawk. This metaphor means transforming consciousness into that of Horus, the redeemer of the soul.

# Egyptian Book of the Dead Chapter 78 – Transforming into a Hawk verses 10-13

**Trans. by Muata Ashby**

Verse 10.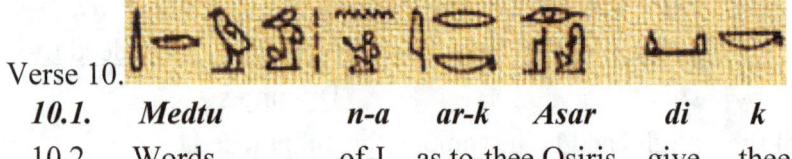
10.1.    *Medtu        n-a     ar-k    Asar     di      k*
10.2.    Words        of-I    as to-thee Osiris   give    thee
10.3.    These words are from me to thee, Osiris: I ask you to please give…

Verse 11.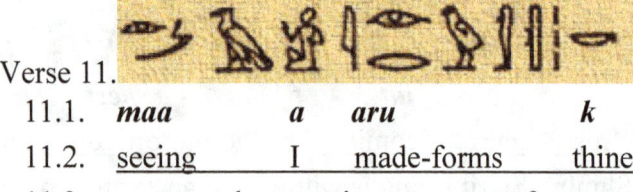
11.1.    *maa        a      aru        k*
11.2.    seeing      I      made-forms    thine
11.3.    …to me the capacity to see your forms…

Verse 12.
12.1.    *Djez-k   seqednu    a      Baiu   k    di     k         pert a        sekhem    a*
12.2.    thine-own  disposed    I      Souls  thine give   thee  going forth/out I     vital energy  I
12.3.    …your own forms, as you manifest in the life of all creatures and as the very soul of Creation itself. Oh Osiris: I ask you to please give me the capacity of going forth/out, when going into the temple for spiritual evolution and coming out transformed; grant to me the capacity of going forth/out with life force vital energy…

Verse 24.

| | | | | | | |
|---|---|---|---|---|---|---|
| 24.1. | er | djeddu | zahu | a | im | zahu | f |
| 24.2. | as to | Djeds city | Glorious Body | I | within | Glorious Body | his |

24.3. …the city of the double djed pillars (ancient Busiris city), the place where the body of the soul resides on earth while the soul resides in heaven, my glorious body, the evolved image of my earthly body, also exists within and through the Glorious Body of he who is the Supreme Glorious Body. Therefore, my body is glorious because his body is glorious, as my glory comes from his glory.

# Egyptian Book of the Dead Chapter 78 – Transforming into a Hawk verses 27-30

**Highlight: I am one of the Akhu created by god from the limbs of god himself**

Verse 27.

| | | | | | |
|---|---|---|---|---|---|
| 27.1. | Nuk a | pu | nuk a | akhu sheps | immy |
| 27.2. | I am | that | I am | a Noble Shining Spirit | within/among |

27.3. I declare that I am that I am. I am an enlightened person possessing Shining Spirit consciousness and I am among…

Verse 28.

| | | | | | |
|---|---|---|---|---|---|
| 28.1. | akhu | qmamu | kheperu | im | Neter hau |
| 28.2. | illumined | created beings | creations (images) | within | Divine body parts Divine |

28.3. …those who are enlightened beings were created and reflections of and within the Divine; even more, they are not just reflections, images of the Divine, but they are composed of the body parts of the Divine!

Verse 29.

| | | | | | | | |
|---|---|---|---|---|---|---|---|
| 29.1. | Nuk | ua | im | nenu | en | akhu | immu | akhu |
| 29.2. | I am | one | in | those | of | Noble Shining Spirits | within | illumined Divine |

29.3. I declare that I am one of those noble spiritually enlightened persons who exist within the Divine as illumined…

Verse 30.
    *30.1.*   qmamu                           en      Tem      djesef
    30.2.   <u>created beings</u>           of      <u>Tem</u>      <u>himself</u>
    30.3.   … beings created by the god of Creation and Completion, Tem himself.

# Egyptian Book of the Dead Chapter 78 – Transforming into a Hawk Verses 58-64

**Trans. by Muata Ashby**

Highlight: I shall not fall through grace of Shu, lord of serpent power and breath-

Verse 58.
    58.1.  An       cher                         her
    58.2.  <u>Not</u>     <u>defeated</u>                 <u>personality</u>
    58.3.  I am not defeated or cast down or vanquished by the grace of the personality known as…

Verse 59.
    *59.1.*  **Shu**     **nuk**     **hetep**     **neb**     **araty**       **oashuty**       **nuk**    **rech**   **akhu**    **iu**
    59.2.  <u>Shu</u>     <u>I am</u>     <u>content</u>   <u>lord</u>   <u>Dual Serpents</u>   <u>worship them</u>   <u>I am</u>  <u>knowledgeable</u> <u>Shining Spirit</u> <u>It is</u>
    59.3.  …Shu, who is the son of Ra and god of air, space, ether and through whom the light of Ra is transferred to the world. I am feeling secure and contented (hetep=harmony beyond duality) with Shu, the lord of the Serpent Power goddesses. I worship them, their wisdom and their serpentine movements as their energies course my body. I have knowledge about akhu, the Divine Shining Spirit. It is…

Verse 60.
    *60.1.*  **nafu**     **f**     **im**     **khat**     **an**     **khesefu**     **ka**     **nesheny**     **ay**     **n-a**
    60.2.  <u>breath</u>   <u>his</u>   <u>in</u>   <u>body</u>   <u>not</u>   <u>rejected</u>   <u>bull</u>   <u>storms</u>   <u>come</u>   <u>of-I</u>
    60.3.  through my physical body with the life force (goddesses) of/in his (Shu's) air that enters my body. By means of this process, I am not rejected by the Bull Generative Life Force, that I receive from God, that would otherwise cause storms of mental delusion, untoward desires and other disturbances. Instead, I come along…

**Below: From 2014 Neterian Conference -Teachings of New Kingdom Pert-M-Heru #8: Djehuty Raises the Hair and Brings the Cleansed Eye -PMH Chap. 17**

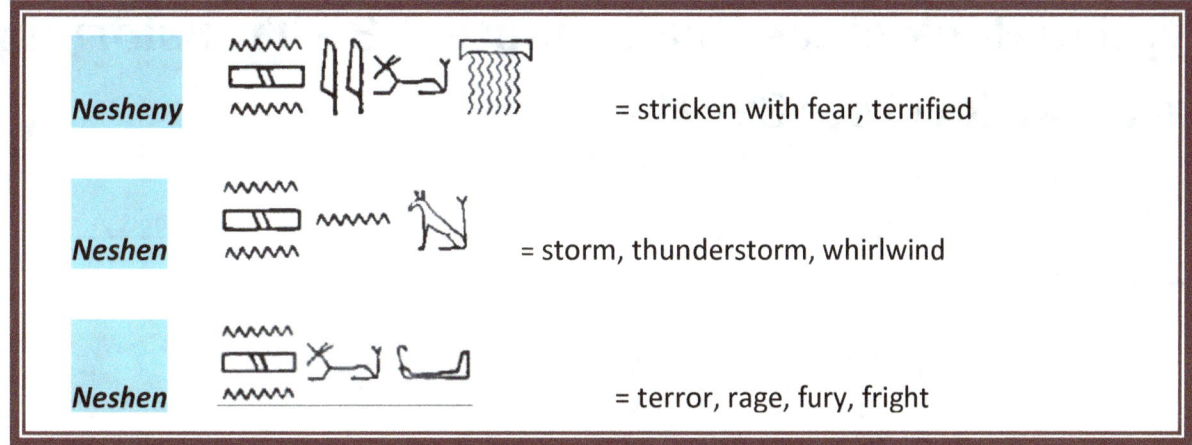

Verse 61.

61.1. mi n-ra im per Ruruty pert n-a im f er per
61.2. like the sun in temple Dual Lion Divinities come forth/out of-I into he as to temple
61.3. …as the sun comes along, shining brightly and powerfully in my lucidity of mind and powerful balanced life forces; I come in this capacity to the temple of the dual lion divinities, Shu and his counterpart Tefnut, the goddess of water, moisture and life force [Sekhem]. Passing through the duality of the Akeru (dual lion divinities Shu and Tefnut of the western horizon, symbolizing yesterday and tomorrow (past and future)) next I am able to come forth/out and move forward on my spiritual journey on to the temple…

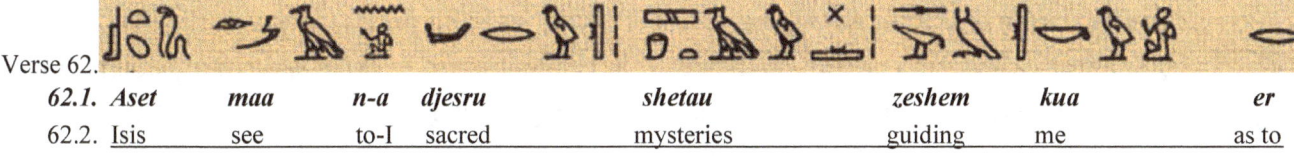

Verse 62.

62.1. Aset maa n-a djesru shetau zeshem kua er
62.2. Isis see to-I sacred mysteries guiding me as to
62.3. …of Goddess Isis and there I am able to see for myself, the sacred mysteries and there I am guided as to the…

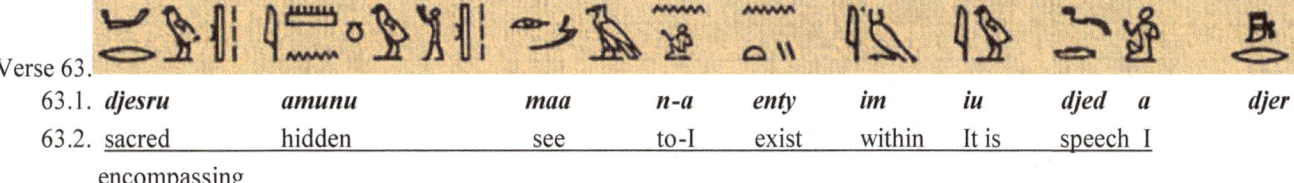

Verse 63.

63.1. djesru amunu maa n-a enty im iu djed a djer
63.2. sacred hidden see to-I exist within It is speech I encompassing
63.3. …hidden meanings of the sacred mysteries; I can see what exists in the temple; it is the words, the wisdom philosophy that encompasses…

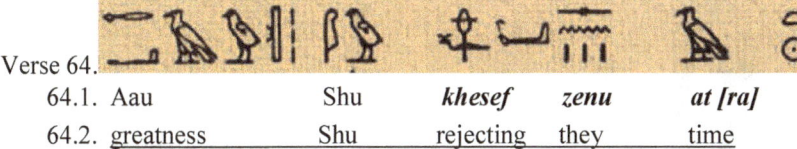

Verse 64.

64.1. Aau Shu khesef zenu at [ra]
64.2. greatness Shu rejecting they time
64.3. …the greatness of the god Shu that reaches to the limits of existence such that even time itself is rejected. Thereby I experience existence beyond time, this is the fruit of the work with breath, the serpent power and the study of the mysteries of the temple, going to and beyond the limits of space and time to discover the nature of reality, beyond my physical body, that renders my consciousness without disturbance and harmonized beyond duality.

# Egyptian Book of the Dead Chapter 78 – Transforming into a Hawk verses 89-91

**Highlight: I have seen Osiris and spoken with him about his soul his beloved prince. A wound is in heart of Set (ego)**

Verse 89.

| | | | | | | | | |
|---|---|---|---|---|---|---|---|---|
| 89.1. | Maa | n-a | Asar | djed a | n-f | er | chetu {mdj} | Ba f |
| 89.2. | See | to-I | Osiris | spoken I | to-him | about | things {scroll} | Soul his |

89.3. May I be able to see Osiris. I have already spoken to him about the intangible things concerning his soul…

Verse 90.

| | | | | | | | | | |
|---|---|---|---|---|---|---|---|---|---|
| 90.1. | pen | ser a | mer n-f | aspu | im | Ab | en zetep | maa | n-a |
| 90.2. | this | elder I | beloved of-his | misery | in | heart | of Set | see | of-I |

90.3. …that is with this elder child of yours, your beloved prince. Having seen Osiris and having conversed with him about soul things, the god Set is suffering in his heart because by communing with Osiris directly in the heart, Set cannot get in the way and cause Setian actions in my heart. My soul, Osiris, is alive and active now, he who is…

Verse 91.

| | | |
|---|---|---|
| 91.1. | neb | baga |
| 91.2. | lord | (soul) stillness |

91.3. …the lord of the stillness of the Soul.

# Verses from the Stele of Abu
**Trans. by Muata Ashby**

## Verses 1-3 previously presented at 2014 Neterian Conference

Verse 1.
- 1.1. En — mert — un — n-a — im — shemsu-f — amakhy
- 1.2. The — love/devotion — being — to-I — in — following — revered
- 1.3. The love for existing to myself as a personality in the following of the revered and holy…

Verse 2.
- 2.1. ari — a — her sesheta — im — hebu — -f — neb — im
- 2.2. doing — I — mysteries — in — festivals — his — all — in
- 2.3. …mysteries and my doing the sacred mysteries as well as participating in all of the festivals and rituals of the God including participating in…

Verse 3.
- 3.1. sektet — –f — neb — djed — en — Amunt — nefert — iu — im
- 3.2. Procession — his — all — words — of — West — Beautiful: — Coming — in…
- 3.3. …all the temple processions.

## Verses 4-7 Below is new for 2018 Neterian Conference and published here for the first time

Verse 4.
- 4.1. hetep — khu — a — Neter — er — zahu — mench
- 4.2. peace — Shining Spirit mine — Divine — as to — glorious body sculpted
- 4.3. …peace, my Divine Shining Spirit Body, of the Divine, that goes to my Glorious Body that has been sculpted through the chiseling process of the temple that allowed my earthly body to be transformed into a Glorious Body…

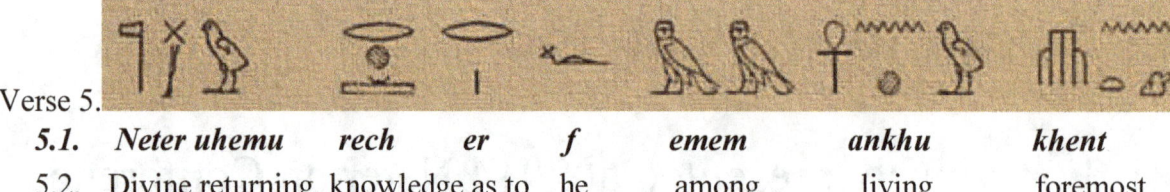

Verse 5.
- 5.1. Neter uhemu rech er f emem ankhu khent
- 5.2. Divine returning knowledge as to he among living foremost
- 5.3. …through the returning of divinity owed to acquiring the knowledge of him, the Divine, gained by being foremost amongst those living on earth…

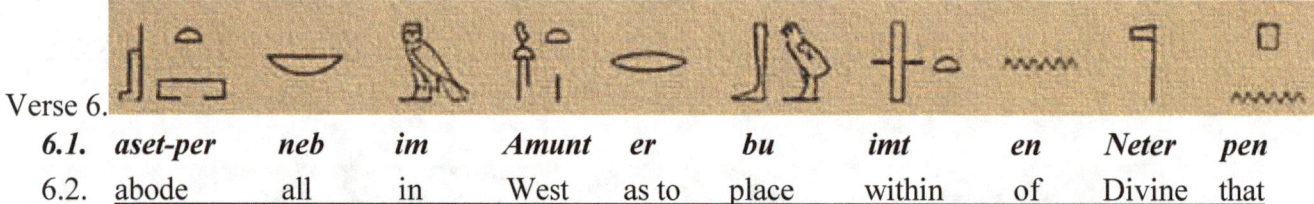

Verse 6.
- 6.1. aset-per neb im Amunt er bu imt en Neter pen
- 6.2. abode all in West as to place within of Divine that
- 6.3. Spending time in all the abodes of the Divine shrines and temples in the west, wherein are to be found the places where the Divine can be found…

Verse 7.
- 7.1. im djer entet k it em hetep aper im chet
- 7.2. in due to encompassing existing thee coming in peace provisioned in things
- 7.3. …within, for the reason of the all-encompassing existence. I came in peace, provisioned with the joy and knowledge and devotion of the spiritual practices composed of the things, the temples, scriptures, rituals and mysteries…

Verses 8-11 below previously published and presented at 2014 Neterian Conference - Folly of Love and Hate-mental polarization that fuels egoism and delusion

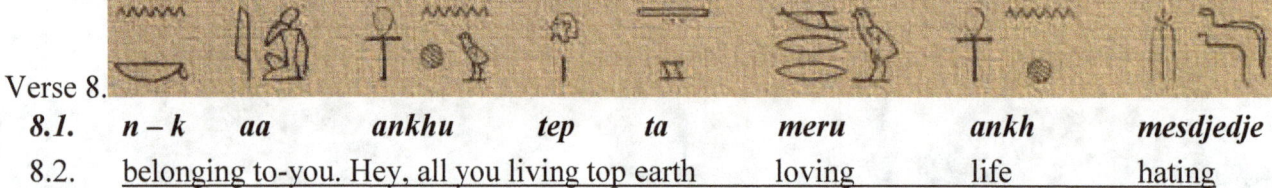

Verse 8.
- 8.1. n – k aa ankhu tep ta meru ankh mesdjedje
- 8.2. belonging to-you. Hey, all you living top earth loving life hating
- 8.3. …that appertain to you. Hey, to all of you people who are alive in your physical bodies and walking on the surface of the earth, who experience love for being alive and hatred for …

Verse 9.

| 9.1. | chepet | im | merr | tjen | oah | tep | ta | djed |
|---|---|---|---|---|---|---|---|---|
| 9.2. | downfall | within | loving | that | planting | on top | earth. | I say… |

9.3. … the inevitable downfall of old age, disease and death and still desiring that, to plant oneself down on the earth plane, living as a physical human being, even while knowing it is temporary enjoyment of pleasures that will end in death; to all of you this is what I have to say:

Verse 10.

| 10.1. | ten | chat | ta | nu | n | amakhy |
|---|---|---|---|---|---|---|
| 10.2. | the | thousands | loaves, | drink, | to | revered |

10.3. You need to offer the thousands of loaves of bread and thousands of jugs of drink to the revered and holy…

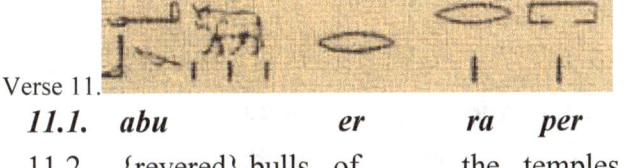

Verse 11.

| 11.1. | abu | er | ra | per |
|---|---|---|---|---|
| 11.2. | {revered} bulls | of | | the temples. |

11.3. Temple mascot symbol of the life-giving generative power of the Divine that is kept at the temples.

## Below: Ancient Egyptian Proverb in harmony with the text above:

"If you seek GOD, you seek for the Beautiful. One is the Path that leads unto GOD - Devotion joined with Wisdom."

-Ancient Egyptian Proverb

# Egyptian Book of the Dead of Hunefer, The source of true happiness

**Trans. by Muata Ashby**

**NOTE:** The following verse from the Book of the Dead of Hunefer is being presented as it contains a fascinating and important message about happiness. It states that happiness is obtained by having a positive outcome when the judgment scales of Goddess Maat determine that a life has been lived in an ethical, virtuous manner. This is in contrast with the messages of modern society that happiness is gained through relationships, possessions, accolades, wealth or power. The following terms for the opposite of happiness denote the dire consequences of the opposite of happiness and by association, the lack of living with ethical conscience. When the heart expands it experiences joy. When the heart contracts due to egoism and pursuit of untoward desires, happiness becomes elusive. True happiness is abiding and not dependent on gaining objects of desire, which are always elusive if not perishable once obtained. Therefore those are not places to find true happiness but only temporary stress relief in expectation of those gains being eventually lost, and with that loss the return of sorrow, frustrations and depression.

Verse 1.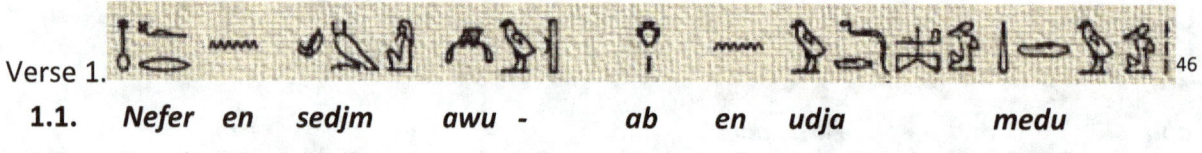

1.1. **Nefer   en   sedjm   awu -   ab   en   udja   medu**
1.2. <u>Good   to   hear   expansion   heart   of   weighing   words</u>
1.3. It is good to hear about the happiness that was experienced when the words of the Osiris initiate were weighed in the scale of Maat against the heart.

 **awu nedjs mwt**—sadness, sorrow, depression [the opposite of expansion of heart].

 **mwt, cheft** -Means death or enemy.

 **nedjs** -means something small, narrow, bereft, illness, bad, etc.

---

[46] Papyrus Hunefer

# Assorted Ancient Egyptian Texts Related to the Book of the Dead
# Pyramid Texts -King Unas– Utterance 222.211b Born of Horus

Translation by Muata Ashby

Verse 211.B

- *211.1.*   mes   k   en   Heru   iu-er   k   en   Set
- *211.2.*   born  thee  of  Horus  child/youth as to thee  of  Set
- *211.3.*   You are born of the God Horus; he is your essential and true nature. As you grow up in the land of the living, the world of time and space you are the adopted child of the God Set, who rears you and socializes you in the ways of worldly thoughts and feelings that allow forgetfulness of the original, essential and true nature.

Verse 212.C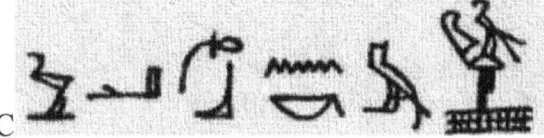

- *212.1.*   uab   n-k   im   amentet
- *212.2.*   Purification   of-thee through west
- *212.3.*   Your purification occurs when you spend time within and though the land of the hidden west, the abode of our enlightened soul, Osiris in the form of Sokkar, the place where the Divine, in the form of Horus, presides, as opposed to the east, where Set presides, the dominion of ignorance and worldliness.

Egyptian Book of the Dead Hieroglyph Translations Volume 4

Pyramid of King Unas – Sakkara, Egypt

Pyramid of King Unas – Sakkara, Egypt
Location of verse 222.211b

# Egyptian Book of the Dead Hieroglyph Translations Volume 4

Pyramid of King Unas – Sakkara, Egypt
Close-up of Location of verse 222.211b

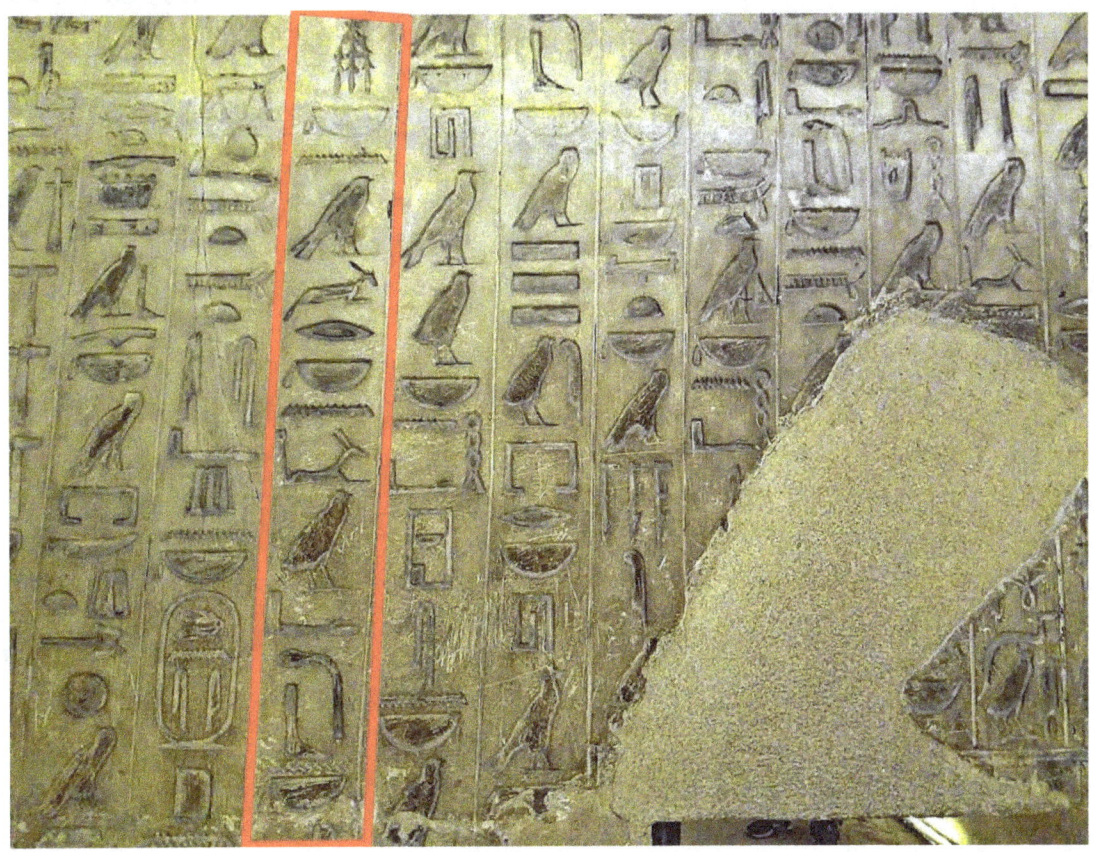

# The Movement of the Serpent Power According to the Ancient Egyptian Funerary Scripture

**NOTE:** The following scripture comes from a set of the Ancient Egyptian embalming ceremonies. In this scripture of Ancient Egyptian hieroglyphic text the movement of the Serpent Power is described. The hieroglyphic text is presented below with an original translation by Dr. Muata Ashby. For more details see the video webinar presentation given by Dr. Ashby on 8/26/17.

## ORIGINAL SERPENT POWER TEXT TRANSLATION BY DR. MUATA ASHBY

Verse 1.

**1.1.** Aiy   n – k   Wadjty   im   Arat   ankh   t {Ntr} urhu   tpy – k am   nebt

**1.2.** Coming to thee  serpent form goddesses living {divine}       anoint   head-thine form

Mistress

**1.3.** The two goddesses of the green life force energy come to you in the form of the living Serpent Goddesses of upper and lower Egypt, forms of Aset and Nebethet and Maati, who govern the duality of time and space, they come to anoint you on your head in the form as mistress...

Verse 2.

**2.1.** Rerat   senu   cha  S her tpy   im   abtetu   uben        {Ntr}S her tehenat   k   im   {mdj[47]}

**2.2.** of fire. They    rise Goddess upon head through eastern shining {Ntr} Goddesses upon

forehead thine through

**2.3.** ...of fire that burns away impurities of mind. These Goddesses rise *{mdj}*, through your subtle body, and your psycho-spiritual consciousness centers, up to your head, one moving through the east (left) side of the body and they project a shining effect as the other one moves towards your forehead through

Verse 3.

**3.1.** Amentetu  an  kheru   cha{mdj} senu her tpy   im   nuu   ra  nebu  mi   u  senu en

**3.2.** Western   not  speaking     rising they upon head thine form theirs day every like goddesses

those of

**3.3.** the western (right) side also and shine there on your head. Not with words or audible sound, but in silence, they rise *{abstract}* upon your head and they stay there all the days, encompassing all time, as they do for their

---

[47]    mdjat -scroll- signifies that the meaning to be assigned to the word is abstract and not mundane

# The Movement of the Serpent Power According to the Ancient Egyptian Funerary Scripture

**NOTE:** The following scripture comes from a set of the Ancient Egyptian embalming ceremonies. In this scripture of Ancient Egyptian hieroglyphic text the movement of the Serpent Power is described. The hieroglyphic text is presented below with an original translation by Dr. Muata Ashby. For more details see the video webinar presentation given by Dr. Ashby on 8/26/17.

## ORIGINAL SERPENT POWER TEXT TRANSLATION BY DR. MUATA ASHBY

Verse 1.

1.1. Aiy    n – k   Wadjty    im   Arat    ankh    t {Ntr}  urhu    tpy – k am    nebt

1.2. Coming to thee  serpent  form  goddesses living  {divine}    anoint   head-thine form

　　　　　　　　　　　　　　　　　　　　　　　　　　　　　　　　　　　　Mistress

1.3. The two goddesses of the green life force energy come to you in the form of the living Serpent Goddesses of upper and lower Egypt, forms of Aset and Nebethet and Maati, who govern the duality of time and space, they come to anoint you on your head in the form as mistress…

Verse 2.

2.1. Rerat   senu   cha  S her tpy   im   abtetu     uben    {Ntr}S her tehenat   k   im {mdj[47]}

2.2. of fire. They    rise Goddess upon head through eastern shining {Ntr} Goddesses upon

　　　　　　　　　　　　　　　　　　　　　　　　　　　　　　　　　　forehead thine through

2.3. …of fire that burns away impurities of mind. These Goddesses rise *{mdj}*, through your subtle body, and your psycho-spiritual consciousness centers, up to your head, one moving through the east (left) side of the body and they project a shining effect as the other one moves towards your forehead through

Verse 3.

3.1. Amentetu   an   kheru   cha{mdj} senu her tpy   im   nuu   ra   nebu mi   u   senu en

3.2. Western   not  speaking    rising they upon head thine form theirs day every like goddesses

　　　　　　　　　　　　　　　　　　　　　　　　　　　　　　　　　　　　　those of

3.3. the western (right) side also and shine there on your head. Not with words or audible sound, but in silence, they rise *{abstract}* upon your head and they stay there all the days, encompassing all time, as they do for their

---

[47]   mdjat -scroll- signifies that the meaning to be assigned to the word is abstract and not mundane

# Egyptian Book of the Dead Hieroglyph Translations Volume 4

Pyramid of King Unas – Sakkara, Egypt
Close-up of Location of verse 222.211b

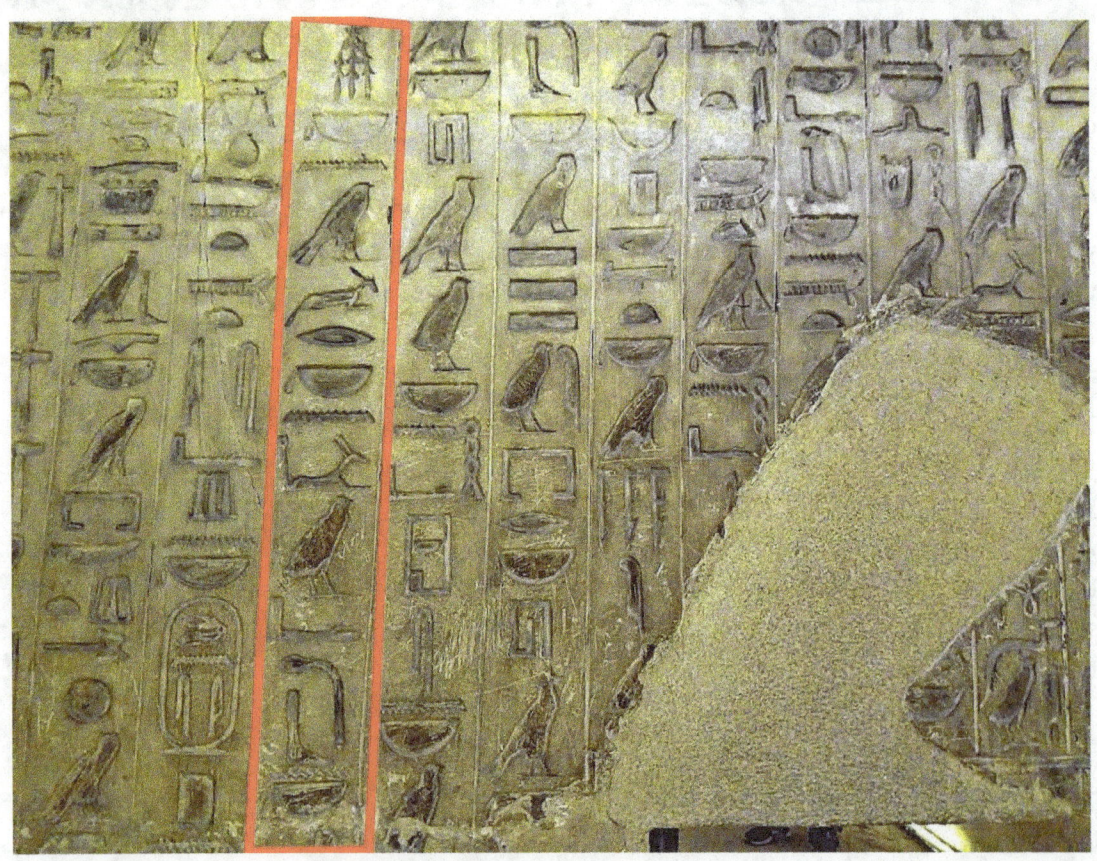

Verse 4.

4.1. Atef {Ntr} S Ra    ar    sent    {det}  neb   im   senu   im   machu    shepsu  {Ntr}
4.2. Father {divine} Ra  by  customary       all   form  theirs   as   illumined   exalted {div}
4.3. father Ra, who is the Creator and Divine Spirit manifesting as Creation, as is their total habitual way, {det} informing conscious awareness, in their abode; from there they speak to you, from within, in their form as the illumination of sages, those venerable Blessed {divine} Spirits.

Verse 5.

5.1. Kheper {mdj} ner iu adjetu k im  ma   bau {Ntr}  aqertu     shesep {mdj} tpy k  cha   S {mdj}
5.2. coming into being Victory through goddesses. It is speaking thee form souls divine blessed lands, receiving head thine rising goddesses
5.3. coming into being {abstract}, as they become spiritually victorious, achieving self-mastery by the grace of the goddesses. It is them speaking to you in the form of divine souls of perfected realms (lands) who, as you, receive { abstract } on the head the rising { abstract } of the goddesses and thus are elevated to divine states of consciousness; (in other words, It is they who give souls perfection, as they work their way, up to the brow, to their dwelling place on the head).

Verse 6.

6.1. S-en   tehenat   tpy k aset-per senu    iu  men {det}    im   tpy   mi   Ra    an
6.2. They   forehead    head thine abode theirs. It is firm {rest}    in    head thine like Ra  not
6.3. They go to the forehead area of your head and there make their firm abode and rest there inside the head firmly establishing themselves on your brow as they do on Ra's brow. Not

Verse 7.

7.1. her    senu    ar – k djeta
7.2. excepting  they  relating – thee forever.
7.3. Allowing any exception, or excluding or being apart from you, not leaving you or going away from you, these goddesses are related to you, not taking away the illumination, the enlightenment they brought and continue to perpetuate by sitting on your brow, the two having joined in your brow, the single abode, as one, non-dual consciousness that sees the transcendent and the mundane time and space reality; they stay there for you forever.

**SUMMARY:** The following section from the Ancient Egyptian Book of the Dead is presented here as a parallel text to the funerary scripture above, presenting a variant of the concept of the movement of the Serpent Goddesses

# Section from Pert-m-Heru Chapter 15

Verse 1.
- 1.1. Neteru     nebu     im     haauyu     {mdj}
- 1.2. Gods and goddesses all    in    celebration
- 1.3. All the gods and goddesses are in a state of exalted celebration and jubilation…

Verse 2.
- 2.1. maa     zen     tu     im     suten     en     pet     Nebt Unnut     menti {mdj} ta
- 2.2. see    the    you    in    royal    of    heaven Mistress Time    establish    on
- 2.3. …upon sight of the image of you as a full royal personality, as ruler over heaven. The goddess Unut, who is mistress of the transcendental moment being established, perched at…

Verse 3.
- 3.1. em  tpy – k     shemaut  - z         Mehit   - z         im     wept - k
- 3.2. inside head yours    south serpent - she        north serpent - she        within brow - thine
- 3.3. …the place inside your head; the southern aspect of Unnut and the northern aspect of Unnut go there.

Verse 4.
- 4.1. Iu     ari  n - z    aset    z    im    hat    k
- 4.2. It is  doing of – she abode hers in  front  thine
- 4.3. In that place on your brow is where the goddess makes her dwelling place, before you, in your foremost place.

Egyptian Book of the Dead Hieroglyph Translations Volume 4

VISUALS SUMMARY: The following slide images, from the live presentation of this scripture, are presented here as supplementary visuals to complement the descriptions in the Serpent Power scripture and the Book of the Dead Chapter 15 Scripture.

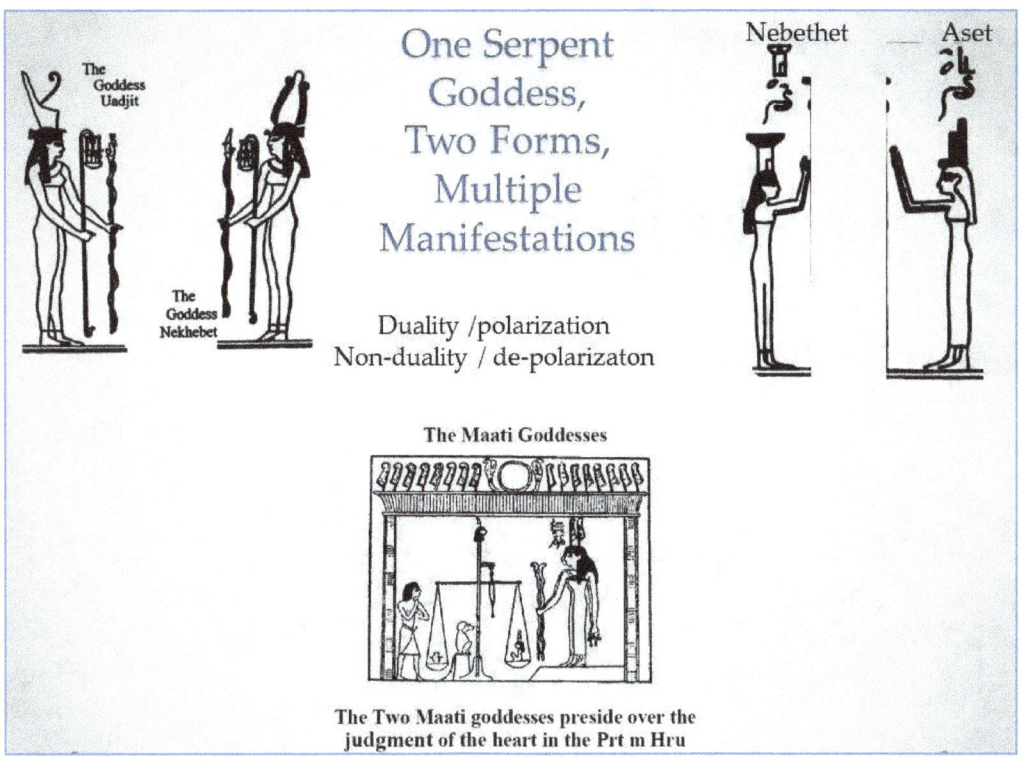

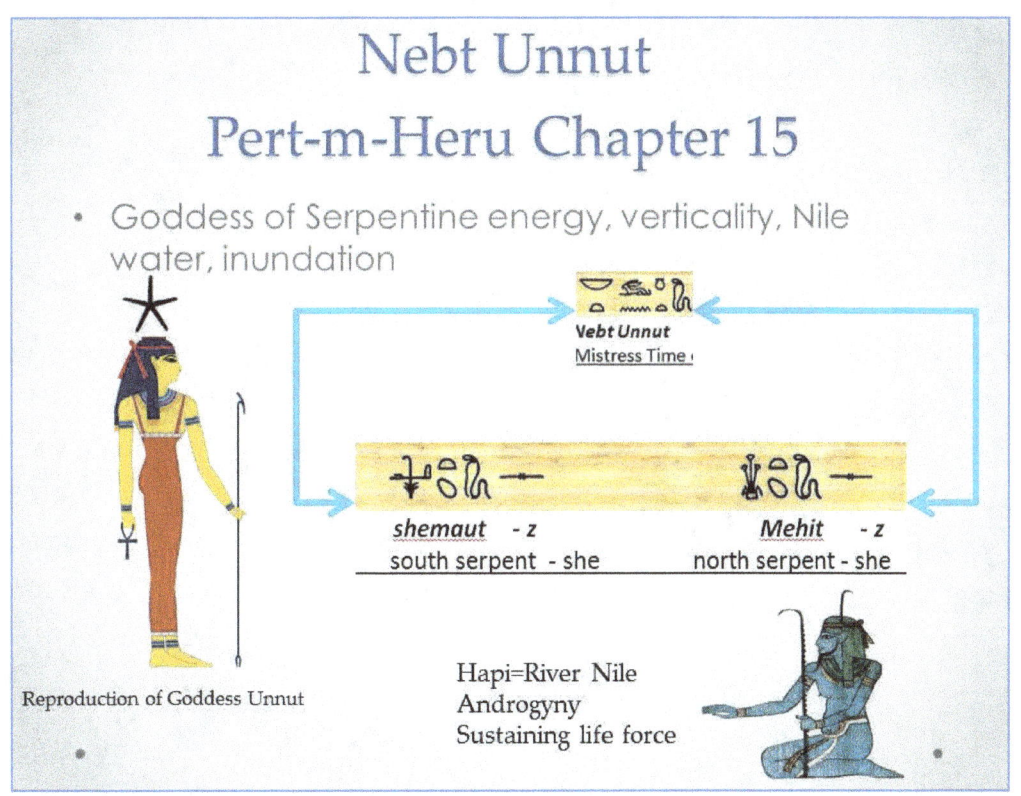

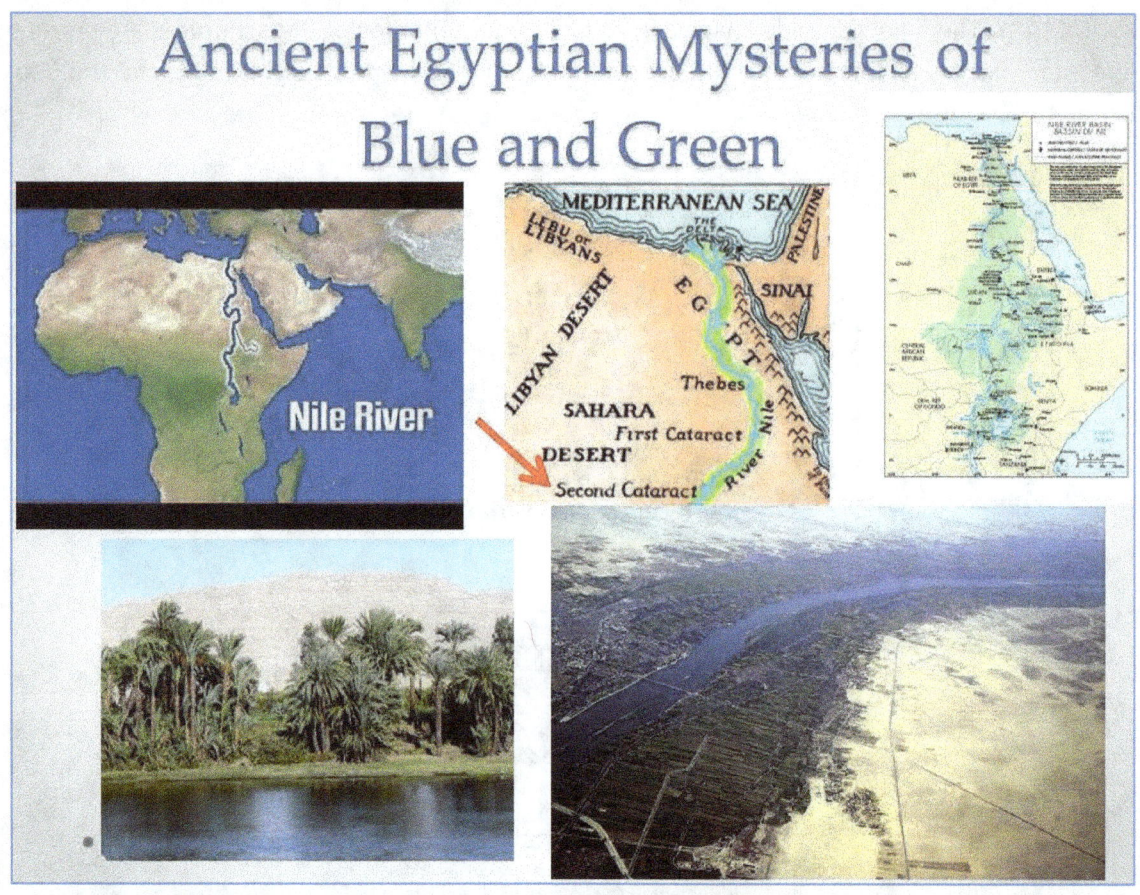
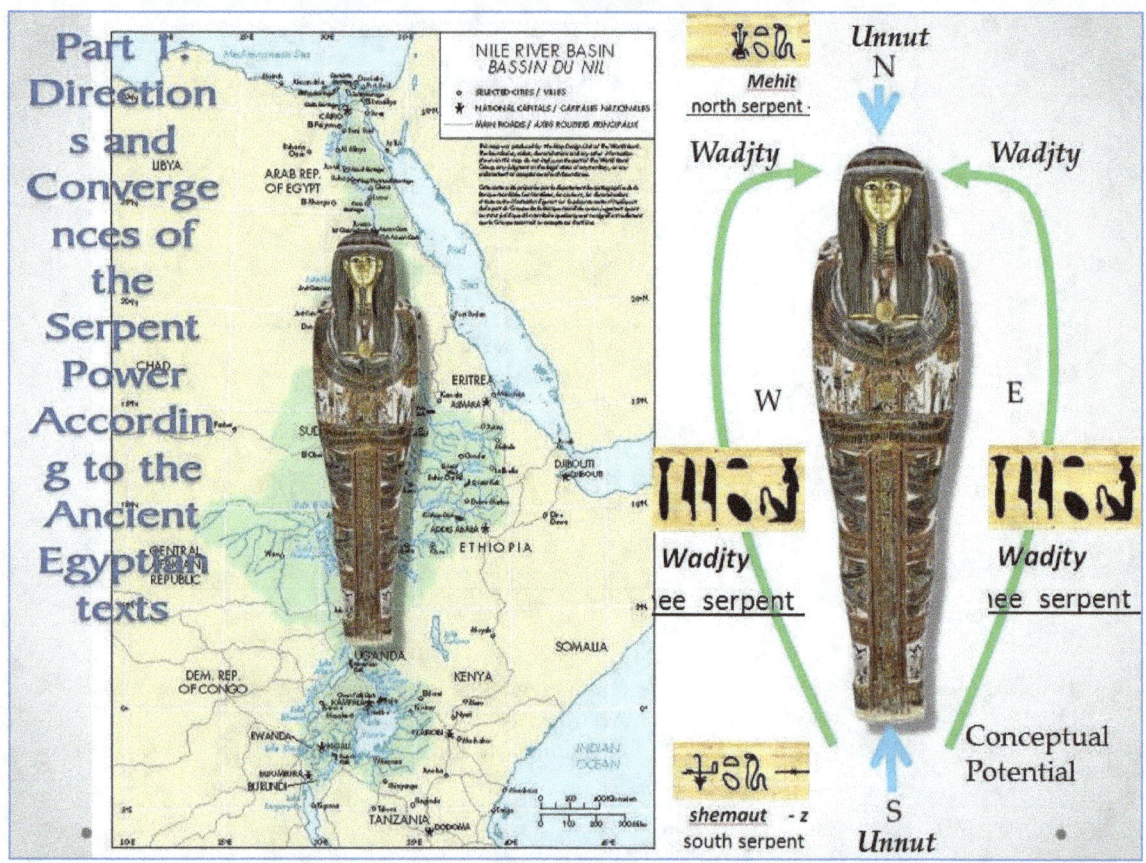

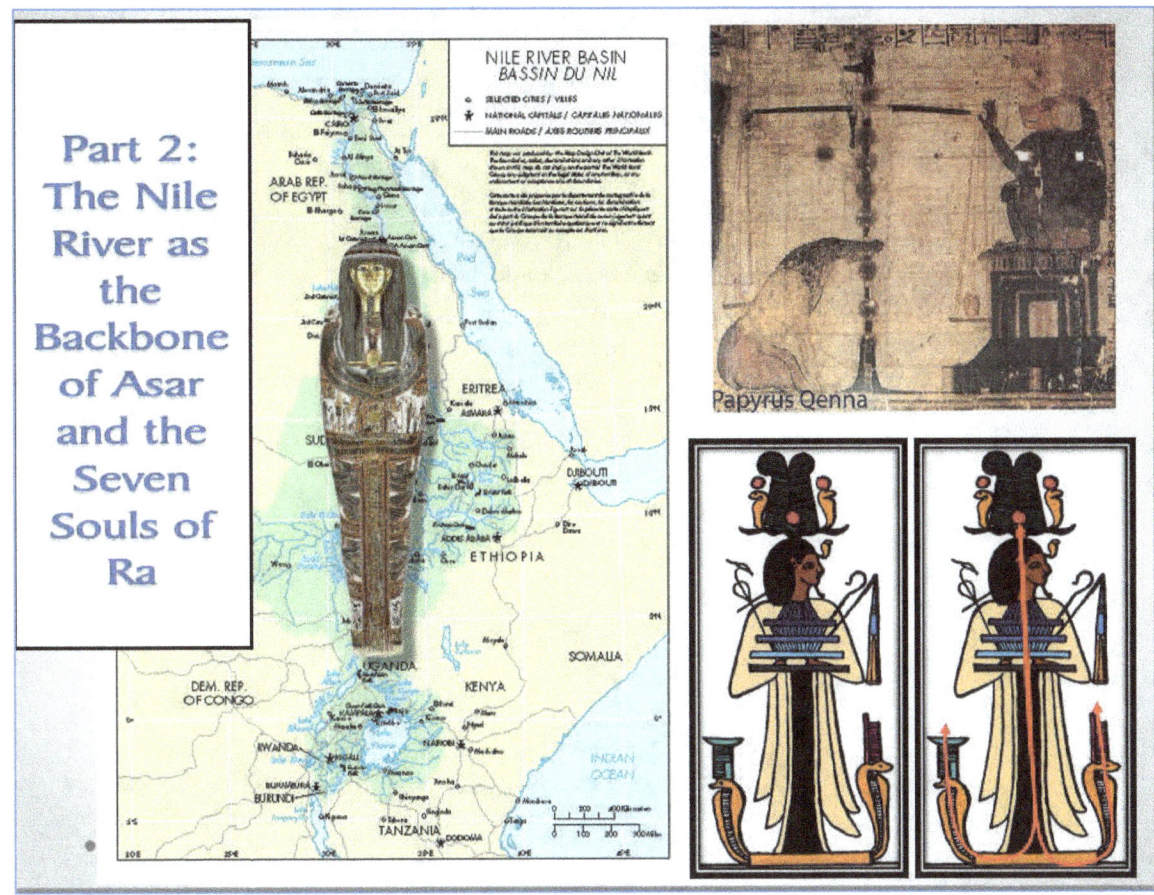
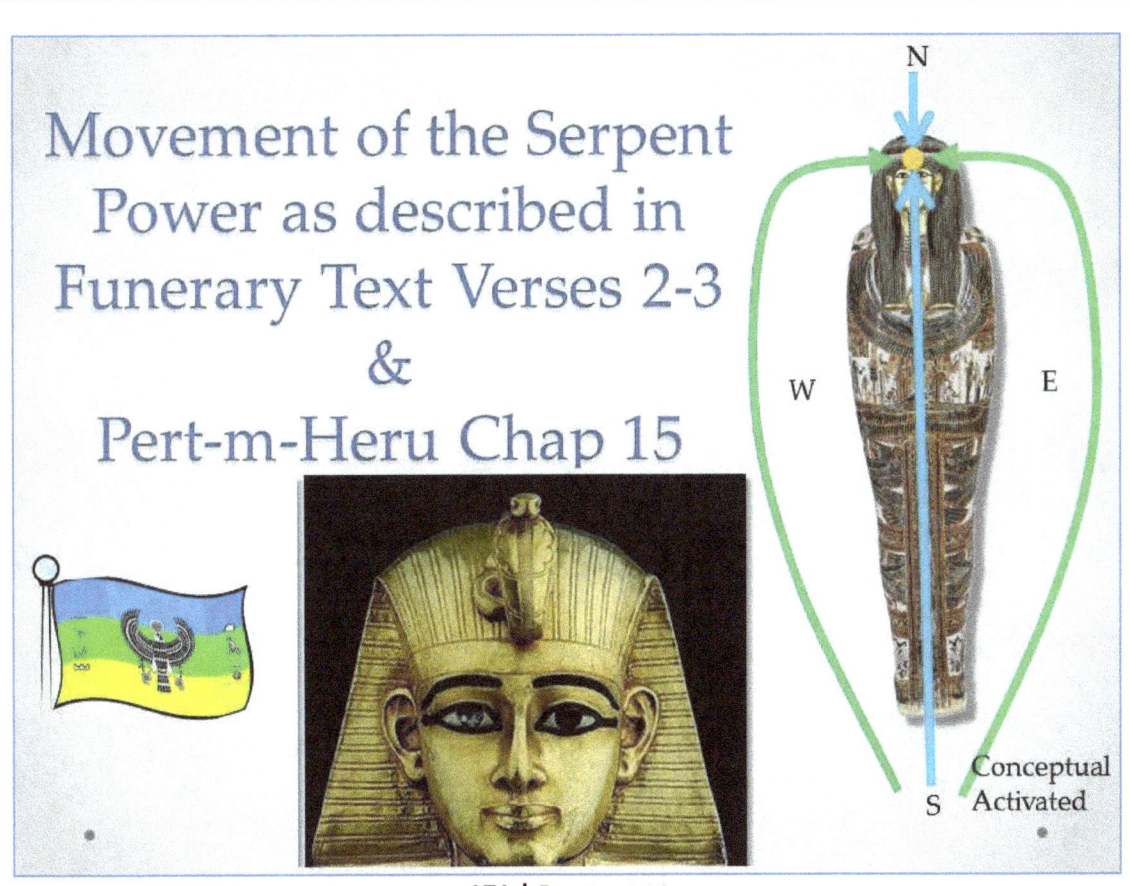

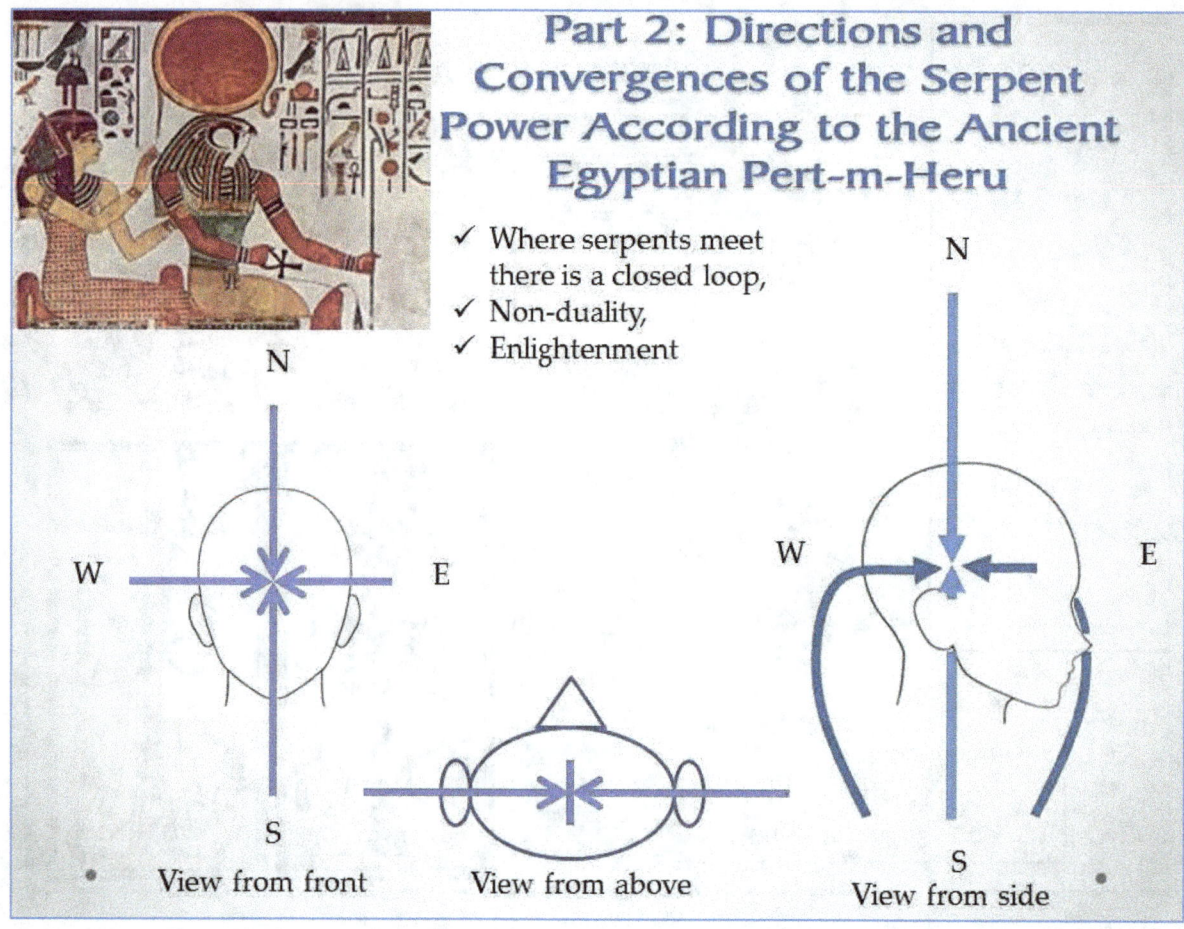

# Hieroglyphic Scripture -Hymn to Goddess Net

– Goddess Neith is the goddess of Creation, on a par with the God Ra and the Transcendental Divine in the form of Neberdjer. Here the aspirant is beseeching the goddess to reveal herself using the metaphor of removing the clothing that she has weaved over the universe that shows it outer forms but not its inner reality.
-Translation by Dr. Muata Ashby

Image of Goddess Net

Verse 1.

| | | | | | | |
|---|---|---|---|---|---|---|
| 1.1. | Ya | Mut | ur | an | sefech | mesu | s |
| 1.2. | Hey! | Mother | Great | Not | loosed | birth | she |

1.3. Hey! Great Mother, the garment that you wear, that covers your body, the underlying substratum of Creation, has not been loosened and removes so we can see your true nature. Therefore, the knowledge of the nature of your true nature is not released.

## Verse 2.

| | | | | | | | | | |
|---|---|---|---|---|---|---|---|---|---|
| 2.1. | Ya | neterit | aaht | m | chenu | n | dua | sheta - s | sen |
| 2.2. | Hey! | Goddess | great | in | private part | of | netherworld | hidden- she | doubly |

2.3. Hey! Great Goddess, who dwells in the secluded section of heaven, who is twice hidden…

## Verse 3.

| | | | | | | | |
|---|---|---|---|---|---|---|---|
| 3.1. | entet | rech | s | ya | netert | renpety | urt | an |
| 3.2. | not | known | she | Hey! | divinity, | time | total-great | not |

3.3. …it is not known where you are. Hey! you who deifies, you who are the great totality, they is not…

## Verse 4.

| | | | | | | |
|---|---|---|---|---|---|---|
| 4.1. | Sefech | tu | qeras | s | ya | sefech | znhu - s |
| 4.2. | Loosen | you | wrappings | she | Hey! | Loosen | bindings/ties fetters she |

4.3. …your garments are not loosened! Hey! Please loosen the knots that are holding your garments on your body, which is the very body of Creation itself.

## Verse 5.

| | | | | | | | |
|---|---|---|---|---|---|---|---|
| 5.1. | Ya | hapt | s | an | erta-tu | wat-a | n | aq |
| 5.2. | Hey! | Concealed | she | not | given | path | of | enter |

5.3. Hey! You, goddess, who are concealed. The path to enter you, to come into the knowledge and experience of you, is not openly given…

## Verse 6.

| | | | | | | | |
|---|---|---|---|---|---|---|---|
| 6.1. | re - s | mait | shesept | ba | n | Asar {net} | chuy | s |
| 6.2. | to she | come see to this | take/accept | soul | of (this) | Osiris {divine} | protect | she |

6.3. …about you. Please come and see about this, take my divine Osiris soul and protect it goddess…

Verse 7.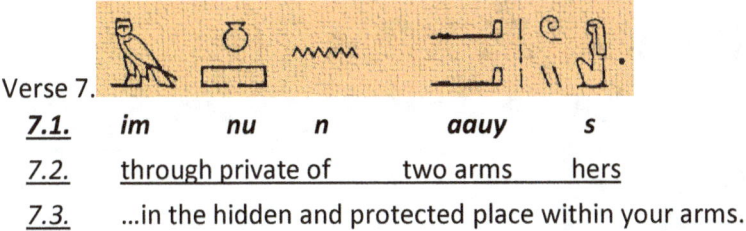

| | | | | | |
|---|---|---|---|---|---|
| **7.1.** | im | nu | n | aauy | s |
| **7.2.** | through private of | | | two arms | hers |
| **7.3.** | ...in the hidden and protected place within your arms. | | | | |

END

# The second HARPER'S SONG FROM THE TOMB OF NEFERHOTEP
# Theban Tomb No. 50

**Translation by Dr. Muata Ashby**

Verse 1.
- **1.1.** Djed en pa hesy     em bent     en Neter in Amun Neferhetep MaaKheru
- 1.2. Speech of the chant through harp    to Divine by Hidden Divine Beautiful Contentment
             Spiritually victorious
- 1.3. These are the words of praise to be chanted and sung, with the harp in praise of the Divine by one who goes by the name "One who is hidden divine and beautifully content", and spiritually victorious.

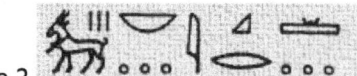
Verse 2.
- **2.1.** zahu nebu aqer    {mdj}
- 2.2. exalted all worthy
- 2.3. …for all present, being exalted, glorified and worthy listeners of this song…

Verse 3.
- **3.1.** Paut neteru nebt ankh
- 3.2. and the Company of Gods and Goddesses Mistress of the land of life present
- 3.3. …and in the presence of the Company of Gods and Goddesses Mistress of the land of life.

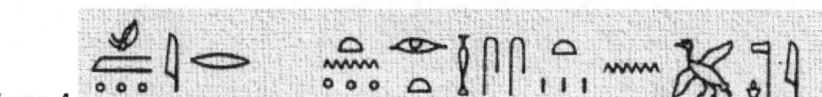
Verse 4.
- **4.1.** Sedjemu ar     tenu arit hess ten en    pa Netera
- 4.2. Listen to     the offering chant yours of the Divine
           /song
- 4.3. Listen and heed these words of chant offerings, a song of praise and devotion to the Divine…

Verse 5.
- **5.1.** im se-oash     en Ba    f mench en zahu aqer
- 5.2. Through cause-worship of soul     his chisel of exalted worthy
- 5.3. …by means of listening to this chant/song of divine worship to his soul, doing this is a chiseling work on the personality that carves away impurities and renders the personality exalted, noble, glorified and worthy…

Verse 6.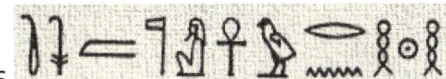
- 6.1. ta im Neter ankhu ren heh
- 6.2. though as divine living name eternity
- 6.3. …however, now having a divine living name that is for eternity instead of having a temporal and ephemeral name such as those who live on earth.

Verse 7.
- 7.1. Se-aau im Amuntet
- 7.2. Causing greatness in the final western abode of all souls.
- 7.3. This practice causes the person in question to experience greatness in the final western abode of all souls.

Verse 8.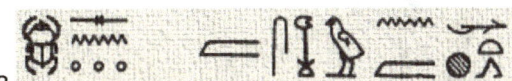
- 8.1. Kheper zenu im sechau en m-necht
- 8.2. Creating they form as memory of form what follows
- 8.3. This works to create a form or kind of memory that manifests in the form of the experience that follows…

Verse 9.
- 9.1. en aay neb-er
- 9.2. of comers all those oncoming
- 9.3. …for all those who approach and come by to listen and assimilate the song.

Verse 10.
- 10.1. Iu sedjm en nen hesu
- 10.2. It is listening to this chant/song
- 10.3. This experience requires listening to the deeper message of this current song…

Verse 11.
- 11.1. enty im asu djer
- 11.2. not in tombs earlier times
- 11.3. …and not blindly following the writings that are in certain tombs from earlier times…

## Verse 12.

**12.1.** se-djedt zenu im se-aah tep-ta
**12.2.** causing-aphorisms form of causing exaltation superior earthly
**12.3.** ...that contain sayings that seem to elevate life on earth as being the superior goal and purpose of existence...

## Verse 13.

**13.1.** im za nedjs Neterchert
**13.2.** while putting down cemetery
**13.3.** ...and in doing that though putting down, denigrating the value of what is expereinced in the cemetery, that is, the experience of the soul beyond the physical body...

## Verse 14.

**14.1.** her ma pu arit im mitet er pa ta ent heh
**14.2.** upon which that doing in likewise as to that earth to eternity
**14.3.** ...and then proceeding to put the same values upon eternity as upon the earth, as if the perishable value of earthly life could be compared to the abiding and transcendental nature of eternity....

## Verse 15.

**15.1.** aqa anty heru
**15.2.** accurately no fears
**15.3.** ...which, if we are going to be accurate, precise and truthful in the comparison, (eternity) is a place/state in which there is nothing to fear.

## Verse 16.

**16.1.** butu f pu hnen
**16.2.** hatefulness he this conflict
**16.3.** In truth, this conflict is hateful to him (the person who experiences it).

## Verse 17.

**17.1.** an unher her su er nu f
**17.2.** not known hostility he as to the he
**17.3.** In that realm of eternity the hostility of one person to another is unheard of, it is unknown, as it has no meaning in the realm of eternity, only in the realm of the living in time and space on earth.

### Verse 12.

**12.1.** se-djedt zenu im se-aah tep-ta
12.2. causing-aphorisms form of causing exaltation superior earthly
12.3. ...that contain sayings that seem to elevate life on earth as being the superior goal and purpose of existence...

### Verse 13.

**13.1.** im za nedjs Neterchert
13.2. while putting down cemetery
13.3. ...and in doing that though putting down, denigrating the value of what is expereinced in the cemetery, that is, the experience of the soul beyond the physical body...

### Verse 14.

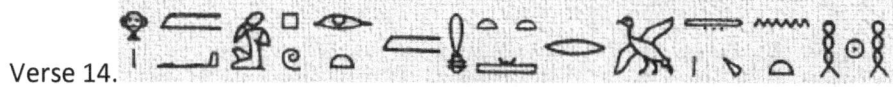

**14.1.** her ma pu arit im mitet er pa ta ent heh
14.2. upon which that doing in likewise as to that earth to eternity
14.3. ...and then proceeding to put the same values upon eternity as upon the earth, as if the perishable value of earthly life could be compared to the abiding and transcendental nature of eternity....

### Verse 15.

**15.1.** aqa anty heru
15.2. accurately no fears
15.3. ...which, if we are going to be accurate, precise and truthful in the comparison, (eternity) is a place/state in which there is nothing to fear.

### Verse 16.

**16.1.** butu f pu hnen
16.2. hatefulness he this conflict
16.3. In truth, this conflict is hateful to him (the person who experiences it).

### Verse 17.

**17.1.** an unher her su er nu f
17.2. not known hostility he as to the he
17.3. In that realm of eternity the hostility of one person to another is unheard of, it is unknown, as it has no meaning in the realm of eternity, only in the realm of the living in time and space on earth.

Verse 6.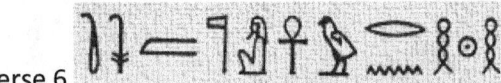
- 6.1.     *ta   im   Neter ankhu  ren  heh*
- 6.2.     though as divine living name eternity
- 6.3.     ...however, now having a divine living name that is for eternity instead of having a temporal and ephemeral name such as those who live on earth.

Verse 7.
- 7.1.     *Se-aau     im   Amuntet*
- 7.2.     Causing greatness in the final western abode of all souls.
- 7.3.     This practice causes the person in question to experience greatness in the final western abode of all souls.

Verse 8.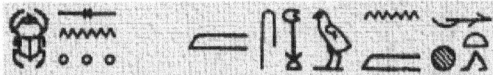
- 8.1.     *Kheper zenu   im   sechau   en m-necht*
- 8.2.     Creating they form as memory of form what follows
- 8.3.     This works to create a form or kind of memory that manifests in the form of the experience that follows...

Verse 9.
- 9.1.     *en   aay     neb-er*
- 9.2.     of   comers  all those oncoming
- 9.3.     ...for all those who approach and come by to listen and assimilate the song.

Verse 10.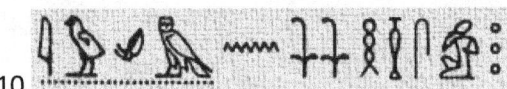
- 10.1.     *Iu   sedjm   en   nen   hesu*
- 10.2.     It is listening to this chant/song
- 10.3.     This experience requires listening to the deeper message of this current song...

Verse 11.
- 11.1.     *enty   im   asu        djer*
- 11.2.     not   in   tombs      earlier times
- 11.3.     ...and not blindly following the writings that are in certain tombs from earlier times...

Verse 18.
**18.1.**   ta   pen   anty   reqa           f
18.2.   territory that no   foes/fiends   he
18.3.   in that special realm of eternity there are no foes, enemies, adversaries to be against a person, as all are one existence there in that realm of unitary consciousness.

Verse 19.
**19.1.**   hau   nu   neb hetep im khenu f   djer   rek   paut   tep
19.2.   family   they all content in within he since time primeval head
19.3.   …the family members and friends and everyone you know or whoever is alive now or who has ever been alive, they have all gone or are going there and this has been so since the time of the beginning…

Verse 20.
**20.1.**   nty   er   kheper   en   heh   en   hehu   er-f   tem
20.2.   there as to created for eternity of eternities coming as to-he completely
20.3.   …and to this place the created beings, those who will be born in the future, will also die and eventually go there to the cemetery and the land beyond, and this goes on for an eternity of eternities; and a person will come to that land completely, entirely, in fullness, without leaving anything behind.

Verse 21.
**21.1.**   an   kheper en   asq         im   tameri
21.2.   not creating of delay   within   land-beloved
21.3.   Why? Because no one can delay their stay on earth even in the beloved land of Egypt; human life is ephemeral and not abiding.

Verse 22.
**22.1.**   an   ua   tem   spr   n-f
22.2.   not   one   stop   approach to-he
22.3.   Not one person can stop their approach to the death state and the experiences beyond mortal life on earth.

Verse 23.

**23.1.** ar aha ari er tu tep-ta zep pen ent resut
23.2. as to  lifetime acting as to you on earth that of dream
23.3. So, realize that an entire lifetime on earth and all the earthly activities, all of that is just a dream, a temporary deviation from the abiding truth of your actual existence.

Verse 24.

**24.1.** djed tu  aay   ad udja en peh  im  urt
24.2. say  you  come sound vital to arrive  in  great-land
24.3. So, let us state it definitively: understanding this wisdom, you, come sound and vital, arrive in the great land, the beautiful west, the final abode of the righteous souls, where there is no terror and nothing to fear, no conflict and no death and there is no end, for it is eternal.

Text of Neferhotep I: Tomb of Neferhotep, Thebes No. 50, North Wall of Passage (Photograph by K. C. Seele)

# Hymn to the Diadem- Bremner-Rhind Papyrus

Translation by Dr. Muata Ashby

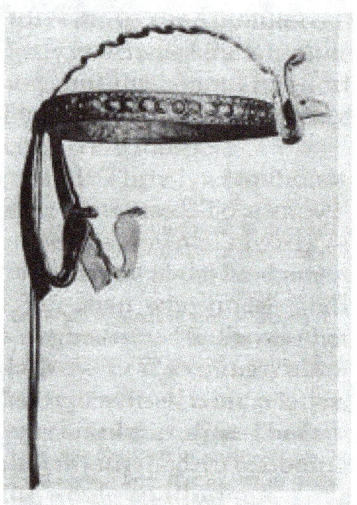

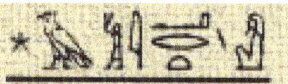

Verse 1.TITLE

    **_1.1._**    **_Dua Araty_**

    _1.2._    Adorations goddesses.

    _1.3._    Adorations to the two goddesses.

Verse 2.

    **_2.1. Res[t]    im hetep    res    sutenyt    urt{y}    im hetep    resut [t]    hetepti_**

    _2.2._ Awaken[fem] in  peace  awaken  royal cobra goddesses great  in  peace  vision[fem] peacefully she

    _2.3._ Awaken, oh goddess, without the agitation of duality. Awaken, oh, you great royal cobra goddesses in the calm of contentment. May she have an awakening vision in the peacefulness of non-duality.

Verse 3.

    **_3.1. Res[t]    im hetep    res    aarat    tept{det}    mehdty    Heru    ab mehdty Neter_**

    _3.2._ Awaken[fem] in  peace  awaken serpent goddess on head {sovereign[48]} northern Horus heart northern

    _3.3._ Awaken, oh goddess, without the agitation of duality. Awaken on the head of the sovereign, the Royal Person, who is in the north, who is the ruler, the representative of Horus, the divinity presiding from the north, the city of Heliopolis (Anu), the innermost being, the heart of the north of Egypt...

---

[48] {crocodile}

# Hymn to the Diadem- Bremner-Rhind Papyrus

Translation by Dr. Muata Ashby

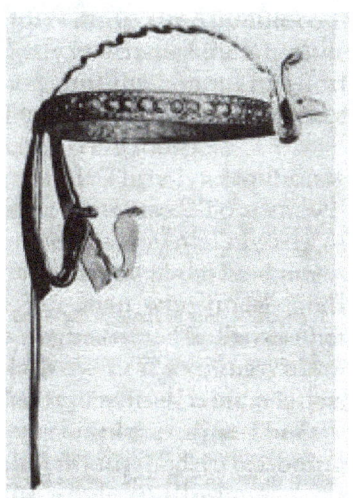

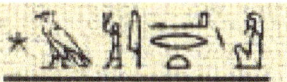

Verse 1.TITLE

- **1.1.** ***Dua Araty***
- 1.2. <u>Adorations goddesses.</u>
- 1.3. Adorations to the two goddesses.

Verse 2.

- **2.1.** ***Res[t]   im   hetep   res   sutenyt   urt{y}   im   hetep   resut [t]   hetepti***
- 2.2. <u>Awaken[fem] in   peace   awaken   royal cobra goddesses great   in   peace   vision[fem] peacefully she</u>
- 2.3. Awaken, oh goddess, without the agitation of duality. Awaken, oh, you great royal cobra goddesses in the calm of contentment. May she have an awakening vision in the peacefulness of non-duality.

Verse 3.

- **3.1.** ***Res[t]   im   hetep   res   aarat   tept{det}   mehdty   Heru   ab mehdty Neter***
- 3.2. <u>Awaken[fem] in   peace   awaken serpent goddess on head {sovereign[48]} northern Horus heart northern</u>
- 3.3. Awaken, oh goddess, without the agitation of duality. Awaken on the head of the sovereign, the Royal Person, who is in the north, who is the ruler, the representative of Horus, the divinity presiding from the north, the city of Heliopolis (Anu), the innermost being, the heart of the north of Egypt…

---

[48] *{crocodile}*

Text of Neferhotep I: Tomb of Neferhotep, Thebes No. 50, North Wall of Passage (Photograph by K. C. Seele)

3.4.
3.5. im hetep    resut[t]    hetepti
3.6. in peace    vision[fem] peacefully she.
3.7. ...be in peace, in the calm of contentment.    Oh, goddess; may she have an awakening vision in the peacefulness of non-duality.

Verse 4.
4.1. Res[t]    im hetep    res    aarat    aarat    shemaut    im hetep    resut[t]    hetepti
4.2. Awaken    in peace    awaken    serpent, serpent goddess southern in peace vision[fem] peacefully she.
4.3. Awaken, oh goddess, without the agitation of duality. Awaken oh, serpent, serpent goddess, you who are the goddess of the south. Oh, goddess, be in peace, in the calm of contentment; may she have an awakening vision in the peacefulness of non-duality.

Verse 5.
5.1. Res[t]    im hetep    res    aarat    mehyt    im hetep resut[t]    hetepti
5.2. Awaken[fem] in peace    awaken serpent goddess northern    in peace vision[fem] peacefully she.
5.3. Awaken, oh goddess, without the agitation of duality. Oh serpent goddess of the north, be in peace, in the calm of contentment; may she have an awakening vision in the peacefulness of non-duality.

Verse 6.
6.1. Res[t]    im hetep    res    Renenutet    im hetep    resut[t]    hetepti
6.2. Awaken[fem] in peace    awaken Goddess harvest    in peace    vision[fem] peacefully she.
6.3. Awaken, oh goddess, without the agitation of duality. Oh goddess of the harvest, Oh nurse of souls as they receive the fruits of their actions; Oh, goddess, be in peace, in the calm of contentment; may she have an awakening vision in the peacefulness of non-duality.

Verse 7.
7.1. Res[t]    im hetep    res    Wadjit    djesert    im hetep    resut[t]    hetepti
7.2. Awaken[fem] in peace    awaken Goddess Holy    in peace    vision[fem] peacefully she.
7.3. Awaken, oh goddess, without the agitation of duality. Oh, holy goddess, be in peace, in the calm of contentment; may she have an awakening vision in the peacefulness of non-duality.

Verse 8.
- **8.1.** Res[t]　　im　hetep　　res　　fat　　huii　tep　usech　ahtyt {Ntr}　im　hetep
- **8.2.** Awaken[fem] in peace　awaken　bear on head strike top of head expand neck　in peace
- **8.3.** Awaken, oh goddess, without the agitation of duality. Awaken and carry the load of wakefulness and endure it on your head; tap the head with it and allow your neck/throat to expand as the cobra goddess does with breath and muscle; be in peace, in the calm of contentment;…

- **8.4.**
- **8.5.** resut[t]　　hetepti
- **8.6.** vision[fem]　peacefully she.
- **8.7.** …may she have an awakening vision in the peacefulness of non-duality.

Verse 9.
- **9.1.** Res[t]　　im　hetep　　res　　selket im hetep　　resut[t]　　hetepti
- **9.2.** Awaken[fem] in peace　awaken　goddess Selket in peace　vision[fem] peacefully she.
- **9.3.** Awaken, oh goddess, without the agitation of duality. Oh goddess of protection and stamina of breath and stillness be in peace, in the calm of contentment; may she have an awakening vision in the peacefulness of non-duality.

Verse 10.
- **10.1.** Res[t]　　im　hetep　　res　　zeshent zenhet Wadjit　im　hetep　resut[t]　　hetepti
- **10.2.** Awaken[fem] in peace　awaken funerary goddess fetter Northern Cobra goddess in　peace　vision[fem]　peacefully she.
- **10.3.** Awaken, oh goddess, without the agitation of duality. Oh funerary goddess of the north, who breaks down the fetters of the personality preventing higher consciousness, be in peace, in the calm of contentment; may she have an awakening vision in the peacefulness of non-duality.

Verse 11.
- **11.1.** Res[t]　　im　hetep　　res　　khentet　sechet　　se-arat im　hetep resut[t]　　hetepti
- **11.2.** Awaken[fem] in peace awaken　foremost　land　cause goddess in　peace vision[fem] peacefully she.
- **11.3.** Awaken, oh goddess, without the agitation of duality. Awaken, you who are the foremost personality, the head of the land; this causes the cobra to be in peace, in the calm of contentment; may she have an awakening vision in the peacefulness of non-duality.

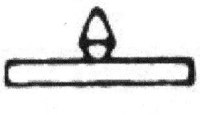

# HETEP

# INDEX

## A

Ab, 93, 94, 95, 113, 158
Abdu, 57, 84
Abraham, 18
Absolute, 29, 30, 32, 38, 61, 68, 72, 76, 97, 101, 192
Africa, 15, 16, 17, 21, 23, 37, 73, 197, 204, 207, 208, 209
African Proverbial Wisdom Teachings, 215
*African Religion*, 192, 199, 200, 203
Akhnaton, 85
Akhus, 91
Alexander the Great, 58
Alexander The Great, 18, 58
Alexandria, 11
Allopathic, 193
Amenta, 198
Amentet, 166, 200
American Heritage Dictionary, Dictionary, 36, 203
American Theocracy, 207
Amma, 87
Amun, 11, 19, 38, 48, 50, 51, 57, 70, 71, 75, 79, 82, 87, 99, 100
Amun-Ra-Ptah, 19, 38, 87
Ancient Egypt, 1, 2, 8, 11, 12, 14, 15, 16, 17, 18, 19, 21, 22, 23, 25, 26, 29, 30, 31, 35, 36, 37, 38, 39, 41, 42, 43, 44, 45, 47, 48, 51, 54, 55, 56, 57, 58, 59, 60, 61, 62, 64, 65, 66, 67, 69, 70, 73, 74, 76, 77, 87, 88, 92, 95, 96, 98, 99, 102, 103, 105, 106, 113, 120, 121, 122, 149, 152, 153, 161, 163, 166, 168, 192, 193, 194, 195, 196, 197, 198, 199, 200, 201, 202, 203, 204, 205, 206, 208, 209, 212, 213, 214, 215, 216, 217, 218, 219, 221
Ancient Egyptian Book of the Dead, 8, 12, 152, 153, 168
Ancient Egyptian Mythology, 47
**Ancient Egyptian Wisdom Texts**, 213
anger, 27, 68, 202
Ani, 67, 124
Ankh, 38, 40
Anu, 18, 19, 57, 79, 80, 199
Anu (Greek Heliopolis), 18, 19, 57, 79, 80, 87, 199
Anubis, 86
Anunian Theology, 75, 79, 80, 199
Apep serpent, 90, 110, 116, 121
Apophis, 90, 110, 116, 121
Arabs, 18, 36
Aramaic, 12
Aristotle, 24, 25
Aryan, 194
Asar, 11, 12, 14, 15, 19, 35, 38, 48, 55, 57, 59, 61, 69, 70, 75, 79, 80, 84, 86, 96, 98, 99, 104, 114, 117, 122, 124, 131, 137, 141, 142, 143, 146, 147, 149, 153, 158, 174, 198, 201
*Asar and Aset*, 198
Asarian Resurrection, 11, 54, 55, 56, 75, 198, 201, 202, 204
Aset, 11, 35, 38, 42, 48, 60, 75, 80, 83, 84, 86, 96, 114, 122, 137, 138, 139, 157, 166, 195, 198, 200, 201
Aset (Isis), 11, 35, 38, 42, 48, 60, 75, 80, 83, 84, 96, 114, 122, 137, 138, 139, 157, 166, 195, 198, 200, 201
Ashanti, 215
Asia, 21, 209
Asia Minor, 209
Asiatic, 126, 127, 206, 208, 209
Aspirant, 43, 142
Assyrians, 213
Astral, 69, 94, 95, 96, 97, 198
Astral Plane, 69, 94, 95, 96, 198
Atheists, 33
Atlantis, 205
**Aton**, 79, 85
Atonism, 85
Attachment, 21
Atum, 48, 70, 98, 99
Augustus, 15, 17
*Ausarian Resurrection*, 11, 56
Austerity, 26
Awakening, 48, 198, 220
Awareness, 45

## B

B, 87
Ba (also see Soul), 71, 93, 94, 95, 96, 97, 100, 118, 131, 132, 133, 136, 141, 142, 143, 146, 149, 158
Being, 25, 35, 38, 50, 57, 64, 69, 70, 76, 77, 79, 86, 87, 94, 95, 98, 99, 117, 119, 147, 154, 200
*Bhagavad Gita*, 25, 55, 59, 213
Bible, 12, 13, 18, 35, 44, 54, 55, 56, 59, 200, 201
Black, 16, 208, 209
Black Africa, 209
Black people, 16
Blackness, 23
Blood, 137
Body, 94, 95, 96, 125, 133, 134, 140, 142, 155, 159, 219
Book of Coming Forth By Day, 8, 11, 12, 36, 48, 69, 98, 198, 199
Book of Enlightenment, 9, 35, 55, 130, 131, 146, 149
Book of the Dead, see also Rau Nu Prt M Hru, 2, 8, 11, 12, 35, 48, 50, 52, 57, 124, 140, 145, 153, 154, 155, 156, 158, 162, 163, 169, 199, 213, 223
Brahman, 61
Breath control, 25
Buddha, 28, 204, 206, 222
Buddha Consciousness, 28
Buddhism, 27, 30, 32, 33, 44, 199, 206
Buddhist, 32, 36, 197, 206
Bull, 156
Byzantine, 17

## C

C, 87
Catholic, 43, 200
Catholic Church, 200
Causal Plane, 69, 94, 95, 96
Chanting, 25
*Child*, 201
China, 61
Christ, 28, 198
Christ Consciousness, 28
Christhood, 97
Christian Church, 43
Christian Yoga, 12, 32, 55
Christianity, 17, 23, 25, 27, 29, 30, 33, 35, 38, 41, 42, 43, 55, 192, 199, 200
Church, 43, 200
Church Fathers, 43
Civilization, 194, 195, 206, 207, 208, 209, 218, 219
coercion, 207
Coffin Texts, 35, 48, 51, 57, 58, 70, 75, 99
**Collapse**, 207, 218, 221
colonialism, 17
colony, 15
color, 16, 211, 214
Color, 211
Company of gods and goddesses, 63
Conflict, 207, 215
Confucianism, 33

Congress, 2
Conscience, 125
Consciousness, 15, 23, 25, 28, 29, 32, 41, 47, 50, 67, 69, 93, 98, 198, 214
Consciousness, human, 21, 28, 51, 67, 72, 101, 193
Constitution, 95
contentment, 70, 98, 143, 222
Contentment (see also Hetep), 73
Coptic, 60, 74, 198
cosmic force, 30, 32, 71, 99, 116, 200, 205
Cosmology, 24
Cow, 83
Creation, 11, 25, 30, 41, 47, 48, 62, 63, 64, 65, 71, 74, 75, 76, 79, 80, 81, 82, 83, 84, 85, 86, 87, 93, 94, 97, 99, 109, 110, 112, 113, 116, 117, 118, 119, 120, 122, 123, 147, 153, 156, 167, 173, 174, 198, 199, 214
cultural ego, 67
cultural egoism, 67
Culture, 73, 197, 205, 210, 219, 220

## D

Death, 42, 207, 218
December, 200
Deism, 26
delusion, 156, 160
Demotic, 15
Denderah, 19, 198
depression, 68, 162
Desire, 97, 215
Detachment, 26
*Devotional Love*, 46, 196
Diet, 193
Diodorus, 15, 16, 18
Discipline, 32, 42
dispassion, 44
Divine Consciousness, 91
*Divine Word*, 68
Djehuti, 38, 48, 50, 68, 86
Dollar, U.S. Dollar, 221
Dream, 72, 100
Dream, REM sleep, 72, 100
Dualism, 26, 27
dualism and egoism, 27
Duality, 27
Duat, 70, 94, 96, 99, 198
Dynastic period, 35, 36, 67

## E

Earth, 94
Edfu, 19, 84, 198
Egoism, 27, 70, 90, 98
Egyptian Book of Coming Forth By Day, 69, 198
Egyptian civilization, 36, 39, 67
Egyptian Mysteries, 8, 36, 41, 51, 105, 121, 194, 202, 203, 215, 217
Egyptian Physics, 200
Egyptian Proverb, 22, 45, 59, 69, 70, 98, 99, 195
Egyptian proverbs, 39, 65, 195
Egyptian religion, 15, 21, 30, 38, 47, 67
Egyptian Religion, 87
Egyptian Yoga, 2, 15, 21, 30, 32, 37, 38, 40, 41, 42, 47, 54, 66, 69, 70, 72, 82, 96, 97, 99, 100, 192, 194, 197, 198, 199
Egyptian Yoga Book Series, 47, 66, 97
Egyptian Yoga see also Kamitan Yoga, 15, 21, 24, 30, 32, 37, 38, 40, 41, 42, 47, 54, 66, 69, 70, 72, 82, 96, 97, 99, 100, 192, 194, 197, 198, 199, 222
Egyptologists, 15, 17, 18, 35, 37, 43, 46, 50, 57, 66, 90, 203, 212
Elements, 69, 93
Empire culture, 207
Enlightenment, 1, 2, 9, 15, 21, 22, 23, 28, 35, 41, 54, 55, 56, 68, 69, 70, 72, 73, 96, 97, 99, 100, 142, 192, 194, 195, 196, 197, 198, 199, 200, 202, 206, 215, 217, 218, 219
Ennead, 86
*ETHICS*, 194, 206, 208, 209, 214
Ethiopia, 15, 16, 215
Ethiopian priests, 15
Eucharist, 66, 198
Europe, 21
evil, 27, 96, 202, 203
Evil, 204
Evolution, theory of, 46, 47, 48
Exercise, 25, 198
Existence, 21
Existing One, 63
Eye, 113, 138, 149, 156
eye of Heru, 66
Eye of Heru, 91, 149
Eye of Horus, 138, 149

## F

**Faith**, 209
Fasting, 25
Feelings, 120
Fiction, 28
Finances, 219
First Intermediate Period, 17
Form, 95, 103
frustration, 21, 22

## G

Galla, 215
Galla culture, 215
Geb, 80, 86, 114, 122, 198
Ghana, 215
Giza, 18, 36
Giza Plateau, 18
global economy, 207
Globalization, 207
Gnostic, 29, 33, 41, 42, 43
Gnostic Christianity, 33, 41, 42, 43
Gnostic Christians, 43
God, 11, 20, 24, 25, 26, 29, 30, 32, 33, 35, 38, 39, 44, 50, 56, 62, 63, 64, 65, 67, 68, 69, 70, 71, 73, 76, 86, 91, 92, 93, 94, 95, 96, 97, 98, 99, 113, 114, 116, 117, 154, 156, 159, 163, 173, 195, 196, 199, 200, 204, 211
Goddess, 60, 68, 75, 76, 79, 83, 92, 114, 157, 162, 166, 173, 174, 200, 211
Goddesses, 64, 76, 80, 82, 83, 86, 88, 142, 166, 168, 197, 203
Gods, 11, 15, 64, 76, 80, 82, 86, 88, 121, 142, 168, 197, 203
gods and goddesses, 30, 31, 36, 50, 62, 63, 64, 66, 115, 117, 131, 146, 168, 199, 203, 205
Good, 162, 204
Gospels, 200
Great Months, 18
Great Year, 18
Greece, 16, 60, 194, 205
greed, 27
Greek philosophers, 17, 25
Greek philosophy, 192
Greeks, 18, 58, 60, 61, 213

## H

Harappans, 38
Harmony, 27, 140
Hate, 160, 215
**Hatha Yoga**, 208
Hathor, 86, 132, 147, 198, 200, 202, 222
hatred, 27
Hatred, 215
Hawk, 152, 153, 154, 155, 156, 158
Health, 193, 200
Heart, 27, 113, 130, 202, 210
Heart (also see Ab, mind, conscience), 113, 130, 202, 210
Heaven, 28, 94, 200
Hebrew, 12, 18
Hekau, 11, 35, 67, 221
Heliopolis, 19, 57
Hermes, 113, 217
Hermes (see also Djehuti, Thoth), 113, 217
Hermetic, 24, 48, 60, 121, 217
Hermetic XE "Hermetic" Texts, 48
Hermeticism, 24, 217
Herodotus, 16, 18

Heru, 10, 11, 13, 17, 35, 36, 37, 38, 40, 46, 47, 48, 50, 51, 52, 54, 55, 57, 66, 67, 69, 75, 79, 80, 84, 122, 127, 130, 134, 135, 139, 148, 149, 150, 153, 156, 163, 168, 198, 199, 200, 201, 204, 213
Heru (see Horus), 10, 11, 13, 17, 35, 36, 37, 38, 40, 46, 47, 48, 50, 51, 52, 54, 55, 57, 66, 67, 69, 75, 79, 80, 84, 122, 127, 130, 134, 135, 139, 148, 149, 150, 153, 156, 163, 168, 198, 199, 200, 201, 204, 213
Hetep, 22, 38, 40, 59
Hetheru, 38, 48, 75, 79, 83, 202
Hetheru (Hetheru, Hathor), 38, 48, 75, 79, 83, 202
Hetkaptah see also Menefer, Memphite, 19, 57
Het-Ka-Ptah, see also Men-nefer, Memphis, 79
Hidden, 11, 38, 72, 100
Hidden God, 11
*Hieroglyphic*, 1, 8, 68, 103, 105, 106, 173, 197, 212, 217
Hieroglyphic Writing, language, 1, 8, 68, 103, 105, 106, 173, 197, 212, 217
Hieroglyphs, 2, 8, 106
Hinayana,, 30
Hindu, 29, 36, 61
Hinduism, 30, 31, 38, 44, 199
Hindus, 203
Hollywood, 43
hope, 43, 210, 212
Horus, 11, 37, 38, 40, 48, 75, 84, 114, 122, 127, 134, 138, 139, 149, 150, 153, 163
Horushood, 28, 69, 98
HUMANITY, 202
Hymns of Amun, 48, 70, 87, 99

I

I, 70, 96, 97, 99
Iamblichus, 213
Ignorance, 21, 94
Ignorance, see also Khemn, 21, 94
illusion, 22, 28, 29, 44, 45, 65, 69, 70, 98, 99
Illusion, 28, 29, 44, 45
Image, 132
India, 16, 17, 24, 25, 29, 37, 38, 42, 61, 194, 195, 196, 197, 206, 208
Indian Yoga, 25, 32, 36, 194
Individual consciousness, 25
Indus, 38, 194
Indus Valley, 38, 194
Initiate, 193
Intuition, 59

Isis, 11, 35, 38, 48, 75, 84, 86, 96, 114, 122, 137, 138, 139, 157, 195, 198, 200, 222, 223
Isis and Osiris, see Asar and Aset, 35
Isis, See also Aset, 11, 35, 84, 114, 122, 137, 138, 139, 157, 195, 198, 200, 222, 223
Islam, 29, 33, 192

J

Jainism, 33
Jesus, 44, 55, 97, 198, 200, 201, 222
Jesus Christ, 198
Jnana Yoga, 42
Joseph, 18
Joy, 73
Judaism, 17, 29, 33, 35, 192

K

Ka, 69, 71, 79, 95, 96, 100, 131, 133, 136
*Kabbalah*, 192
Kamit, 17, 18, 23, 36, 73, 76, 77, 83, 84
Kamit (Egypt), 17, 18, 23, 36, 73, 76, 77, 83, 84, 203
Kamitan, 54, 74, 76, 78, 194, 205
Kant, 25
Karma, 196
Kemetic, 8, 23, 24, 54, 58, 60, 61, 62, 63, 65, 66, 92, 94, 206, 210, 216, 219, 222
Khaibit, 95, 97, 149
Khat, 69, 70, 71, 94, 95, 96, 98, 100, 133
*Khemn, see also ignorance*, 203
Khu, 11, 67, 95, 97, 113
*King*, 12, 17, 55, 201, 204
Kingdom, 17, 28, 38, 44, 54, 57, 60, 67, 200
Kingdom of Heaven, 28, 200
KMT (Ancient Egypt). See also Kamit, 16, 23
Know Thyself, 28, 40
Knowledge, 23, 69, 98
Koran, 59
Krishna, 201
Kybalion, 121, 217

L

Latin, 26
Liberation, 28, 69, 98
Libyans, 17
Life, 40, 156, 197, 204, 209, 211, 214
Life Force, 40, 156, 197
Listening, 41, 42, 46, 79
Lotus, 22, 40
Love, 46, 160, 196, 222

Lower Egypt, 37, 40, 63

M

M, 96
Maakheru, 65
Maat, 42, 54, 57, 68, 71, 75, 86, 100, 162, 196, 200, 202, 205, 210, 213, 215, 216, 217, 218, 219
*MAAT*, 51, 195
Maat Philosophy, 202, 205, 210, 217, 218
Maati, 68, 166
*MAATI*, 196
Malawi, 215
Manetho, 18, 36
Manetho, see also History of Manetho, 18, 36
Mantras, 11
martial law, 58
Marxism, 20
Matter, 72, 100, 200
Matthew, 44
media, 35, 72, 100, 207
Meditating, 42
Meditation, 2, 25, 26, 41, 46, 193, 195, 197, 223
Medu Neter, 68, 203, 221
Mehurt, 83
Memphis, 19, 57
Memphite Theology, 57, 70, 75, 81, 99, 200, 223
Mental agitation, 27
Meskhenet, 96, 196
Metamorphosis, 27
Metaphor, 133
Metaphysics, 24, 25, 200, 214
Metu Neter, 39, 51, 67
Middle East, 192
Middle Kingdom, 17, 54, 57, 60
Middle Kingdom XE "Middle Kingdom" Period, Ancient Egypt, 57
Min, 198
Mind, 130, 133, 219
Modern science, 25, 26
Moksha, 28
Monism, 29, 31, 33
Monotheism, 29
Monotheistic, 30
Moon, 16
Mortals, 47
Moses, 18
Muhammad, 43
mummy, 11
Music, 20, 28, 211
Mut, 61, 173
Mysteries, 8, 11, 36, 41, 51, 60, 87, 105, 121, 194, 202, 203, 213, 215, 217, 223
Mysterious, 11

mystical experience, 12, 26
mystical philosophy, 25, 31, 37, 43, 47, 54, 59, 66, 207, 213
Mysticism, 13, 26, 30, 31, 34, 55, 60, 194, 195, 199, 200, 202, 206, 208, 209
Myth of Creation, 48
Mythology, 2, 15, 20, 21, 28, 37, 47
Mythology is a lie, 28

## N

Nature, 74
Neberdjer, 38, 61, 87, 94, 110, 116, 117, 154, 173, 192
Nebertcher, 38, 71, 87, 100
Nebethet, see also Nebthet, 122, 166
Nebthet, 80
Nebthet, see also Nebethet, 115
Nefer, 38, 40, 48, 162
Nefertem, 81
Negative Confessions, 51
Nehast, 91, 203
neo-con, 207
Nephthys, 86, 115, 122
Net, goddess, 75, 83, 112, 173
Neter, 11, 15, 24, 27, 30, 32, 33, 38, 39, 47, 51, 54, 64, 67, 68, 71, 73, 74, 76, 77, 79, 85, 91, 100, 121, 141, 145, 155, 159, 160, 196, 198, 203, 204, 207, 212, 215, 220, 221
Neterian, 8, 79, 83, 90, 91, 156, 159, 160, 203, 204, 206, 219, 220, 222
Neterianism, 76, 217, 220
Neter-khert, see also Cemetery, 145
Neters, 36, 39
Neteru, 38, 63, 74, 76, 77, 78, 90, 91, 168, 203
Netherworld, 50, 96, 131
New Kingdom, 17, 60, 67, 82, 85, 156
New Testament, 12
Nigeria, 215
*Nile flood*, 13
Nile River, 17, 73
Nile Valley, 16
Nine, 95
Nirvana, 28, 69, 98
non-dualism, 27
Non-dualistic, 27
North East Africa . See also Egypt Ethiopia
    Cush, 16
North East Africa. See also Egypt Ethiopia
    Cush, 16
Nubian, 17
Nubians, 16, 73
Nun, 79
Nun (primeval waters-unformed matter), 79

Nun (See also Nu), 79
Nut, 80, 86, 114, 122, 198

## O

Ocean, 70, 71, 72, 94, 99, 100, 101, 118
Octavian, 17
Old Kingdom, 17, 57, 60
*Old Kingdom XE "Old Kingdom" XE "Kingdom" Period*, 57
Old Testament, 12
Om, 223
Ontology, 24
Orion Star Constellation, 200
Orthodox, 43, 59, 203
Osiris, 11, 19, 35, 38, 48, 57, 61, 69, 75, 84, 86, 96, 98, 104, 114, 117, 122, 124, 131, 132, 134, 137, 141, 142, 143, 146, 147, 149, 150, 153, 158, 162, 163, 174, 198, 204, 223

## P

Pa Neter, 71, 100
Palermo Stone, 18
Panentheism, 30
Pantheism, 30
Papyrus of Any, 48, 75
Papyrus of Turin, 18
Patañjali, 25
Paut, 63, 64
Pautti, 71, 99
**Peace**, 215, 217, 218, 219, 223
Peace (see also Hetep), 73, 215, 217, 218, 219, 223
Pepi II, 48
Persia, 16
Persians, 17, 58, 213
Pert Em Heru, See also Book of the Dead, 13, 35, 36, 40, 199
Pert em Hru, 34, 35
Pharaoh, 219
phenomenal universe, 25
Philae, 19, 198
Philosophy, 2, 15, 17, 21, 23, 24, 29, 30, 31, 32, 36, 37, 38, 39, 40, 41, 48, 54, 61, 69, 70, 72, 74, 94, 96, 97, 99, 100, 105, 192, 194, 195, 199, 200, 202, 205, 206, 208, 209, 210, 217, 218, 219
Phoenix, 131
Physical, 69, 71, 94, 95, 96, 100, 140
Physical body, 71, 100
Physical Plane, 69
physical world, 62, 65
Plato, 25
polytheism, 31
Polytheism, 29, 30
pressure, 44
*Priest*, 18

priests and priestesses, 51, 52, 105, 198, 204
Priests and Priestesses, 77, 194, 204
Primeval Divinity, 63, 64
Primeval time, 63
Primeval Waters, 71, 100, 118
*Proverbial Wisdom*, 215
Psyche, 24, 25
Psychology, 20, 24, 25, 29, 121, 200, 217
psychomythology, 113
Psycho-Mythology, 20
Ptah, 19, 38, 57, 75, 79, 81, 87, 200
Ptahotep, 48, 67, 75
Ptahotep, Sage, 48, 67
Ptolemy, Greek ruler, 17
Puranas, 38
Pure Consciousness, 69, 93, 98
Pyramid, 13, 35, 36, 43, 48, 50, 51, 52, 53, 54, 57, 58, 59, 66, 133, 136, 163
Pyramid of Unas, 48
Pyramid Texts, 13, 35, 36, 43, 48, 50, 51, 52, 53, 54, 57, 58, 59, 66, 133, 136, 163
Pyramids, 36
Pythagoras, 57

## Q

quantum physics, 27
Quantum Physics, 20
*Queen*, 204

## R

Ra, 18, 19, 38, 48, 57, 60, 64, 70, 75, 79, 80, 82, 86, 87, 90, 93, 96, 99, 104, 110, 112, 113, 116, 120, 121, 124, 131, 132, 137, 141, 146, 147, 149, 156, 167, 173, 198
racism, 215
**Racism**, 215
*Realization*, 195
Reflecting, 42
Reflection, 44, 46
relativity, 25, 70, 99
Relegare, 26
Religion, 11, 15, 21, 23, 24, 26, 28, 30, 31, 36, 37, 38, 44, 47, 55, 74, 87, 91, 192, 194, 195, 198, 199, 200, 201, 203, 204, 205, 206, 208, 209, 220, 222
Ren, 70, 94, 95, 98, 124
Renunciation, 26
resurrection, 11, 12, 27, 39, 55
Resurrection, 11, 12, 28, 54, 55, 56, 69, 75, 98, 134, 198, 200, 201, 202, 204
resurrection from the grave, 43
Righteous action, 23
ritual, 12, 47, 50, 51, 55

Ritual, 13, 30, 31, 47, 55, 66, 74, 202
Ritualism, 33
Rituals, 11, 25, 200
Roman, 17, 41, 43, 48, 57, 59, 60, 75, 213
Roman Catholic, 41
Romans, 18, 58, 213
Rome, 17, 205

## S

Saa (spiritual understanding faculty), 71, 100
Sages, 13, 20, 31, 41, 45, 51, 56, 59, 60, 62, 69, 94, 95, 98, 192, 198, 199, 202, 205, 222
Sahu, 94, 95, 97
Saints, 45, 199, 222
Saints and Sages, 45
Sakkara, 14
salvation, 27
Salvation, 27, 28, 33, 39, 69, 98
Salvation . See also resurrection, 28, 33, 39, 69, 98
Salvation, See also resurrection, 28, 33, 39, 69, 98
Samkhya, 32
Sanskrit, 25, 37
Scroll, 10
Sebai, 85, 206, 211, 217, 220
Second Intermediate Period, 17
*secret*, 11, 15
See also Ra-Hrakti, 18, 19, 38, 48, 57, 60, 64, 70, 93, 96, 99, 104, 110, 112, 113, 116, 120, 121, 124, 131, 132, 137, 141, 146, 147, 149, 156, 167, 173, 198
See Nat, 112, 173
Sekhem, 94, 95, 149, 157
Sekhet Yaru, 59
Sekhmet, 87
Self (see Ba, soul, Spirit, Universal, Ba, Neter, Heru)., 2, 11, 21, 22, 23, 24, 25, 28, 31, 33, 36, 37, 38, 39, 40, 42, 44, 45, 47, 64, 65, 66, 69, 70, 71, 90, 92, 94, 95, 96, 97, 98, 99, 100, 110, 194, 195, 196, 198, 202, 211
Self (seeBasoulSpiritUniversal BaNeterHorus)., 2, 11, 21, 22, 24, 25, 28, 31, 33, 36, 37, 38, 39, 40, 42, 44, 45, 47, 64, 65, 66, 69, 70, 71, 94, 95, 96, 97, 98, 99, 100
*Self-knowledge*, 39, 40
Self-realization, 28
Sema, 1, 2, 28, 37, 38, 40, 204, 215, 218, 221
Sema Tawi, 221
Serpent, 94, 156, 166, 168, 169
Serpent Power, 94, 156, 166, 169

Serpent Power (see also Kundalini and Buto), 94, 156, 166, 169
Serpent Power see also Kundalini Yoga, 94, 156, 166, 169
Set, 37, 38, 40, 80, 86, 87, 90, 114, 122, 127, 134, 158, 163, 204
Seti I, 197
*Setian*, 38, 127, 158
*Sex*, 198
sexism, 215
**Sexism**, 215
Shabaka, 48, 70, 99
Shabaka Inscription, 48, 70, 99
Shadow, 149
*Shedy*, 193
Sheps, 147
Shetai, 11
Shetaut Neter, 11, 15, 24, 27, 30, 32, 33, 47, 51, 54, 73, 74, 79, 198, 203, 204, 207, 215, 220, 221
Shetaut Neter See also Egyptian Religion, 11, 15, 24, 27, 30, 32, 33, 47, 51, 54, 73, 74, 79, 198, 203, 204, 207, 215, 220, 221
Shu, 86
Shu (air and space), 80, 86, 113, 114, 122, 156, 157
Signs, 1, 2
Sirius, 18, 200
Skeptics, 25
skin, 16
slavery, 56, 203
Sma, 37, 38
Smai, 24, 26, 37, 40
Smai Tawi, 24, 26, 37
society, 16, 17, 18, 25, 44, 48, 56, 67, 126, 162, 193, 203, 205, 210, 214, 215, 216, 218, 221
Society, 217, 218, 221
Soul, 15, 39, 43, 50, 54, 71, 93, 94, 100, 122, 124, 132, 133, 140, 141, 142, 143, 146, 147, 149, 158, 204, 219
Sphinx, 18, 39
Spirit, 26, 39, 51, 79, 92, 112, 117, 119, 131, 137, 138, 141, 146, 147, 149, 154, 155, 156, 159, 167
Spiritual discipline, 193
Spiritual transformation, 43
Spiritual Transformation, 27
Spirituality, 47, 194, 210, 220, 222
stages of religion, 30
Story of Sinuhe, 96
Study, 41, 63, 67
Sublimation, 198
Sufism, 33
Sufism, see also Sufi, 33
Superpower, 207
Superpower Syndrome, 207
Superpower Syndrome Mandatory Conflict Complex, 207

Supreme Being, 25, 38, 50, 57, 64, 69, 70, 76, 77, 79, 80, 81, 82, 83, 84, 85, 86, 87, 94, 95, 98, 99, 200
Supreme Divinity, 42

## T

*TANTRA*, 198
*TANTRA YOGA*, 198
Tantric Yoga, 46
Tao, 28, 59, 61
Taoism, 27, 33, 36, 44, 192
Tawi, 24, 26, 37, 221
Tefnut, 80, 86
Tefnut (moisture), 80, 86, 114, 122, 157
Tem, 38, 86, 156
Temple, 42, 48, 57, 67, 161, 198, 202, 220
Temple of Aset, 42, 48, 84, 198
The Absolute, 192
The Bhagavad Gita, 55
**The Black**, 208, 209
The God, 67, 80, 83, 197, 223
The Gods, 80, 197
The Gospel of Philip, 43
the Gospel of Thomas, 97
The Hidden One, 11
The Pyramid Texts, 36, 57
The Self, 24, 96
*The Word*, 35
Theban Theology, 57, 75, 87, 192
Thebes, 19, 57, 87, 192, 197
**Theocracy**, 207
Theology, 57, 70, 99, 134, 192, 199, 200
Thoth, 113
Time, 36, 71, 100, 168
time and space, 32, 65, 68, 71, 99, 117, 118, 163, 166, 167, 203
Tomb, 197
Tomb of Seti I, 197
**Tradition**, 79, 80, 81, 82, 83, 84, 85
transcendental reality, 38, 44, 203
Transcendental Self, 36
Tree, 30, 214
Tree of Life, 214
Triad, 193
Trinity, 19, 38, 72, 81, 82, 84, 87, 101, 198
True happiness, 162
Truth, 65, 72, 101

## U

Unas, 48
Understanding, 1, 2, 203, 217, 218
*union*, 15, 36, 38, 40, 69, 96, 98
Union with the Divine, 32, 47
United States of America, 207

Universal Ba, 71, 93, 94, 95, 96, 100
Universal consciousness, 25, 29
Universal Consciousness, 25, 41, 198
*Upanishads*, 25, 38, 199, 213
Upper Egypt, 37, 40
Ur, 80
Uraeus, 94

## V

Vedanta, 24, 27, 29, 32, 33, 41, 42
Vedantic. See also Vedanta, 24, 27
Vedas, 38
Vedic, 194
**Violence**, 215

## W

Waking, 69, 70, 96, 98, 99
wars, 12, 17, 58
Waset, 19, 57, 79, 192
Washington, George, 60

Wealth, Money, 44, 219
Western civilization, 17
Western Culture, 90
Western religions, 29
Western, West, 25, 147, 159, 160
White, 218
Whitehead, 25
Who am I, 20, 41
Wisdom, 42, 46, 47, 48, 74, 75, 134, 161, 195, 197, 212, 213, 215, 219
Wisdom (also see Djehuti), 42, 46, 47, 48, 74, 75
Wisdom (also see Djehuti, Aset), 42, 46, 47, 48, 74, 75, 134, 161, 195, 197, 212, 213, 215, 219
Wisdom teachings, 25, 42
World Ba, 71, 100
World War II, 207

## Y

Yoga, 2, 12, 15, 20, 21, 23, 24, 25, 26, 27, 28, 29, 30, 31, 32, 36, 37, 38, 39, 40, 41, 42, 44, 46, 47, 54, 65, 66, 69, 70, 72, 96, 97, 99, 100, 192, 193, 194, 195, 197, 198, 199, 200, 202, 204, 206, 208, 209, 222
Yoga of Devotion (see Yoga of Divine Love), 46, 222
Yoga of Meditation, 46
Yoga of Righteous . See also Karma Yoga, 23
Yoga of Righteous. See also Karma Yoga, 23
Yoga of Wisdom, 42
Yoga of Wisdom (see also Jnana Yoga), 42, 46
Yoga Philosophy, 29
Yogic, 36, 48, 208, 215
Yoruba, 215

## Z

Zoroastrianism, 33

# Other Books From C M Books

P.O.Box 570459

Miami, Florida, 33257

(305) 378-6253 Fax: (305) 378-6253

**Prices subject to change.**

1.     *EGYPTIAN YOGA: THE PHILOSOPHY OF ENLIGHTENMENT* An original, fully illustrated work, including hieroglyphs, detailing the meaning of the Egyptian mysteries, tantric yoga, psycho-spiritual and physical exercises. Egyptian Yoga is a guide to the practice of the highest spiritual philosophy which leads to absolute freedom from human misery and to immortality. It is well known by scholars that Egyptian philosophy is the basis of Western and Middle Eastern religious philosophies such as *Christianity, Islam, Judaism,* the *Kabala*, and Greek philosophy, but what about Indian philosophy, Yoga and Taoism? What were the original teachings? How can they be practiced today? What is the source of pain and suffering in the world and what is the solution? Discover the deepest mysteries of the mind and universe within and outside of yourself. 8.5" X 11" ISBN: 1-884564-01-1 Soft $19.95

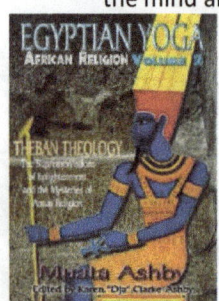

2.     *EGYPTIAN YOGA: African Religion Volume 2-* Theban Theology U.S. In this long awaited sequel to *Egyptian Yoga: The Philosophy of Enlightenment* you will take a fascinating and enlightening journey back in time and discover the teachings which constituted the epitome of Ancient Egyptian spiritual wisdom. What are the disciplines which lead to the fulfillment of all desires? Delve into the three states of consciousness (waking, dream and deep sleep) and the fourth state which transcends them all, Neberdjer, "The Absolute." These teachings of the city of Waset (Thebes) were the crowning achievement of the Sages of Ancient Egypt. They establish the standard mystical keys

for understanding the profound mystical symbolism of the Triad of human consciousness. ISBN 1-884564-39-9 $23.95

3.   *THE KEMETIC DIET: GUIDE TO HEALTH, DIET AND FASTING* Health issues have always been important to human beings since the beginning of time. The earliest records of history show that the art of healing was held in high esteem since the time of Ancient Egypt. In the early 20th century, medical doctors had almost attained the status of sainthood by the promotion of the idea that they alone were "scientists" while other healing modalities and traditional healers who did not follow the "scientific method' were nothing but superstitious, ignorant charlatans who at best would take the money of their clients and at worst kill them with the unscientific "snake oils" and "irrational theories". In the late 20th century, the failure of the modern medical establishment's ability to lead the general public to good health, promoted the move by many in society towards "alternative medicine". Alternative medicine disciplines are those healing modalities which do not adhere to the philosophy of allopathic medicine. Allopathic medicine is what medical doctors practice by an large. It is the theory that disease is caused by agencies outside the body such as bacteria, viruses or physical means which affect the body. These can therefore be treated by medicines and therapies  The natural healing method began in the absence of extensive technologies with the idea that all the answers for health may be found in nature or rather, the deviation from nature. Therefore, the health of the body can be restored by correcting the aberration and thereby restoring balance. This is the area that will be covered in this volume. Allopathic techniques have their place in the art of healing. However, we should not forget that the body is a grand achievement of the spirit and built into it is the capacity to maintain itself and heal itself. Ashby, Muata ISBN: 1-884564-49-6             $28.95

4.   INITIATION INTO EGYPTIAN YOGA Shedy: Spiritual discipline or program, to go deeply into the mysteries, to study the mystery teachings and literature profoundly, to penetrate the mysteries. You will learn about the mysteries of initiation into the teachings and practice of Yoga and how to become an Initiate of the mystical sciences. This insightful manual is the first in a series which introduces you to the goals of daily spiritual and yoga practices: Meditation, Diet, Words of Power and the ancient wisdom teachings. 8.5" X 11" ISBN 1-884564-02-X   Soft Cover $24.95  U.S.

5. ***THE AFRICAN ORIGINS OF CIVILIZATION, RELIGION AND YOGA SPIRITUALITY AND ETHICS PHILOSOPHY*** HARD COVER EDITION Part 1, Part 2, Part 3 in one volume 683 Pages Hard Cover First Edition Three volumes in one. Over the past several years I have been asked to put together in one volume the most important evidences showing the correlations and common teachings between Kamitan (Ancient Egyptian) culture and religion and that of India. The questions of the history of Ancient Egypt, and the latest archeological evidences showing civilization and culture in Ancient Egypt and its spread to other countries, has intrigued many scholars as well as mystics over the years. Also, the possibility that Ancient Egyptian Priests and Priestesses migrated to Greece, India and other countries to carry on the traditions of the Ancient Egyptian Mysteries, has been speculated over the years as well. In chapter 1 of the book *Egyptian Yoga The Philosophy of Enlightenment,* 1995, I first introduced the deepest comparison between Ancient Egypt and India that had been brought forth up to that time. Now, in the year 2001 this new book, *THE AFRICAN ORIGINS OF CIVILIZATION, MYSTICAL RELIGION AND YOGA PHILOSOPHY,* more fully explores the motifs, symbols and philosophical correlations between Ancient Egyptian and Indian mysticism and clearly shows not only that Ancient Egypt and India were connected culturally but also spiritually. How does this knowledge help the spiritual aspirant? This discovery has great importance for the Yogis and mystics who follow the philosophy of Ancient Egypt and the mysticism of India. It means that India has a longer history and heritage than was previously understood. It shows that the mysteries of Ancient Egypt were essentially a yoga tradition which did not die but rather developed into the modern day systems of Yoga technology of India. It further shows that African culture developed Yoga Mysticism earlier than any other civilization in history. All of this expands our understanding of the unity of culture and the deep legacy of Yoga, which stretches into the distant past, beyond the Indus Valley civilization, the earliest known high culture in India as well as the Vedic tradition of Aryan culture. Therefore, Yoga culture and mysticism is the oldest known tradition of spiritual development and Indian mysticism is an extension of the Ancient Egyptian mysticism. By understanding the legacy which Ancient Egypt gave to India the mysticism of India is better understood and by comprehending the heritage of Indian Yoga, which is rooted in Ancient Egypt the Mysticism of Ancient Egypt is also better understood. This expanded understanding allows us to prove the underlying kinship of humanity, through the common symbols, motifs and philosophies which are not disparate and confusing teachings but in reality expressions of the same study of truth through metaphysics and mystical realization of Self. (HARD COVER) ISBN: 1-884564-50-X   $45.00 U.S.   81/2" X 11"

6. *AFRICAN ORIGINS BOOK 1 PART 1* African Origins of African Civilization, Religion, Yoga Mysticism and Ethics Philosophy-Soft Cover $24.95 ISBN: 1-884564-55-0

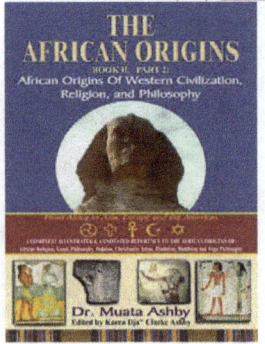

7. *AFRICAN ORIGINS BOOK 2 PART 2* African Origins of Western Civilization, Religion and Philosophy (Soft) -<u>Soft Cover</u> $24.95 ISBN: 1-884564-56-9

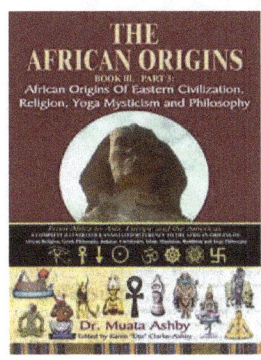

8. *EGYPT AND INDIA* A<small>FRICAN</small> O<small>RIGINS OF</small> *Eastern Civilization, Religion, Yoga Mysticism and Philosophy*-<u>Soft Cover</u> $29.95 (Soft) ISBN: 1-884564-57-7

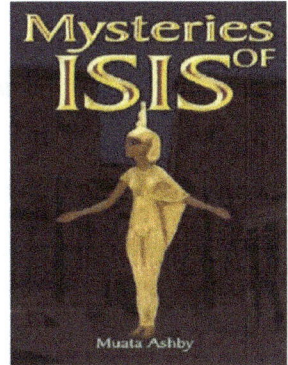

9. THE MYSTERIES OF ISIS: **The Ancient Egyptian Philosophy of Self-Realization** - There are several paths to discover the Divine and the mysteries of the higher Self. This volume details the mystery teachings of the goddess Aset (Isis) from Ancient Egypt- the path of wisdom. It includes the teachings of her temple and the disciplines that are enjoined for the initiates of the temple of Aset as they were given in ancient times. Also, this book includes the teachings of the main myths of Aset that lead a human being to spiritual enlightenment and immortality. Through the study of ancient myth and the illumination of initiatic understanding the idea of God is expanded from the mythological comprehension to the metaphysical. Then this metaphysical understanding is related to you, the student, so as to begin understanding your true divine nature. ISBN 1-884564-24-0  $22.99

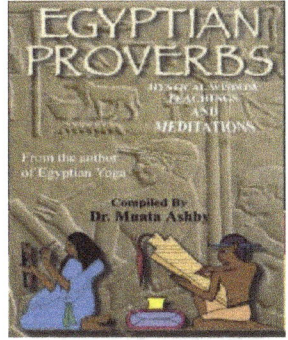

10. EGYPTIAN PROVERBS:  collection of —Ancient Egyptian Proverbs and Wisdom Teachings -How to live according to MAAT Philosophy. Beginning Meditation. All proverbs are indexed for easy searches. For the first time in one volume, ——Ancient Egyptian Proverbs, wisdom teachings and meditations, fully illustrated with hieroglyphic text and symbols. EGYPTIAN PROVERBS is a unique collection of knowledge and wisdom which you can put into practice today and transform your life. $14.95 U'S          ISBN: 1-884564-00-3

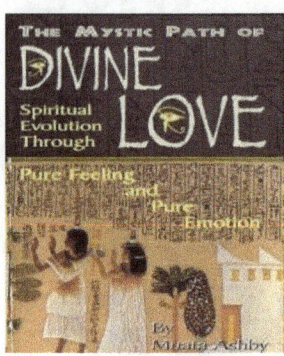

11. **GOD OF LOVE: THE PATH OF DIVINE LOVE** *The Process of Mystical Transformation and The Path of Divine Love* This Volume focuses on the ancient wisdom teachings of "Neter Merri" –the Ancient Egyptian philosophy of Divine Love and how to use them in a scientific process for self-transformation. Love is one of the most powerful human emotions. It is also the source of Divine feeling that unifies God and the individual human being. When love is fragmented and diminished by egoism the Divine connection is lost. The Ancient tradition of Neter Merri leads human beings back to their Divine connection, allowing them to discover their innate glorious self that is actually Divine and immortal. This volume will detail the process of transformation from ordinary consciousness to cosmic consciousness through the integrated practice of the teachings and the path of Devotional Love toward the Divine. 5.5"x 8.5" ISBN 1-884564-11-9 $22.95

12. **INTRODUCTION TO MAAT PHILOSOPHY: Spiritual Enlightenment Through the Path of Virtue** Known commonly as Karma in India, the teachings of MAAT contain an extensive philosophy based on ariu (deeds) and their fructification in the form of shai and renenet (fortune and destiny, leading to Meskhenet (fate in a future birth) for living virtuously and with orderly wisdom are explained and the student is to begin practicing the precepts of Maat in daily life so as to promote the process of purification of the heart in preparation for the judgment of the soul. This judgment will be understood not as an event that will occur at the time of death but as an event that occurs continuously, at every moment in the life of the individual. The student will learn how to become allied with the forces of the Higher Self and to thereby begin cleansing the mind (heart) of impurities so as to attain a higher vision of reality. ISBN 1-884564-20-8   $22.99

13. **MEDITATION** *The Ancient Egyptian Path to Enlightenment* Many people do not know about the rich history of meditation practice in Ancient Egypt. This volume outlines the theory of meditation and presents the Ancient

Egyptian Hieroglyphic text which give instruction as to the nature of the mind and its three modes of expression. It also presents the texts which give instruction on the practice of meditation for spiritual Enlightenment and unity with the Divine. This volume allows the reader to begin practicing meditation by explaining, in easy to understand terms, the simplest form of meditation and working up to the most advanced form which was practiced in ancient times and which is still practiced by yogis around the world in modern times. ISBN 1-884564-27-7  $22.99

14. *THE GLORIOUS LIGHT MEDITATION* TECHNIQUE OF ANCIENT EGYPT New for the year 2000. This volume is based on the earliest known instruction in history given for the practice of formal meditation. Discovered by Dr. Muata Ashby, it is inscribed on the walls of the Tomb of Seti I in Thebes Egypt. This volume details the philosophy and practice of this unique system of meditation originated in Ancient Egypt and the earliest practice of meditation known in the world which occurred in the most advanced African Culture. ISBN: 1-884564-15-1 $16.95 (PB)

15. *THE SERPENT POWER: The Ancient Egyptian Mystical Wisdom of the Inner Life Force.*    This Volume specifically deals with the latent life Force energy of the universe and in the human body, its control and sublimation. How to develop the Life Force energy of the subtle body. This Volume will introduce the esoteric wisdom of the science of how virtuous living acts in a subtle and mysterious way to cleanse the latent psychic energy conduits and vortices of the spiritual body. ISBN 1-884564-19-4   $22.95

16. *EGYPTIAN YOGA The Postures of The Gods and Goddesses* Discover the physical postures and exercises practiced thousands of years ago in Ancient Egypt which are today known as Yoga exercises. Discover the history of the postures and how they were transferred from Ancient Egypt in Africa to India through Buddhist Tantrism. Then

practice the postures as you discover the mythic teaching that originally gave birth to the postures and was practiced by the Ancient Egyptian priests and priestesses. This work is based on the pictures and teachings from the Creation story of Ra, The Asarian Resurrection Myth and the carvings and reliefs from various Temples in Ancient Egypt 8.5" X 11"  ISBN 1-884564-10-0  Soft Cover $21.95     Exercise video   $20

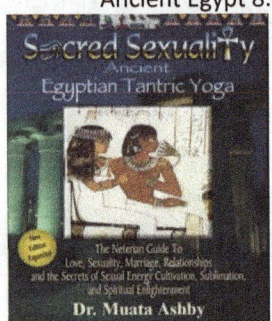

17. *SACRED SEXUALITY: ANCIENT EGYPTIAN TANTRA YOGA:  The Art of Sex* Sublimation and Universal Consciousness This Volume will expand on the male and female principles within the human body and in the universe and further detail the sublimation of sexual energy into spiritual energy. The student will study the deities Min and Hathor, Asar and Aset, Geb and Nut and discover the mystical implications for a practical spiritual discipline. This Volume will also focus on the Tantric aspects of Ancient Egyptian and Indian mysticism, the purpose of sex and the mystical teachings of sexual sublimation which lead to self-knowledge and Enlightenment.  ISBN 1-884564-03-8      $24.95

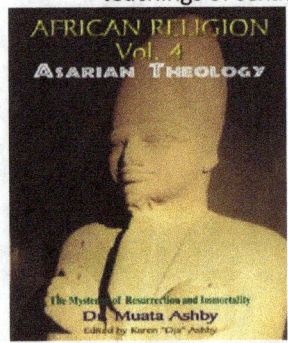

18. *AFRICAN RELIGION Volume 4: ASARIAN THEOLOGY: RESURRECTING OSIRIS* The path of Mystical Awakening and the Keys to Immortality NEW REVISED AND EXPANDED EDITION!   The Ancient Sages created stories based on human and superhuman beings whose struggles, aspirations, needs and desires ultimately lead them to discover their true Self. The myth of Aset, Asar and Heru is no exception in this area. While there is no one source where the entire story may be found, pieces of it are inscribed in various ancient Temples walls, tombs, steles and papyri.  For the first time available, the complete myth of Asar, Aset and Heru has been compiled from original Ancient Egyptian, Greek and Coptic Texts. This epic myth has been richly illustrated with reliefs from the Temple of Heru at Edfu, the Temple of Aset at Philae, the Temple of Asar at Abydos, the Temple of Hathor at Denderah and various papyri, inscriptions and reliefs.   Discover the myth which inspired the teachings of the *Shetaut Neter* (Egyptian Mystery System - Egyptian Yoga) and the Egyptian Book of Coming Forth By Day. Also, discover the three levels of Ancient Egyptian Religion, how to understand the mysteries of the Duat or Astral World and how to discover the abode of the Supreme in the Amenta,  *The Other World*    The ancient religion of Asar, Aset and Heru, if properly understood, contains all of the elements necessary to lead the sincere aspirant to attain immortality through inner self-discovery.  This volume presents the entire myth and explores the main mystical themes and rituals associated with the myth for understating human existence, creation and the way to achieve spiritual emancipation - *Resurrection*. The Asarian myth is so powerful that it influenced and is still having an effect on the major world religions. Discover the origins and mystical meaning of the Christian Trinity, the Eucharist ritual and the ancient origin of the birthday of Jesus Christ. Soft Cover ISBN: 1-884564-27-5  $24.95

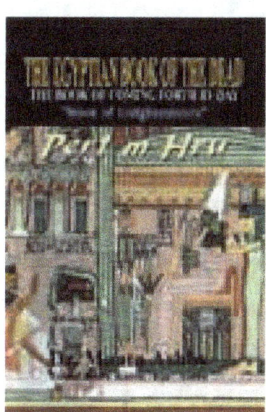

19. *THE EGYPTIAN BOOK OF THE DEAD MYSTICISM OF THE PERT EM HERU* " I Know myself, I know myself, I am One With God!–From the Pert Em Heru "The Ru Pert em Heru" or "Ancient Egyptian Book of The Dead," or "Book of Coming Forth By Day" as it is more popularly known, has fascinated the world since the successful translation of Ancient Egyptian hieroglyphic scripture over 150 years ago. The astonishing writings in it reveal that the Ancient Egyptians believed in life after death and in an ultimate destiny to discover the Divine. The elegance and aesthetic beauty of the hieroglyphic text itself has inspired many see it as an art form in and of itself. But is there more to it than that? Did the Ancient Egyptian wisdom contain more than just aphorisms and hopes of eternal life beyond death? In this volume Dr. Muata Ashby, the author of over 25 books on Ancient Egyptian Yoga Philosophy has produced a new translation of the original texts which uncovers a mystical teaching underlying the sayings and rituals instituted by the Ancient Egyptian Sages and Saints. "Once the philosophy of Ancient Egypt is understood as a mystical tradition instead of as a religion or primitive mythology, it reveals its secrets which if practiced today will lead anyone to discover the glory of spiritual self-discovery. The Pert em Heru is in every way comparable to the Indian Upanishads or the Tibetan Book of the Dead."  $28.95     ISBN# 1-884564-28-3  Size: 8½" X 11

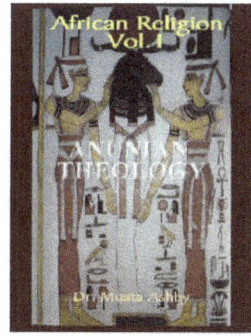

20. *African Religion VOL. 1- ANUNIAN THEOLOGY THE MYSTERIES OF RA* The Philosophy of Anu and The Mystical Teachings of The Ancient Egyptian Creation Myth Discover the mystical teachings contained in the Creation Myth and the gods and goddesses who brought creation and human beings into existence. The Creation myth of Anu is the source of Anunian Theology but also of the other main theological systems of Ancient Egypt that also influenced other world religions including Christianity, Hinduism and Buddhism. The Creation Myth holds the key to understanding the universe and for attaining spiritual Enlightenment. ISBN: 1-884564-38-0  $19.95

21. *African Religion VOL 3: Memphite Theology: MYSTERIES OF MIND* Mystical Psychology & Mental Health for Enlightenment and Immortality based on the Ancient Egyptian Philosophy of Menefer -Mysticism of Ptah, Egyptian Physics and Yoga Metaphysics and the Hidden properties of Matter. This volume uncovers the mystical psychology of the Ancient Egyptian wisdom teachings centering on the philosophy of the Ancient Egyptian city of Menefer (Memphite Theology). How to understand the mind and how to control the senses and lead the mind to health, clarity and mystical self-discovery. This Volume will also go deeper into the philosophy of God as creation and will explore the concepts of modern science and how they correlate with ancient teachings. This Volume will lay the ground work for the understanding of the philosophy of universal consciousness and the initiatic/yogic insight into who or what is God? ISBN 1-884564-07-0    $22.95

22. AFRICAN RELIGION VOLUME 5: THE GODDESS AND THE EGYPTIAN MYSTERIESTHE PATH OF THE GODDESS THE GODDESS PATH The Secret Forms of the Goddess and the Rituals of Resurrection The Supreme Being may be worshipped as father or as mother. *Ushet Rekhat* or *Mother Worship*, is the spiritual process of worshipping the Divine in the form of the Divine Goddess. It celebrates the most important forms of the Goddess including *Nathor, Maat, Aset, Arat, Amentet and Hathor* and explores their mystical meaning as well as the rising of *Sirius*, the star of Aset (Aset) and the new birth of Hor (Heru). The end of the year is a time of reckoning, reflection and engendering a new or renewed positive movement toward attaining spiritual Enlightenment. The Mother Worship devotional meditation ritual, performed on five days during the month of December and on New Year's Eve, is based on the Ushet Rekhit. During the ceremony, the cosmic forces, symbolized by Sirius - and the constellation of Orion ---, are harnessed through the understanding and devotional attitude of the participant. This propitiation draws the light of wisdom and health to all those who share in the ritual, leading to prosperity and wisdom.    $14.95 ISBN 1-884564-18-6

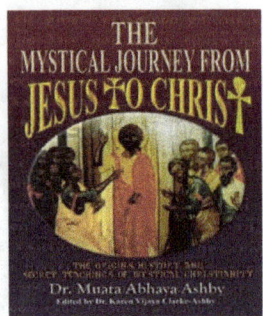

23. THE MYSTICAL JOURNEY FROM JESUS TO CHRIST Discover the ancient Egyptian origins of Christianity before the Catholic Church and learn the mystical teachings given by Jesus to assist all humanity in becoming Christlike. Discover the secret meaning of the Gospels that were discovered in Egypt. Also discover how and why so many Christian churches came into being. Discover that the Bible still holds the keys to mystical realization even though its original writings were changed by the church. Discover how to practice the original teachings of Christianity which leads to the Kingdom of Heaven. $24.95    ISBN# 1-884564-05-4 size: 8½" X 11"

24.  *THE STORY OF ASAR, ASET AND HERU:* An Ancient Egyptian Legend (For Children)   Now for the first time, the most ancient myth of Ancient Egypt comes alive for children. Inspired by the books *The Asarian Resurrection: The Ancient Egyptian Bible* and *The Mystical Teachings of The Asarian Resurrection, The Story of Asar, Aset and Heru* is an easy to understand and thrilling tale which inspired the children of Ancient Egypt to aspire to greatness and righteousness.  If you and your child have enjoyed stories like *The Lion King* and *Star Wars you will love The Story of Asar, Aset and Heru.* Also, if you know the story of Jesus and Krishna you will discover than Ancient Egypt had a similar myth and that this myth carries important spiritual teachings for living a fruitful and fulfilling life.  This book may be used along with *The Parents Guide To The Asarian Resurrection Myth: How to Teach Yourself and Your Child the Principles of Universal Mystical Religion.* The guide provides some background to the Asarian Resurrection myth and it also gives insight into the mystical teachings contained in it which you may introduce to your child. It is designed for parents who wish to grow spiritually with their children and it serves as an introduction for those who would like to study the Asarian Resurrection Myth in depth and to practice its teachings. 8.5" X 11"   ISBN: 1-884564-31-3   $12.95

25.  *THE PARENTS GUIDE TO THE AUSARIAN RESURRECTION MYTH:*  How to Teach Yourself and Your Child  the Principles of Universal Mystical Religion.   This insightful manual brings for the timeless wisdom of the ancient through the Ancient Egyptian myth of Asar, Aset and Heru and the mystical teachings contained in it for parents who want to guide their children to understand and practice the teachings of mystical spirituality. This manual may be used with the children's storybook *The Story of Asar, Aset and Heru* by Dr. Muata Abhaya Ashby.   ISBN: 1-884564-30-5   $16.95

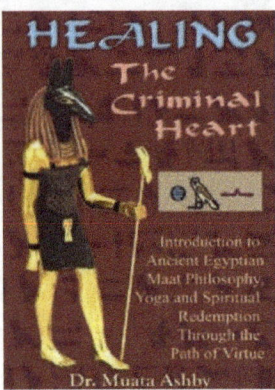

26. *HEALING THE CRIMINAL HEART.* Introduction to Maat Philosophy, Yoga and Spiritual Redemption Through the Path of Virtue   Who is a criminal? Is there such a thing as a criminal heart? What is the source of evil and sinfulness and is there any way to rise above it? Is there redemption for those who have committed sins, even the worst crimes? Ancient Egyptian mystical psychology holds important answers to these questions. Over ten thousand years ago mystical psychologists, the Sages of Ancient Egypt, studied and charted the human mind and spirit and laid out a path which will lead to spiritual redemption, prosperity and Enlightenment.    This introductory volume brings forth the teachings of the Asarian Resurrection, the most important myth of Ancient Egypt, with relation to the faults of human existence: anger, hatred, greed, lust, animosity, discontent, ignorance, egoism jealousy, bitterness, and a myriad of psycho-spiritual ailments which keep a human being in a state of negativity and adversity    ISBN: 1-884564-17-8   $15.95

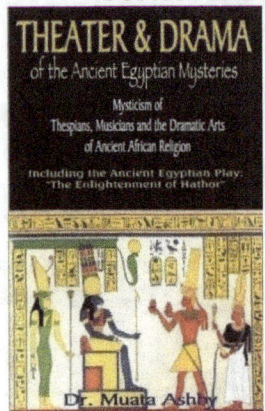

27. *TEMPLE RITUAL OF THE ANCIENT EGYPTIAN MYSTERIES--THEATER & DRAMA OF THE ANCIENT EGYPTIAN MYSTERIES*: Details the practice of the mysteries and ritual program of the temple and the philosophy an practice of the ritual of the mysteries, its purpose and execution. Featuring the Ancient Egyptian stage play-"The Enlightenment of Hathor' Based on an Ancient Egyptian Drama, The original Theater -Mysticism of the Temple of Hetheru 1-884564-14-3  $19.95   By Dr. Muata Ashby

28. GUIDE TO PRINT ON DEMAND: SELF-PUBLISH FOR PROFIT, SPIRITUAL FULFILLMENT AND SERVICE TO HUMANITY Everyone asks us how we produced so many books in such a short time. Here are the secrets to writing and producing books that uplift humanity and how to get them printed for a fraction of the regular cost. Anyone can become an author even

if they have limited funds. All that is necessary is the willingness to learn how the printing and book business work and the desire to follow the special instructions given here for preparing your manuscript format. Then you take your work directly to the non-traditional companies who can produce your books for less than the traditional book printer can. ISBN: 1-884564-40-2    $16.95 U. S.

29.    *Egyptian Mysteries: Vol. 1,* Shetaut Neter What are the Mysteries? For thousands of years the spiritual tradition of Ancient Egypt, *Shetaut Neter,* "The Egyptian Mysteries," "The Secret Teachings," have fascinated, tantalized and amazed the world. At one time exalted and recognized as the highest culture of the world, by Africans, Europeans, Asiatics, Hindus, Buddhists and other cultures of the ancient world, in time it was shunned by the emerging orthodox world religions. Its temples desecrated, its philosophy maligned, its tradition spurned, its philosophy dormant in the mystical *Medu Neter,* the mysterious hieroglyphic texts which hold the secret symbolic meaning that has scarcely been discerned up to now.   What are the secrets of *Nehast* {spiritual awakening and emancipation, resurrection}. More than just a literal translation, this volume is for awakening to the secret code *Shetitu* of the teaching which was not deciphered by Egyptologists, nor could be understood by ordinary spiritualists. This book is a reinstatement of the original science made available for our times, to the reincarnated followers of Ancient Egyptian culture and the prospect of spiritual freedom to break the bonds of *Khemn,* "ignorance," and slavery to evil forces: *Såaa* . ISBN: 1-884564-41-0    $19.99

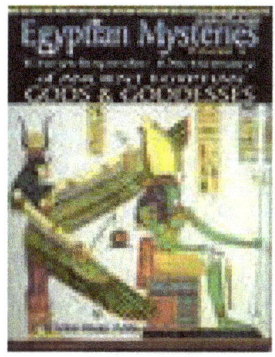

30.    *EGYPTIAN MYSTERIES VOL 2:* Dictionary of Gods and Goddesses This book is about the mystery of neteru, the gods and goddesses of Ancient Egypt (Kamit, Kemet). Neteru means "Gods and Goddesses." But the Neterian teaching of Neteru represents more than the usual limited modern day concept of "divinities" or "spirits." The Neteru of Kamit are also metaphors, cosmic principles and vehicles for the enlightening teachings of Shetaut Neter (Ancient Egyptian-African Religion). Actually they are the elements for one of the most advanced systems of spirituality ever conceived in human history. Understanding the concept of neteru provides a firm basis for spiritual evolution and the pathway for viable culture, peace on earth and a healthy human society.    Why is it important to have gods and goddesses in our lives? In order for spiritual evolution to be possible, once a human being has accepted that there is existence after death and there is a transcendental being who exists beyond time and space knowledge, human beings need a connection to that which transcends the ordinary experience of human life in time and space and a means to understand the transcendental reality beyond the mundane reality. ISBN: 1-884564-23-2    $21.95

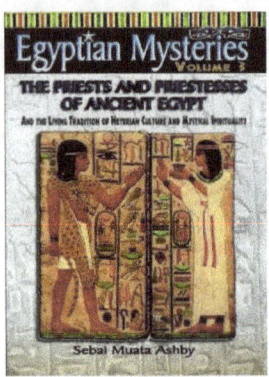

31. **EGYPTIAN MYSTERIES VOL. 3** The Priests and Priestesses of Ancient Egypt This volume details the path of Neterian priesthood, the joys, challenges and rewards of advanced Neterian life, the teachings that allowed the priests and priestesses to manage the most long lived civilization in human history and how that path can be adopted today; for those who want to tread the path of the Clergy of Shetaut Neter. ISBN: 1-884564-53-4 $24.95

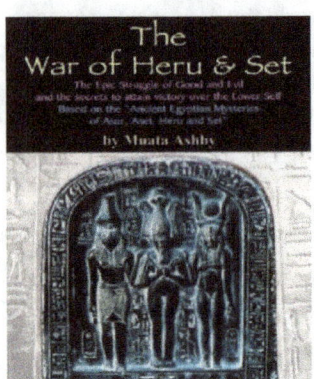

32. *The War of Heru and Set:* The Struggle of Good and Evil for Control of the World and The Human Soul This volume contains a novelized version of the Asarian Resurrection myth that is based on the actual scriptures presented in the Book Asarian Religion (old name –Resurrecting Osiris). This volume is prepared in the form of a screenplay and can be easily adapted to be used as a stage play. Spiritual seeking is a mythic journey that has many emotional highs and lows, ecstasies and depressions, victories and frustrations. This is the War of Life that is played out in the myth as the struggle of Heru and Set and those are mythic characters that represent the human Higher and Lower self. How to understand the war and emerge victorious in the journey o life? The ultimate victory and fulfillment can be experienced, which is not changeable or lost in time. The purpose of myth is to convey the wisdom of life through the story of divinities who show the way to overcome the challenges and foibles of life. In this volume the feelings and emotions of the characters of the myth have been highlighted to show the deeply rich texture of the Ancient Egyptian myth. This myth contains deep spiritual teachings and insights into the nature of self, of God and the mysteries of life and the means to discover the true meaning of life and thereby achieve the true purpose of life. To become victorious in the battle of life means to become the King (or Queen) of Egypt.Have you seen movies like The Lion King, Hamlet, The Odyssey, or The Little Buddha? These have been some of the most popular movies in modern times. The Sema Institute of Yoga is dedicated to researching and presenting the wisdom and culture of ancient Africa. The Script is designed to be produced as a motion picture but may be addapted for the theater as well. $21.95   copyright 1998 By Dr. Muata Ashby ISBN 1-8840564-44-5

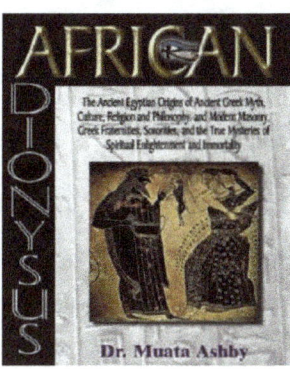

33. *AFRICAN DIONYSUS: FROM EGYPT TO GREECE:* The Kamitan Origins of Greek Culture and Religion ISBN: 1-884564-47-X   From Egypt to Greece   This insightful manual is a reference to Ancient Egyptian mythology and philosophy and its correlation to what later became known as Greek and Rome mythology and philosophy. It outlines the basic tenets of the mythologies and shoes the ancient origins of Greek culture in Ancient Egypt. This volume also documents the origins of the Greek alphabet in Egypt as well as Greek religion, myth and philosophy of the gods and goddesses from Egypt from the myth of Atlantis and archaic period with the Minoans to the Classical period. This volume also acts as a resource for Colleges students who would like to set up fraternities and sororities based on the original Ancient Egyptian principles of Sheti and Maat philosophy.  ISBN: 1-884564-47-X $22.95 U.S.

34. THE FORTY TWO  PRECEPTS OF MAAT,  THE PHILOSOPHY OF  RIGHTEOUS ACTION AND THE  ANCIENT EGYPTIAN WISDOM TEXTS ADVANCED STUDIES   This manual is designed for use with the 1998 Maat Philosophy Class conducted by Dr. Muata Ashby. This is a detailed study of Maat Philosophy. It contains a compilation of the 42 laws or precepts of Maat and the corresponding principles which they represent along with the teachings of the ancient Egyptian Sages relating to each. Maat philosophy was the basis of Ancient Egyptian society and government as well as the heart of Ancient Egyptian myth and spirituality. Maat is at once a goddess, a cosmic force and a living social doctrine, which promotes social harmony and thereby paves the way for spiritual evolution in all levels of society. ISBN: 1-884564-48-8   $16.95 U.S.

**35.     THE SECRET LOTUS: Poetry of Enlightenment**
Discover the mystical sentiment of the Kemetic teaching as expressed through the poetry of Sebai Muata Ashby. The teaching of spiritual awakening is uniquely experienced when the poetic sensibility is present. This first volume contains the poems written between 1996 and 2003. **1-884564--16 -X  $16.99**

**36.  The Ancient Egyptian Buddha: The Ancient Egyptian Origins of Buddhism**
This book is a compilation of several sections of a larger work, a book by the name of African Origins of Civilization, Religion, Yoga Mysticism and Ethics Philosophy. It also contains some additional evidences not contained in the larger work that demonstrate the correlation between Ancient Egyptian Religion and Buddhism. This book is one of several compiled short volumes that has been compiled so as to facilitate access to specific subjects contained in the larger work which is over 680 pages long. These short and small volumes have been specifically designed to cover one subject in a brief and low cost format. This present volume, The Ancient Egyptian Buddha: The Ancient Egyptian Origins of Buddhism, formed one subject in the larger work; actually it was one chapter of the larger work. However, this volume has some new additional evidences and comparisons of Buddhist and Neterian (Ancient Egyptian) philosophies not previously discussed. It was felt that this subject needed to be discussed because even in the early 21st century, the idea persists that Buddhism originated only in India independently. Yet there is ample evidence from ancient writings and perhaps more importantly, iconographical evidences from the Ancient Egyptians and early Buddhists themselves that prove otherwise. This handy volume has been designed to be accessible to young adults and all others who would like to have an easy reference with documentation on this important subject. This is an important subject because the frame of reference with which we look at a culture depends strongly on our conceptions about its origins. in this case, if we look at the Buddhism as an Asiatic religion we would treat it

and it's culture in one way. If we id as African [Ancient Egyptian] we not only would see it in a different light but we also must ascribe Africa with a glorious legacy that matches any other culture in human history and gave rise to one of the present day most important religious philosophies. We would also look at the culture and philosophies of the Ancient Egyptians as having African insights that offer us greater depth into the Buddhist philosophies. Those insights inform our knowledge about other African traditions and we can also begin to understand in a deeper way the effect of Ancient Egyptian culture on African culture and also on the Asiatic as well. We would also be able to discover the glorious and wondrous teaching of mystical philosophy that Ancient Egyptian Shetaut Neter religion offers, that is as powerful as any other mystic system of spiritual philosophy in the world today. ISBN: 1-884564-61-5     $28.95

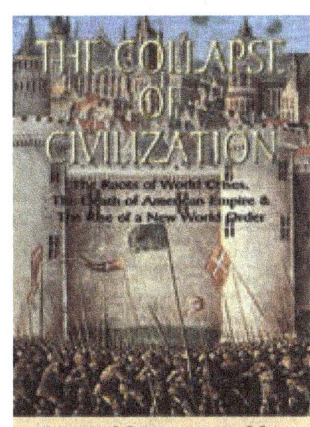

37. **The Death of American Empire: Neo-conservatism, Theocracy, Economic Imperialism, Environmental Disaster and the Collapse of Civilization**

This work is a collection of essays relating to social and economic, leadership, and ethics, ecological and religious issues that are facing the world today in order to understand the course of history that has led humanity to its present condition and then arrive at positive solutions that will lead to better outcomes for all humanity. It surveys the development and decline of major empires throughout history and focuses on the creation of American Empire along with the social, political and economic policies that led to the prominence of the United States of America as a Superpower including the rise of the political control of the neo-con political philosophy including militarism and the military industrial complex in American politics and the rise of the religious right into and American Theocracy movement. This volume details, through historical and current events, the psychology behind the dominance of western culture in world politics through the "Superpower Syndrome Mandatory Conflict Complex" that drives the Superpower culture to establish itself above all others and then act hubristically to dominate world culture through legitimate influences as well as coercion, media censorship and misinformation leading to international hegemony and world conflict. This volume also details the financial policies that gave rise to American prominence in the global economy, especially after World War II, and promoted American preeminence over the world economy through Globalization as well as the environmental policies, including the oil economy, that are promoting degradation of the world ecology and contribute to the decline of America as an Empire culture. This volume finally explores the factors pointing to the decline of the American Empire economy and imperial power and what to expect in the aftermath of American prominence and how to survive the decline while at the same time promoting policies and social-economic-religious-political changes that are needed in order to promote the emergence of a beneficial and sustainable culture. **$25.95soft**  1-884564-25-9, Hard Cover **$29.95**  1-884564-45-3

### 38. The African Origins of Hatha Yoga: And its Ancient Mystical Teaching

The subject of this present volume, The Ancient Egyptian Origins of Yoga Postures, formed one subject in the larger works, African Origins of Civilization Religion, Yoga Mysticism and Ethics Philosophy and the Book Egypt and India is the section of the book African Origins of Civilization. Those works contain the collection of all correlations between Ancient Egypt and India. This volume also contains some additional information not contained in the previous work. It was felt that this subject needed to be discussed more directly, being treated in one volume, as opposed to being contained in the larger work along with other subjects, because even in the early 21st century, the idea persists that the Yoga and specifically, Yoga Postures, were invented and developed only in India. The Ancient Egyptians were peoples originally from Africa who were, in ancient times, colonists in India. Therefore it is no surprise that many Indian traditions including religious and Yogic, would be found earlier in Ancient Egypt. Yet there is ample evidence from ancient writings and perhaps more importantly, iconographical evidences from the Ancient Egyptians themselves and the Indians themselves that prove the connection between Ancient Egypt and India as well as the existence of a discipline of Yoga Postures in Ancient Egypt long before its practice in India. This handy volume has been designed to be accessible to young adults and all others who would like to have an easy reference with documentation on this important subject. This is an important subject because the frame of reference with which we look at a culture depends strongly on our conceptions about its origins. In this case, if we look at the Ancient Egyptians as Asiatic peoples we would treat them and their culture in one way. If we see them as Africans we not only see them in a different light but we also must ascribe Africa with a glorious legacy that matches any other culture in human history. We would also look at the culture and philosophies of the Ancient Egyptians as having African insights instead of Asiatic ones. Those insights inform our knowledge bout other African traditions and we can also begin to understand in a deeper way the effect of Ancient Egyptian culture on African culture and also on the Asiatic as well. When we discover the deeper and more ancient practice of the postures system in Ancient Egypt that was called "Hatha Yoga" in India, we are able to find a new and expanded understanding of the practice that constitutes a discipline of spiritual practice that informs and revitalizes the Indian practices as well as all spiritual disciplines. $19.99 ISBN 1-884564-60-7

### 39. The Black Ancient Egyptians

# Egyptian Book of the Dead Hieroglyph Translations Volume 4

This present volume, The Black Ancient Egyptians: The Black African Ancestry of the Ancient Egyptians, formed one subject in the larger work: The African Origins of Civilization, Religion, Yoga Mysticism and Ethics Philosophy. It was felt that this subject needed to be discussed because even in the early 21st century, the idea persists that the Ancient Egyptians were peoples originally from Asia Minor who came into North-East Africa. Yet there is ample evidence from ancient writings and perhaps more importantly, iconographical evidences from the Ancient Egyptians themselves that proves otherwise. This handy volume has been designed to be accessible to young adults and all others who would like to have an easy reference with documentation on this important subject. This is an important subject because the frame of reference with which we look at a culture depends strongly on our conceptions about its origins. in this case, if we look at the Ancient Egyptians as Asiatic peoples we would treat them and their culture in one way. If we see them as Africans we not only see them in a different light but we also must ascribe Africa with a glorious legacy that matches any other culture in human history. We would also look at the culture and philosophies of the Ancient Egyptians as having African insights instead of Asiatic ones. Those insights inform our knowledge bout other African traditions and we can also begin to understand in a deeper way the effect of Ancient Egyptian culture on African culture and also on the Asiatic as well. ISBN 1-884564-21-6   $19.99

**40. The Limits of Faith: The Failure of Faith-based Religions and the Solution to the Meaning of Life**

Is faith belief in something without proof? And if so is there never to be any proof or discovery? If so what is the need of intellect? If faith is trust in something that is real is that reality historical, literal or metaphorical or philosophical? If knowledge is an essential element in faith why should there by so much emphasis on believing and not on understanding in the modern practice of religion? This volume is a compilation of essays related to the nature of religious faith in the context of its inception in human history as well as its meaning for religious practice and relations between religions in modern times. Faith has come to be regarded as a virtuous goal in life. However, many people have asked how can it be that an endeavor that is supposed to be dedicated to spiritual upliftment has led to more conflict in human history than any other social factor? ISBN 1884564631 SOFT COVER - $19.99, ISBN 1884564623 HARD COVER -$28.95

41. **Redemption of The Criminal Heart Through Kemetic Spirituality and Maat Philosophy**

Special book dedicated to inmates, their families and members of the Law Enforcement community. ISBN: 1-884564-70-4

$5.00

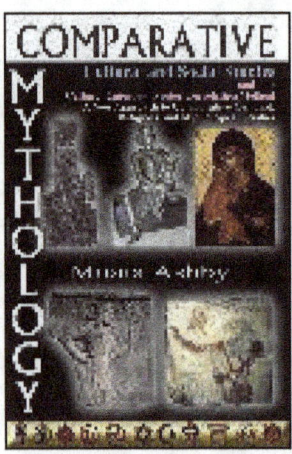

**42. COMPARATIVE MYTHOLOGY**

What are Myth and Culture and what is their importance for understanding the development of societies, human evolution and the search for meaning? What is the purpose of culture and how do cultures evolve? What are the elements of a culture and how can those elements be broken down and the constituent parts of a culture understood and compared? How do cultures interact? How does enculturation occur and how do people interact with other cultures? How do the processes of acculturation and cooptation occur and what does this mean for the development of a society? How can the study of myths and the elements of culture help in understanding the meaning of life and the means to promote understanding and peace in the world of human activity? This volume is the exposition of a method for studying and comparing cultures, myths and other social aspects of a society. It is an expansion on the Cultural Category Factor Correlation method for studying and comparing myths, cultures, religions and other aspects of human culture. It was originally introduced in the year 2002. This volume contains an expanded treatment as well as several refinements along with examples of the application of the method. the apparent. I hope you enjoy these art renditions as serene reflections of the mysteries of life.  ISBN:  1-884564-72-0

Book price $21.95

43. **CONVERSATION WITH GOD: Revelations of the Important Questions of Life**

$24.99 U.S.

This volume contains a grouping of some of the questions that have been submitted to Sebai Dr. Muata Ashby. They are efforts by many aspirants to better understand and practice the teachings of mystical spirituality. It is said that when sages are asked spiritual questions they are relaying the wisdom of God, the Goddess, the Higher Self, etc. There is a very special quality about the Q & A process that does not occur during a regular lecture session. Certain points come out that would not come out otherwise due to the nature of the process which ideally occurs after a lecture. Having been to a certain degree enlightened by a lecture certain new questions arise and the answers to these have the effect of elevating the teaching of the lecture to even higher levels. Therefore, enjoy these exchanges and may they lead you to enlightenment, peace and prosperity. Available Late Summer 2007 ISBN: 1-884564-68-2

44. **MYSTIC ART PAINTINGS**

(with Full Color images) This book contains a collection of the small number of paintings that I have created over the years. Some were used as early book covers and others were done simply to express certain spiritual feelings; some were created for no purpose except to express the joy of color and the feeling of relaxed freedom. All are to elicit mystical awakening in the viewer. Writing a book on philosophy is like sculpture, the more the work is rewritten the reflections and ideas become honed and take form and become clearer and imbued with intellectual beauty. Mystic music is like meditation, a world of its own that exists about 1 inch above ground wherein the musician does not touch the ground. Mystic Graphic Art is meditation in form, color, image and reflected image which opens the door to the reality behind the apparent. I hope you enjoy these art renditions and my reflections on them as serene reflections of the mysteries of life, as visual renditions of the philosophy I have written about over the years. ISBN 1-884564-69-0     $19.95

**45. ANCIENT EGYPTIAN HIEROGLYPHS FOR BEGINNERS**

This brief guide was prepared for those inquiring about how to enter into Hieroglyphic studies on their own at home or in study groups. First of all you should know that there are a few institutions around the world which teach how to read the Hieroglyphic text but due to the nature of the study there are perhaps only a handful of people who can read fluently. It is possible for anyone with average intelligence to achieve a high level of proficiency in reading inscriptions on temples and artifacts; however, reading extensive texts is another issue entirely. However, this introduction will give you entry into those texts if assisted by dictionaries and other aids. Most Egyptologists have a basic knowledge and keep dictionaries and notes handy when it comes to dealing with more difficult texts. Medtu Neter or the Ancient Egyptian hieroglyphic language has been considered as a "Dead Language." However, dead languages have always been studied by individuals who for the most part have taught themselves through various means. This book will discuss those means and how to use them most efficiently. ISBN 1884564429 **$28.95**

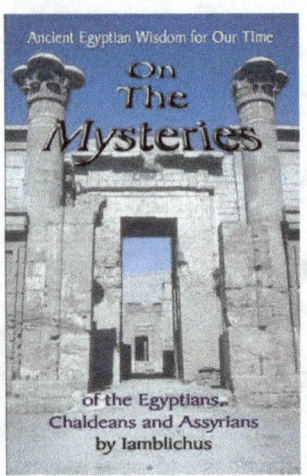

**46. ON THE MYSTERIES: Wisdom of An Ancient Egyptian Sage -with Foreword by Muata Ashby**

This volume, On the Mysteries, by Iamblichus (Abamun) is a unique form or scripture out of the Ancient Egyptian religious tradition. It is written in a form that is not usual or which is not usually found in the remnants of Ancient Egyptian scriptures. It is in the form of teacher and disciple, much like the Eastern scriptures such as Bhagavad Gita or the Upanishads. This form of writing may not have been necessary in Ancient times, because the format of teaching in Egypt was different prior to the conquest period by the Persians, Assyrians, Greeks and later the Romans. The question and answer format can be found but such extensive discourses and corrections of misunderstandings within the context of a teacher - disciple relationship is not usual. It therefore provides extensive insights into the times when it was written and the state of practice of Ancient Egyptian and other mystery religions. This has important implications for our times because we are today, as in the Greco-Roman period, also besieged with varied religions and new age philosophies as well as social strife and war. How can we understand our times and also make sense of the forest of spiritual traditions? How can we cut through the cacophony of religious fanaticism, and ignorance as well as misconceptions about the mysteries on the other in order to discover the true purpose of religion and the secret teachings that open up the mysteries of life and the way to enlightenment and immortality? This book, which comes to us from so long ago, offers us transcendental wisdom that applied to the world two thousand years ago as well as our world today. ISBN 1-884564-64-X    $25.95

**47. The Ancient Egyptian Wisdom Texts -Compiled by Muata Ashby**

The Ancient Egyptian Wisdom Texts are a genre of writings from the ancient culture that have survived to the present and provide a vibrant record of the practice of spiritual evolution otherwise known as religion or yoga philosophy in Ancient Egypt. The principle focus of the Wisdom Texts is the cultivation of understanding, peace, harmony, selfless service, self-control, Inner fulfillment and spiritual realization. When these factors are cultivated in human life, the virtuous qualities in a human being begin to manifest and sinfulness, ignorance and negativity diminish until a person is able to enter into higher consciousness, the coveted goal of all civilizations. It is this virtuous mode of life which opens the door to self-discovery and spiritual enlightenment. Therefore, the Wisdom Texts are important scriptures on the subject of human nature, spiritual psychology and mystical philosophy. The teachings presented in the Wisdom Texts form the foundation of religion as well as the guidelines for conducting the affairs of every area of social interaction including commerce, education, the army, marriage, and especially the legal system. These texts were sources for the famous 42 Precepts of Maat of the Pert-m-Heru (Book of the Dead), essential regulations of good conduct to develop virtue and purity in order to attain higher consciousness and immortality after death.  ISBN1-884564-65-8    $18.95

**48. THE KEMETIC TREE OF LIFE**

**THE KEMETIC TREE OF LIFE: Newly Revealed Ancient Egyptian Cosmology and Metaphysics for Higher Consciousness** The Tree of Life is a roadmap of a journey which explains how Creation came into being and how it will end. It also explains what Creation is composed of and also what human beings are and what they are composed of. It also explains the process of Creation, how Creation develops, as well as who created Creation and where that entity may be found. It also explains how a human being may discover that entity and in so doing also discover the secrets of Creation, the meaning of life and the means to break free from the pathetic condition of human limitation and mortality in order to discover the higher realms of being by discovering the principles, the levels of existence that are beyond the simple physical and material aspects of life. This book contains color plates  **ISBN: 1-884564-74-7  $27.95 U.S.**

**49-MATRIX OF AFRICAN PROVERBS: The Ethical and Spiritual Blueprint**

This volume sets forth the fundamental principles of African ethics and their practical applications for use by individuals and organizations seeking to model their ethical policies using the Traditional African values and concepts of ethical human behavior for the proper sustenance and management of society. Furthermore, this book will provide guidance as to how the Traditional African Ethics may be viewed and applied, taking into consideration the technological and social advancements in the present. This volume also presents the principles of ethical culture, and references for each to specific injunctions from Traditional African Proverbial Wisdom Teachings. These teachings are compiled from varied Pre-colonial African societies including Yoruba, Ashanti, Kemet, Malawi, Nigeria, Ethiopia, Galla, Ghana and many more. ISBN 1-884564-77-1

50- **Growing Beyond Hate: Keys to Freedom from Discord, Racism, Sexism, Political Conflict, Class Warfare, Violence, and How to Achieve Peace and Enlightenment**---INTRODUCTION: WHY DO WE HATE? Hatred is one of the fundamental motivating aspects of human life; the other is desire. Desire can be of a worldly nature or of a spiritual, elevating nature. Worldly desire and hatred are like two sides of the same coin in that human life is usually swaying from one to the other; but the question is why? And is there a way to satisfy the desiring or hating mind in such a way as to find peace in life? Why do human beings go to war? Why do human beings perpetrate violence against one another? And is there a way not just to understand the phenomena but to resolve the issues that plague humanity and could lead to a more harmonious society? Hatred is perhaps the greatest scourge of humanity in that it leads to misunderstanding, conflict and untold miseries of life and clashes between individuals, societies and nations. Therefore, the riddle of Hatred, that is, understanding the sources of it and how to confront, reduce and even eradicate it so as to bring forth the fulfillment in life and peace for society, should be a top priority for social scientists, spiritualists and philosophers. This book is written from the perspective of spiritual philosophy based on the mystical wisdom and sema or yoga philosophy of the Ancient Egyptians. This philosophy, originated and based in the wisdom of Shetaut Neter, the Egyptian Mysteries, and Maat, ethical way of life in society and in spirit, contains Sema-Yogic wisdom and understanding of life's predicaments that can allow a human being of any ethnic group to understand and overcome the causes of hatred, racism, sexism, violence and disharmony in life, that plague human society. ISBN: 1-884564-81-X

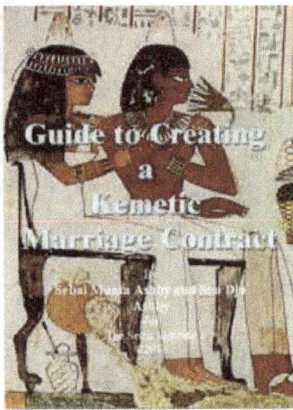

52. Guide to Creating a Kemetic Marriage Contract

This marital contract guide reflects actual Ancient Egyptian Principles for Kemetic Marriage as they are to be applied for our times. The marital contract allows people to have a framework with which to face the challenges of marital relations instead of relying on hopes or romantic dreams that everything will workout somehow; in other words, love is not all you need. The latter is not an evolved, mature way of handling one of the most important aspects of human life. Therefore, it behooves anyone who wishes to enter into a marriage to explore the issues, express their needs and seek to avoid costly mistakes, and resolve conflicts in the normal course of life or make sure that their rights and dignity will be protected if any eventuality should occur. Marital relations in Ancient Egypt were not like those in other countries of the time and not like those of present day countries. The extreme longevity of Ancient Egyptian society, founded in Maat philosophy, allowed the social development of marriage to evolve and progress to a high level of order and balance. Maat represents truth, righteous, justice and harmony in life. This meant that the marital partner's rights were to be protected with equal standing before the law. So there was no disparity between rights of men or rights of women. Therefore, anyone who wants to enter into a marriage based on Kemetic principles must first and foremost adhere to this standard...equality in the rights of men and women. This guide demonstrates procedures for following the Ancient Egyptian practice of formalizing marriage with a contract that spells out the important concerns of each partner in the marital relationship, based on Maatian principles [of righteous, truth, harmony and justice] so that the rights and needs of each partner may be protected within the marriage. It also allows the partners to think about issues that arise out of the marital relations so that they may have a foundation to fall back on in the event that those or other unforeseen issues arise and cause conflict in the relationship. By having a document of expressed concerns, needs and steps to be taken to address them, it is less likely that issues which affect the relationship in a negative way will arise, and when they do, they will be better handled, in a more balanced, just and amicable way.

EBOOK ISBN: 978-1-937016-59-3, HARDCOPY BOOK ISBN: 1-884564-82-8

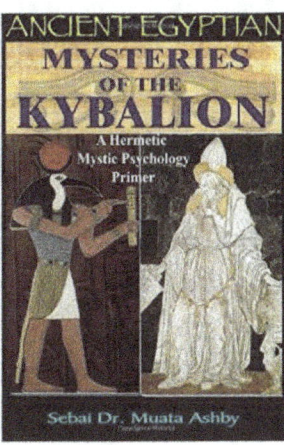

## 53-Ancient Egyptian Mysteries of The Kybalion: A Hermetic Mystic Psychology Primer Paperback – November 28, 2014

This Volume is a landmark study by a renouned mystic philosopher, Sebai Dr. Muata Ashby. It is study not just to philosophize but to be practiced for the purpose of attaining enlightenment. The book is divided into three sections. Part 1 INTRODUCTION presents a brief history of Hermeticism, its origins in the Ancient Egyptian Mysteries (Neterianism) the Kybalion and the origins of the personality known as Hermes Trismegistus. Part 2 presents the essential teachings of the Kybalion text, a set of MAXIMS, without interpretation. Part 3 presents glosses (commentary and explanation) on the essential teachings of the Kybalion based on the philosophy of the Ancient Egyptian Mysteries as determined by Sebai Dr. Muata Ashby based on studies and translations of original Ancient Egyptian Hieroglyphic texts; the source from which the Kybalion teaching is derived. The Glosses are an edited and expanded version of Lessons given by Sebai Dr. Muata Ashby in the form of lectures on the teachings of the Kybalion.

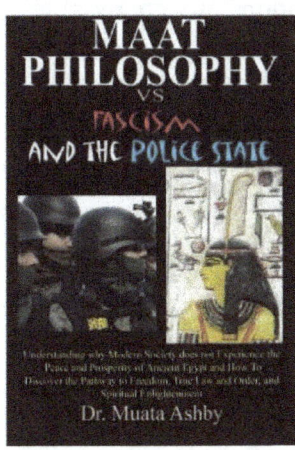

## 54-Maat Philosophy Versus Fascism and the Police State: Understanding why Modern Society does not Experience the Peace and Prosperity of Ancient Egypt ... Law and Order, and Spiritual Enlightenment Paperback – January 1, 2014

Understanding why Modern Society does not Experience the Peace and Prosperity of Ancient Egypt and How To Discover the Pathway to Freedom, True Law and Order, and Spiritual Enlightenment. Understanding the Corporate State and How Maatian Philosophy can Leads to Freedom, Prosperity and Enlightenment

55- MALFEASANCE & IMMORALITY: An Analysis of the World Economic Crash of 2008, the Corrupt Political and Financial Institutions that Caused it and Strategies to Survive the Future Collapse of the Economy

The following is a first ever publication, by the Sema Institute, of a �White Paper�. The term is defined as: A white paper is an authoritative report or guide that often addresses issues and how to solve them. White papers are used to educate readers and help people make decisions. They are often used in politics and business. This paper serves as an update to the book Dollar Crisis: The Collapse of Society and Redemption Through Ancient Egyptian Fiscal & Monetary Policy (2008). That book was a continuation and expansion of issues presented in the book The Collapse of Civilization and the Death of American Empire (2006). Those books contained a detailed analysis of economic and political as well as social issues and how Maat Philosophy could offer insights into the nature of the problem, its sources and possible solutions as well as a means to develop an economic system (Fiscal and Monetary policies) that can work for all members of society. This paper contains an analysis of economic events and possible future outcomes based on those events as well as ideas individuals or groups may use in order to develop plans of action to deal with the possible detrimental events that may occur in the near and intermediate future. It serves as an update to the previous publications. This paper is divided into two parts. The first section is a summary which contains the conclusions of each section of Part 2. This was done so that the reader may have a quick and easy understanding of what is happening with the economy and finally, the actions that should be considered to meet the challenges ahead

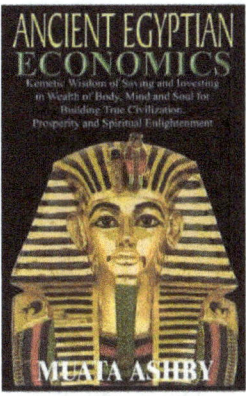

56- ANCIENT EGYPTIAN ECONOMICS

Ancient Egyptian Economics: Kemetic Wisdom of Saving and Investing in Wealth of Body, Mind and Soul for Building True Civilization, Prosperity and Spiritual Enlightenment------Question: Why has the subject of finances and economics become important, I thought the spiritual teachings and Ancient Egyptian Philosophy and money were separate? Answer: Finances and money are an integral part of Ancient Egyptian culture as an instrument for promoting Maat ethics in the form of the well-being of the 'hekat'. The hekat are the people and the "Heka" is the Pharaoh. The Pharaoh was like a shepherd leading a flock and moneys were controlled righteously to promote the welfare of the people. In that tradition we have applied the philosophy of maatian economics to promote the well-being of those who are following this path as well as those who may read the books so they may avoid financial trouble as much as possible and have better capacity to practice the teachings. In order to have a successful life, human beings need a certain amount of money and wealth, but money and wealth are not the goal. They are a foundation that enables the true goal of life, enlightenment, to be realized. Therefore, we are only fulfilling the duty of transmitting wisdom about wealth to promote Maat, righteousness, truth and well-being, for all. This volume explores the mysteries of wealth based on the teachings of the sages of Ancient Egypt and the means to promote prosperity that allows a person to create the conditions for discovering inner peace and spiritual enlightenment. HTP-Peace

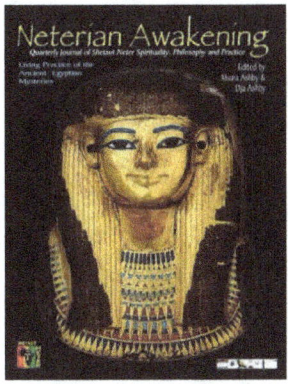

57- NETERIAN AWAKENING Journal of Neterian Culture Vol 1-12 In one Volume

This is a single file containing 12 volumes of The Neterian Awakening Journal. The Neterian Awakening Journal was a publication where the culture and community of Shetaut Neter spirituality was explored. In it Sebai Dr. Muata Ashby and Dr. Dja Ashby along with members of the Temple of Shetaut Neter presented articles, festival reviews, Questions and Answer columns and many other important aspects of Neterian culture and spirituality beyond those presented in other volumes of the book series that are useful in understanding the practice of Neterian Spirituality and the path to achieving a �Neterian Spiritual Awakening.� Part of its mission was: To promote the study of Shetaut Neter (Neterianism, Neterian Religion) as a spiritual path. Instruct the serious followers of Shetaut Neter spirituality who would like to receive literature in between the publication of major books that will fill the needs of their daily spiritual practice. Neterian Awakening Journal explores the varied aspects of Shetaut Neter spirituality not covered in the books. NAJ provides a forum for the development of a Neterian Community of those who wish to follow the Neterian Spiritual Path of African Religious Culture

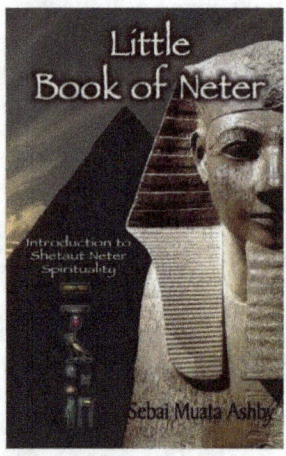

58- Little Book of Neter: Introduction to Shetaut Neter Spirituality and Religion Paperback – June 7, 2007

The Little Book of Neter is a summary of the most important teachings of Shetaut Neter for all aspirants to have for easy reference and distribution. It is designed to be portable and low cost so that all can have the main teachings of Shetaut Neter at easy access for personal use and also for sharing with others the basic tenets of Neterian spirituality.

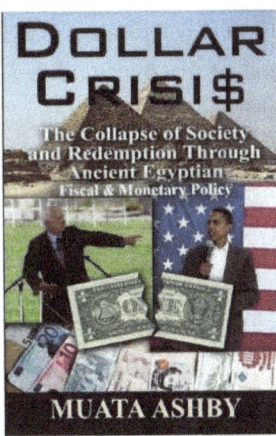

59- Dollar Crisis: The Collapse of Society and Redemption Through Ancient Egyptian Monetary Policy by Muata Ashby (2008-07-24)

This book is about the problems of the US economy and the imminent collapse of the U.S. Dollar and its dire consequences for the US economy and the world. It is also about the corruption in government, economics and social order that led to this point. Also it is about survival, how to make it through this perhaps most trying period in the history of the United States. Also it is about the ancient wisdom of life that allowed an ancient civilization to grow beyond the destructive corruptions of ignorance and power so that the people of today may gain insight into the nature of their condition, how they got there and what needs to be done in order to salvage what is left and rebuild a society that is sustainable, beneficial and an example for all humanity.

60- Devotional Worship Book of Shetaut Neter: Medu Neter song, chant and hymn book for daily practice [Paperback] [2007] (Author) Muata Ashby Paperback – 2007

Ushet Hekau Shedi Sema Tawi Uashu or Ushet means "to worship the Divine," "to propitiate the Divine." Ushet is of two types, external and internal. When you go to pilgrimage centers, temples, spiritual gatherings, etc., you are practicing external worship or spiritual practice. When you go into your private meditation room on your own and your utter words of power, prayers and meditation you are practicing internal worship or spiritual practice. Ushet needs to be understood as a process of not only an outer show of spiritual practice, but it is also a process of developing love for the Divine. Therefore, Ushet really signifies a development in Devotion towards the Divine. This practice is also known as sma uash or Yoga of Devotion. Ushet is the process of discovering the Divine and allowing your heart to flow towards the Divine. This program of life allows a spiritual aspirant to develop inner peace, contentment and universal love, and these qualities lead to spiritual enlightenment or union with the Divine. It is recommended that you see the book "The Path of Divine Love" by Dr. Muata Ashby. This volume will give details into this form of Sema or Yoga.

**61- Initiation Into Egyptian Yoga and Neterian Religion Workbook for Beginning and Advancing Aspirants**

What is Initiation? The great personalities of the past known to the world as Isis, Hathor, Jesus, Buddha and many other great Sages and Saints were initiated into their spiritual path but how did initiation help them and what were they specifically initiated into? This volume is a template for such lofty studies, a guidebook and blueprint for aspirants who want to understand what the path is all about, its requirements and goals, as they work with a qualified spiritual guide as they tread the path of Kemetic Spirituality and Yoga disciplines. This workbook helps by presenting the fundamental teachings of Egyptian Yoga and Neterian Spirituality with questions and exercises to help the aspirant gain a foundation for more advanced studies and practices

62. EGYPTIAN BOOK OF THE DEAD HIEROGLYPH TRANSLATIONS SERIES

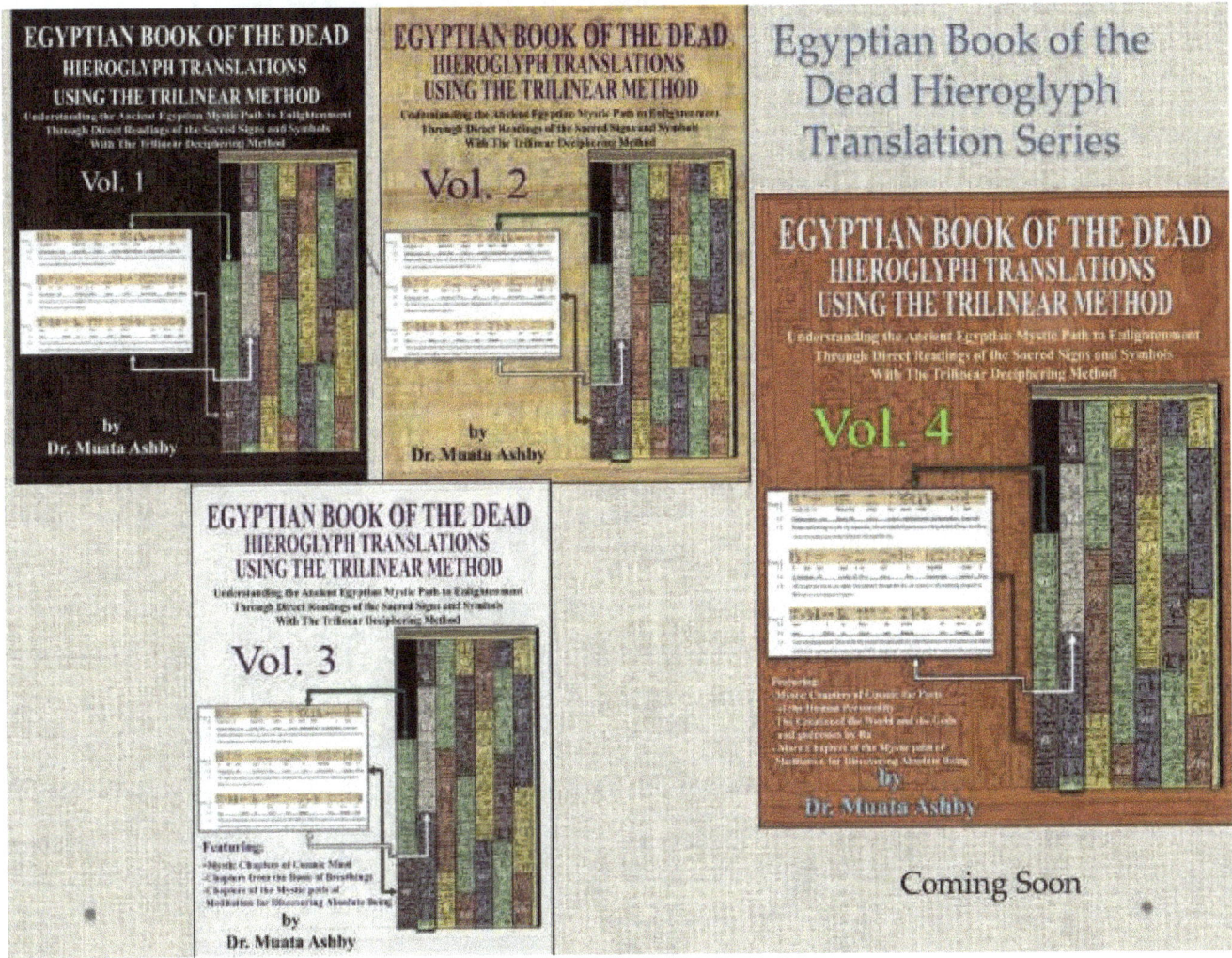

---

[i] After 1570 B.C.E they would evolve into a more unified text, the Egyptian Book of the Dead.

[ii] See the book *The Egyptian Book of the Dead* by Muata Ashby

[iii] See the Book Memphite Theology by Muata Ashby

[iv] See the Books, *The Goddess Path, Mysteries of Isis, Glorious Light Meditation, Memphite Theology* and *Resurrecting Osiris* by Muata Ashby

[v] See the Book Resurrecting Osiris by Muata Ashby

[vi] (Prt M Hru 9:4)